Language and Literacy
in the Early Years

Marian R. Whitehead was until recently a Senior Lecturer in Education at Goldsmiths College, University of London, with responsibility for organizing and teaching M.A. degrees in Language and Literature and Early Childhood Education. She has published extensively on literacy, literature and bilingualism and is a co-editor of the journal *Early Years*. She now combines writing with language and early years consultancy work.

LANGUAGE AND LITERACY IN THE EARLY YEARS
Second Edition

Marian R. Whitehead

P·C·P
Paul Chapman
Publishing Ltd

Copyright © 1997 Marian R. Whitehead
All rights reserved

Paul Chapman Publishing Ltd
144 Liverpool Road
London
N1 1LA

British Library Cataloguing in Publication Data
Whitehead, Marian R.
  Language and literacy in the early years. – 2nd ed.
  1. Language and languages – Study and teaching (Elementary)
  2. Language acquisition   3. Literacy
  I. Title
  407

ISBN 1 85396 341 0

Typeset by Dorwyn Ltd
Printed and bound in Great Britain

A B C D E F G H 9 8 7

Contents

For Jim – and a fine city –
with love.

Preface to Second Edition

In an introduction to the first edition of this book I noted the extensive 'books-about-language' industry and justified my contribution on the grounds that few of these books addressed the professional interests and priorities of early years teachers and students. Since then there has been a huge increase in the numbers and quality of 'language and literacy in the early years' books and I am gratified that the first edition of this book was in the vanguard of such a significant development.

During the past seven years research studies of language, literacy and child development have also continued to emerge and many of their insights are reflected in this new edition. But the greatest changes since this book was first published have occurred in the sphere of education and schooling. The world of education has been turned upside down and early years education is going through particularly traumatic upheavals.

A statutory national curriculum for the years of compulsory schooling is now in place; a set of desirable learning outcomes for children on entry to compulsory education exists (creating a pre-national curriculum for children in playgroups, nursery schools and classes and other under-5s settings); and base-line assessment of children in the first half-term of primary school is coming (in effect, tests for 4-year-olds). Furthermore, the short-lived national system of nursery vouchers for all 4-year-olds has drawn a wider spectrum of providers into early years education and made many infant teachers responsible for the care and education of children who are just 4 years of age.

All the recent curriculum and initial teacher-training legislation contains requirements and guidelines for language and literacy, making this book more relevant than ever before – and in need of considerable modifications. It must now speak to a wider range of practitioners and early years settings and cannot assume a readership of teachers working in schools.

This widening of the notion of what constitutes an early years practitioner and an early years setting can be a liberating challenge and I have approached it as such. However, the dangers of settling for simplified views of language, literacy and early years education are in evidence everywhere. This book continues to reject quick-fix approaches to language and narrow prescriptive rules for teaching it – and teaching children – and re-asserts the complexity and the joy involved in supporting young children's development as speakers, writers and readers. The call for a second edition indicates that early years educators in many settings agree with me about the complexity of their task and approach it with undiminished professionalism and commitment. I am proud to count myself one of them.

Marian R. Whitehead
Norwich, March 1997

Introduction

The focus of this book is on children from 0–8 and particularly on those attend-ing a wide range of early years group settings providing care and education.

In the terminology of the current legislation, this book is concerned with the language provision and curriculum for under-5s and the years, reception, 1, 2 and 3. However, the early years of education are not restricted to formal schooling and books about this stage must also focus on children's pre-school and out-of-school learning and experiences.

Language and literacy are areas of study that continue to produce new research findings and stimulating theories, and certainly justify regular review and re-appraisal. Furthermore, early language and literacy learning are often seen as patterns or 'models' for a great range of human learning strategies and achievements. Language and literacy demonstrate the complex interweaving of the personal and the public, the private and the social, the idiosyncratic and the conventional, that characterizes all learning. Language also affects the whole of education for, even when it is not the particular focus of planned teaching and learning, it is the means and the channel for teaching and learning.

The role of the professional educator involves looking at the theories put forward by linguists, reviewing some of the trends in linguistic research and making informed decisions about their possible implications for practice. Pro-fessional educators have to be their own researchers in their own settings, their own policy-makers and their own curriculum planners. It is never a simple matter of transferring carefully controlled laboratory findings to busy, com-plex group settings in any area of early-years curriculum planning. Teachers, students and other early years professionals need the appropriate information and insights to begin to answer such difficult questions as: 'What is educational linguistics?' 'What use is it?' 'What do we do about the claims of the re-searcher?' These are practitioners' questions and they must be answered by professional educators. This book attempts to outline the kinds of knowledge about language from which practitioners might evolve sound and appropriate educational practices.

Early-years education appears to be an under-valued area of specialism threatened by narrow curriculum control and bureaucracy, but its particular contribution to many research areas and to education in general should be recognized. Much of the work in early-years education has been a source of original thinking and flexible practices. Fresh and unconventional studies of the origins of children's later achievements in mathematical and scientific thinking, logic and topology began in early-years research. In particular, the roots of language and of literacy have been investigated in research based in kindergarten, nursery and early-years classes in several countries. Good early-years practices are more likely to be grounded in educational theories, principles and rigorous research than in pragmatic responses to political, economic and social pressures.

After the justifications comes the business of actually approaching this book. In this case it might be helpful to think of it as similar to a visit to a nursery or primary school during the working day. It takes some time to get through the gates, across the playground, down the corridor or across the hall, and into a classroom to meet the thinking, talking and learning children. Part I describes these routes into early years settings. The first chapter, on linguistics, might seem at times like a rather dull expanse of deserted tarmac, even though this has been marked out for children's play and games and there is even a hint of a garden that adds a bit of unrestrained nature to the scene. Chapter 2, on sociolinguistics, is like the entrance area and corridors of a nursery or school. There are signs of human organization and hierarchies, evidence of conflicts and successes, and the first glimpses of rooms full of a great variety of children and adults. Chapter 3 introduces us to the children and allows us to observe them closely, to assess what they can do already and to evaluate what they are presently attempting to do. We also have the opportunity to relate these activities to the early years educator's thinking, planning and provision for the language curriculum (Chapter 4).

Part II of the book focuses on literacy and might, if we continue the metaphor, be equated with ceasing to be a visitor and accepting the invitation to become a teacher of literacy.

Chapters 1, 2, 3, 5, 6 and 7 contain lists of summary statements about the topics and research covered and these may be useful as discussion points in professional training sessions. Extensive lists of further reading are provided at the end of each chapter and Chapters 1, 2, 3, 5, 6 and 7 also have teaching and learning suggestions for the practitioner. Chapters 4 and 8 omit these because they are entirely focused on the professional implications of Parts I and II of the book.

Part I

Language and learning

1

Linguistics: the study of language

The discipline of linguistics can be likened to a pathway which is being cut through the dark and mysterious forest of language. Different parts of the forest have been explored at different times, so we can depict the path as a winding one.

Aitchison, 1987, p. 29

The brief, non-specialist introduction to linguistics that follows can be no more than an invitation to walk along the winding linguistic pathway described by Aitchison and to appreciate its skilful construction, while admiring the interesting areas of the language forest it has opened up. The value of this metaphorical way of discussing linguistics and language is its emphasis on the vastness and mystery of human language, and the far from fully explored state of knowledge about it. Knowledge about language is a frequently used phrase in contemporary educational debates and the issues it raises for language study in the curriculum are addressed in Chapter 4. These first three chapters aim to establish not so much a body of knowledge but more a healthy respect for the mystery, complexity and beauty of language.

This seems an entirely proper aim for a book focused on early childhood: early-years educators are the professionals closest to young children's discoveries and happy accidents in their first language learning. Indeed, early-childhood educators are well placed to appreciate children's language learning, particularly the determination and ingenuity with which they set about tackling the linguistic unknown – sometimes head on and sometimes by devious routes. One way for teachers to comprehend the sheer scale of young children's linguistic achievements is to attempt a little linguistic learning for themselves. Other gains include the clearing away of some common misunderstandings about language and the establishment of basic ground-rules for further talking and reading about the nature of language. Furthermore, if we, the practitioners, are at ease with the main concepts and specialist terminology of linguistics, we are less likely to be misled by dubious claims about language and learning and by questionable educational implications. The following discussion formulates some working generalizations about linguistics and considers modern approaches to grammar.

Linguistics

The study of language (one simple way of defining linguistics) has probably been pursued in various forms for thousands of years. Humankind has puzzled over the proliferation of many different languages: we might call this the Tower of Babel problem. Earlier generations were fascinated by what we could call the 'roots' issue – when and where did human language originate? People have even speculated about which language God, or the gods, spoke and which language totally isolated and untutored babies would first utter naturally. Clearly, ordinary people as well as philosophers, teachers and linguists have persistently asked, what is language and how does it work?

For centuries the proposed answers to these questions were highly prescriptive, that is, they were cast in the form of rules and assertions about which language was best, the ways in which it ought to be used and which ideals and models of linguistic perfections should be emulated. It is not surprising that traditional prescriptive linguists frequently promoted the superiority of their own particular form of language use. As we will see later, this tradition of linguistic partiality is deeply rooted in communities and in the attitudes of individuals. For example, it is noticeably difficult for many monolinguals (who speak only one language) to take seriously other ways of naming, organizing and thinking about the world, apart from their own linguistic practice. Furthermore, any attacks on these language loyalties can lead to passionate and violent reactions, as linguistic conflicts and riots all over the world often demonstrate.

At the personal level, the language of home and early socialization is an intimate part of our sense of self, and any attack on our first language can be insulting, disturbing and alienating. One of the reasons for the huge numbers of bilingual and multilingual speakers in the world is the desire to preserve the languages and the traditions of the home and cultural group, while living and working within another language community.

If prescriptive linguistics was frequently entangled with issues of national power and individual identity, it was also responsible for claims that some languages were best or even God-given. Latin and Greek were usually held to be the ideal languages for Western Christianity: they were the voices of spiritual aspirations, because they were used by the Church, and of learning, because of the history of the development of writing. Here we have one probable source for the almost superstitious respect for literacy that still permeates contemporary societies – often to the detriment of other human arts and skills, including spoken language. Religion, learning and literacy were firmly linked to the classical languages and, subsequently, to those European languages that could possibly claim Latinate grammars and classically derived vocabularies. Other languages and the spoken tongues of ordinary people were thought to be vulgar or even primitive.

This brief historical note highlights the style and the long-lasting influence of the prescriptive linguistic tradition that was still dominant in the early decades of the twentieth century. Indeed, we are living in the shadow of this approach. This set of inherited linguistic beliefs still perpetuates restrictive notions of correctness and the sort of linguistic table manners that undermine serious attempts to understand human language.

Saussure and Modern Linguistics

Modern linguistics originated alongside the other modern social sciences (notably psychology and sociology) in the latter half of the nineteenth century, although it had little impact until this century. One man, Ferdinand de Saussure, is usually credited as the founding father of linguistics but his ideas were only published in 1915, after his death, as reconstructed lecture notes (Saussure, 1974). Despite this haphazard publication, Saussure's work radically challenged traditional approaches to language studies and outlined a methodology and an analysis of linguistics that remains the basis of modern linguistic science.

Saussure's work proposed a complete rejection of prescriptive judgements and unfounded and fruitless speculations about the origins of language. In their place he suggested a scientific approach to analysing and understanding the nature of human language as it exists and as it is used. In order to clear the ground for this more scientific study of language, Saussure formulated a set of linguistic distinctions, or definitions.[1] First, he proposed a way of reducing the potential confusion that exists in our ways of referring to the many aspects of language by the one term 'language'. Linguists must clearly distinguish in their studies between the concept of language as the known system of norms and rules of a specific tongue (for example, Welsh or Gujerati), and actual manifestations of language in daily use – that is, utterances or written examples using these or any other languages.

Saussure happened to be a French speaker and his original choice of French terminology for these distinctions, *langue* for language system and *parole* for specific usage, are still commonly used by linguists. Any book about grammar or modern linguistics is generally a study of langue, but an investigation of the languages and dialects used by inner-city schoolchildren would be predominantly a study of parole. The qualifiers, 'generally' and 'predominantly', are important because even the latter inner-city example would lead to some kind of analysis of the language system that had been acquired by the particular speakers. Saussure's distinctions are not absolute categories but working hypotheses.

Saussure's next great insight was that any language is a total system – a structure of elaborately interrelated elements and relationships. This emphasis on the relationships and the rules that link the elements of a language has led to all approaches since Saussure being broadly defined as 'structural linguistics'. For the modern linguist, the social or political significance of any particular language is always secondary to the prime aim of analysing and describing how it works, and what sets of rules and relationships are significant in its operation.

One final distinction made in Saussure's work is the synchronic and diachronic division he formulated in order to clarify the differing concerns and emphases possible in linguistic studies. Synchronic approaches form the major part of modern linguistics and are concerned with the current state of the language. In other words, a synchronic study is like a detailed snapshot of the language, the langue as it exists and is being used in samples of parole. The diachronic approach is focused on the historical evolution of a language and was very popular in Europe in the nineteenth century. Such studies are not entirely irrelevant for the modern linguist, but they must be kept clearly separate from claims about a language as it is now. Views of what has happened to a language over centuries may unduly influence and falsify attempts to describe the current state of the language – as when older adults complain that young people do not talk properly.

What has emerged most clearly from Saussure's radical re-shaping of the study of language is a scientific concern to observe languages objectively, to propose theories about their systems and to attempt to reconstruct and describe them accurately. This descriptive linguistics, as it is sometimes called, was further developed and used very practically in North America in the first half of this century. The new insights about linguistics coincided with attempts to salvage something of the dead or dying American Indian cultures. As the tribal ways of life disintegrated, their languages died with them. However, some anthropologists and linguists employed the new scientific methodology to collect, record, analyse and describe the many languages of the North and South American continents. This body of research created new scientific procedures for collecting unknown languages 'in the field', using phonetic systems of notation as well as recordings and photographs. The work also developed a useful technique of relying on the ordinary 'insiders' of a language and culture as linguistic informants.

This kind of approach has been taken up by most later researchers and used in the study of child language and language variety. The modern researcher tests the plausibility of any hypothesis about the nature of an utterance or a linguistic form by trying it out on a native speaker. In other words, the ordinary speaker–listener's knowledge of the particular language system they use is the reality against which the professional linguist must test any theories.

In emphasizing the existence of ordinary knowledge of language, linguists simply claim that the native speaker (adult or child) knows one or more language systems at a deeply intuitive level. Modern linguists do not claim that this kind of knowledge is explicit or easily accessible to self-conscious analysis and descriptions of any kind. However, we know that we 'know' language because we produce it and comprehend it fairly effortlessly and frequently, under many different circumstances and in a great variety of situations. Furthermore, we self-correct our own minor slips of the tongue and the pen and confidently reject any incorrect (that is, ungrammatical) forms of our languages we happen to encounter. Faced with foreign speakers or infants we strive to make sense of their intended meanings despite errors, misunderstandings and inaccurate pronunciations. All of these facts are evidence for the existence or psychological reality of individual linguistic knowledge.

Psycholinguistics, Sociolinguistics and Applied Linguistics

Psycholinguistics
Linguistics is a social science. It is concerned with the description and understanding of human ability developed in social settings alongside other individuals and, indeed, learnt from them. Studies of language that concentrate on the strictly observable, audible and measurable are bound to produce limited and distorted accounts of language. In order to overcome some of the

weaknesses in the partial view, which tended to dominate the early years of modern language study, a branch of linguistics has emerged known as psycholinguistics.

Psycholinguistics is the shared area of psychology and linguistics, and it studies language as a major manifestation of human thinking and learning. As such, it is of central interest to educators and the source of our current knowledge about how language is first acquired in infancy, and how language, thinking and learning are related. It is usually the case that people are clear that language is for communication with others, that it has an obvious social dimension, but they are often less consciously aware of its personal function in thinking and self-directing.

Sociolinguistics

Language is, nevertheless, a central medium of social communication, cultural cohesion and dissemination. It is the tool, the manner and the matter of much of our socialization in infancy. A so-called scientific linguistics, which ignored the totality of the human settings in which language is shared with others and learnt in interaction with them, would be a rather distorted science. Sociolinguistics is the branch of language studies that seeks to explore these complex areas of linguistics and sociology. Language and its social contexts are of major significance in educational studies, particularly because homes, early years group settings and schools are very different contexts in which children learn to use and develop their languages.

Sociolinguistics illuminates another central aspect of language and language learning that has implications for group care and education: language is a social creation, the voice of a community, but it becomes a highly personal possession and a way of thinking. We cannot understand language and, by implication, learning and thinking, unless we keep both the social and the psychological factors in focus.

Applied linguistics

The claim referred to previously is typical of an educational approach to linguistics: it is an example of 'applied' linguistics, the use of linguistic findings for practical social activities. Pure linguists pursue strictly linguistic ends, such as refining even more detailed and accurate descriptions of language or languages, but there are many other applications of linguistics, apart from the educational.

In the medical sphere, linguistics provides help with the study and treatment of language disorders caused by congenital or accidental brain damage or disease. Language disorder and retardation also occur in children and adults who have a variety of abnormalities in the organs of voice production or have some specific sensory impairment such as degrees of deafness. These complex problems are well beyond the scope of this book but progress in dealing with them has been enhanced by detailed linguistic knowledge of phonology and verbal thinking.

The application of linguistics has always been associated with the work of anthropologists, who study remote and unknown languages and cultures, but this approach has in recent years been transferred and adapted to the long-term and in-depth study of distinctive groups and communities existing within a larger community or society.

One of the newer off-shoots of applied linguistics is the study of artificial languages and the creation of voices for robots and computers. In the past, ideological and pedagogical theories also promoted artificial languages, such as Esperanto and 'basic' forms of English. These ventures have remained fairly limited but the best-known application of linguistics is also the most obvious: the use of linguistic knowledge in the teaching of natural languages in educational institutions. It is still the case that the teaching of English and other languages in schools is associated with arguments about the formal teaching of grammar and, as this debate has been revived by the National Curriculum legislation, it will be useful to consider grammar next.

- Linguistics is the study of language.
- Modern linguistics is descriptive and scientific in its approach and can be contrasted with traditional approaches that were prescriptive.
- Prescriptive linguistics emphasized notions of correctness and ideals for good language use that were based on a respect for classical languages and formal written texts.
- Modern linguistic science primarily studies spoken language forms, it describes a language in terms of its structures and relationships. These are the internalized sets of rules that govern its use by native speakers.
- Psycholinguistics is the study of language as it relates to human thinking and learning, particularly the capacity to learn a first natural language in infancy.
- Sociolinguistics is the study of language as it is used and modified by varied social contexts.
- Applied linguistics is the use of language knowledge in practical social settings: educational linguistics is one example, although there are significant applications for linguistics in medicine, information technology and anthropology.

Grammars

It would seem that grammar has a bad name among the majority of people who are not professional linguists. However, this is nothing new: many attempts have been made to sweeten the pill. In the early 1800s the paths of grammar were 'strewed with flowers' (Opie and Opie, 1980, p. 46) as well as jolly rhymes and exquisitely colourful engravings. In the 1970s and 1980s there was a steady flow of books, as well as radio and television programmes, that assured us that grammar and language study can be funny, fascinating and even sexy! These are nearly always well-researched and linguistically serious guides, but they have to fight a general fear of grammar by using such devices as cartoons, jokey sentences and glossy formats. Boredom and anxiety are in fact reactions to the half-understood prescriptive or traditional grammar discussed in the previous section. This grammar may be a largely discredited ideal based on Latin, but it is only fully rejected by linguists and students of linguistics. It is even reappearing in textbooks and workbooks published to support

National Curriculum English. The identification of learning, high culture and power with grammar and classical languages has deep roots in Britain's history, political life and establishment culture.

Issues centred on language and power are returned to in the next chapter, as the relevant concern here is the apparent vacuum left by the discreditation of prescriptive grammar. In reality, there is no vacuum – modern linguistics offers a rich and complex range of grammars, and the plural is intentional. There are several differing hypotheses about the structure or grammar of human languages but it is possible to make some valid points about the important characteristics they all share. It is these general features that may have the most relevance and interest for educators.

First, the grammars are all descriptive: they set out to describe the complex sets of relations or rules that link the sounds of a language, or its written symbols, with the meanings or messages intended. In attempting to describe a grammar, the linguist behaves like a scientist and observes, records and hypothesizes. A modern grammar is always open to challenge and modification, and this makes the study of modern grammars highly provisional and demanding.

Second, all modern grammars describe far more than the surface of a language – that which is heard or seen in writing. The traditional prescriptive approach placed great emphasis on the written form and analysed that into categories derived from Latin. Modern descriptive grammars identify and describe at least three major levels of a language and thus they can be said to be richer and more complex models of language than the traditional prescriptive ideal. At this particular point in the linguistic forest it looks as if the path of grammar is strewn with numbers and levels rather than flowers, but a sense of the several levels involved in any modern grammar is distinctive and significant. At the very least it gives us some sense of pride and respect for our own complex linguistic skills. It should also help the professional early-years educator approach child language and language development with delight in the accomplishments, and a scientific desire to know more about the processes.

Phonology, Syntax and Semantics

The three major levels of a language that modern grammars describe are phonology, syntax and semantics. Lexis, more commonly referred to as vocabulary, is sometimes added to this basic list. Lexis refers to all the words in the definitive dictionaries of a written language or the stock of words available to an oral-language community. This is not intended to suggest that we all know all the words of our first languages; nor does it follow that measuring or assessing anyone's vocabulary is an easy matter. It would seem that we all operate an active vocabulary of words we use regularly and confidently, as well as having a passive vocabulary of words and meanings we understand but are not likely to use frequently. This is a sobering and significant thought for educators and administrators who talk glibly of assessing a child's vocabulary.

Phonology

Phonology is concerned with the organization and patterning of sounds in a language. It includes such important indicators of meaning as intonation and the use of stress or emphasis. This patterning of sounds and stress occurs in all languages, but the actual patterns vary greatly between languages. Most of us become aware that different languages have very different 'tunes', and it is possible to recognize a language by its sound, pitch and rhythms without identifying, or even being capable of identifying, any of its words. Fluent speakers of English can, for example, play the 'football-results game': predicting wins, draws and defeats before they are announced. This is done by assessing the degrees of rising and falling intonation patterns used by the speaker. However, we all use the same skill on a daily basis to identify questions or statements in shared conversations: the distinctive rising tone of questions and the drop in pitch at the end of a statement are common features of English phonology.

The stressed parts of an utterance may be of considerable significance in early language learning: important words are often stressed particularly in conversations with foreigners, infants and young children. Among the words most likely to be emphasized are nouns, verbs and adjectives, and these powerful language labels emerge frequently and very early in a child's first language learning among English speakers.

Phonology also describes and charts the possible varieties of speech sounds, for example, the pronunciation differences between speakers of the same language. In the social sphere this often ceases to be merely a matter of objective scientific description and the values, attitudes and plain prejudices that surround accents are returned to in the next chapter.

One of the most valuable achievements of modern phoneticians has been the gradual evolution of an International Phonetic Alphabet (IPA), which is used throughout the world to write down the sounds of any language and which is particularly useful in transcribing the speech of young children and infants.

The inclusion of phonology as a major element in modern grammars emphasizes the primacy of the spoken forms of language in modern linguistic science. However, it is important that ideas about 'phonetics' are not simply equated or confused with the study of phonology. Phonetics is closer to being a form of applied linguistics and focuses on the actual production of sounds by the physical vocal system. Knowledge about what the tongue, palate and vocal cords can do to shape the out-going breath can be used to help second, and subsequent, language learners articulate a new set of sounds. However, we might note here that rather partial and distorted versions of phonetic knowledge have also been applied to the teaching of reading for many years. This limited approach is how being replaced by carefully researched insights about young children's development of phonological awareness (Chapter 6).

Syntax

Syntax is that level of language concerned with words and the modification of their forms, such as adding '-s' for many plurals and '-ed' for some past tenses of verbs, as well as the organization of words in meaningfully ordered combinations. This is, of course, the area with which traditional prescriptive grammars were concerned, and some modern studies still use the word 'grammar' in a very specific way when referring to syntax only. Traditional views of syntax are still very influential in non-specialist discussion about grammar. For example, the following comments appeared in a serious daily newspaper: 'To deprive a child of grammar is to impose the same handicap as would be if he were left in ignorance of the multiplication tables.'[2] At this point we should note that this is a linguistically nonsensical claim expressed in pretentious and rather confusing syntax. A child – he *or* she – deprived of grammar, would not only be speechless but also incapable of communicating meanings by any other means.

Studies of syntax also highlight the possible variations within the same language that can exist in lexical items (vocabulary), word order, and ways of indicating tenses, possession, number, and so on. These meaningful grammatical varieties of a language are known as dialects and are discussed in the following chapter.

Modern approaches to grammar go well beyond naming the parts of a sentence at the surface level of who did what to whom. This concern to go beyond the rather linear surface descriptions of language at its most obvious takes us to the level of language known as semantics.

Semantics

Semantics is the study of meaning in a language and it touches on the most complex issues, even to the extent of bringing linguistics closer to a form of philosophy. At the simplest level, however, it is clear that meaning in language is partly derived from the syntax – the literal meaning of these words in this order: 'I am wearing a pink T-shirt'. On the other hand, an utterance's meaning can be clear in context but its literal meaning very strange. Thus a specific setting (for example, an early years classroom) makes the following extraordinary request perfectly meaningful: 'Would green table line up at the door, please?'

Semantics is also affected by historical changes in human relationships and circumstances, as well as changes in word usage and syntactic patterns. This only becomes obvious when we consider the dramatic changes in word meaning affecting such terms as 'nice', 'mistress', 'gay' or 'ain't'. Indeed, the chequered histories of these items are often only known to historical scholars and archivists, or students of literature and linguists.

There is a tendency for most people of a particular generation to believe that words and phrases have always meant what they currently mean. The complexity of semantics increases when we consider differing cultures and languages and realize that the same world can be categorized, labelled and described in many ways. Cultures even divide up the colour spectrum differently and they vary enormously in the ways in which they classify and name food, floor coverings and pets: one person's best friend can be another's dinner! However, meanings and acceptable translations are shaped and communicated across cultures far more frequently than these comments have suggested, but translations do require more conscious effort than everyday interactions in a setting of known and shared assumptions.

Language and Mind

The important point to remember about the complex sets of relationships and rules known as phonology, syntax and semantics is that they are all involved in the modern linguist's approach to describing the grammar of a language.

Furthermore, there is one very significant reason for asking educators to take a general interest in modern grammars: when linguists attempt to describe the grammar of a particular language, or make claims about the basic components of all human languages, they are trying to describe the human mind. Modern linguistics is, in essence, a tentative science of thinking and learning. It is tentative because it is not suggesting that it has any absolute answers. Indeed, the proliferation of modern grammars and the constant changes and modifications they all undergo point to the current state of flux in this frontier science. At this point the language forest is dense and at its most mysterious.

The boldest claims about language and the nature of the human mind have been made by the American linguist, Noam Chomsky, and, although his work has inspired a considerable body of research, it is still the subject of disagreements and counter-claims. Chomsky's approach is based on his view that some kind of universal grammar is genetically pre-programmed in the human mind. This claim implies that all human languages share some deep underlying similarities and these 'universals' are reflected in the individual's linguistic 'competence' or innate ability to use and understand language. It would be hard to dismiss this claim in the face of the remarkable acquisition of language by all infants in all times and in all cultures and countries. Barring appalling cruelty or massive physical impairment, babies become skilled linguistic communicators in the first two or three years of life, without professional structured teaching. Current research, now disseminated in a witty and informal style by Pinker (1994), supports this innate hypothesis with the bold claim that there is a 'language instinct' in the human species.

Of course, this innate linguistic disposition, originally described by Chomsky as a Language Acquisition Device (LAD), must be triggered into activity by the child's involvement in a particular social and linguistic world. This human-language context will be the determinant (in ways we do not yet fully understand) of the language choices that individual competence reveals. Chomsky has used the term 'performance' to describe the actual utterances and written manifestations that demonstrate our 'competence' in various languages. As individuals, even as linguists, none of us is able to analyse fully and describe all the rules and structures of our linguistic knowledge, but we use and operate this knowledge effectively and comparatively effortlessly. Indeed, linguists claim that our daily 'performances' are only a very partial reflection of our competence and this holds a salutary warning for carers and educators! It is all too easy to believe that children's linguistic performances in group settings and schools are the sum total of their competence. There is a body of educational research evidence that suggests that the early years group situation rarely taps as much of young children's linguistic competence as a routine day at home with an adult care-giver and siblings (Wells, 1981; Tizard and Hughes, 1984). This becomes a worrying issue as we move into an era of baseline assessment of children at the start of statutory schooling.

The two levels of competence and performance are closely reflected in Chomsky's grammatical descriptions of language structures and rules. For any sample of language, he describes both a surface structure, which is the spoken or written performance, and a deep structure of basic meanings and core ideas. Over the years he has worked on the problem of what connects the two levels:

that is, how are deep structures transformed into surface manifestations of linguistic performance? This search for satisfactory descriptions and explanatory models of the rules we all operate so successfully is at the forefront of current debates in linguistics, and well beyond the scope of this book.

- Language is rule-governed, it is organized, produced and made meaningful by the rules of grammar. A grammar is a set of rules that describe but do not prescribe language.
- Language is creative: we can put together the basic elements of sounds, words, meanings and letter symbols, according to the rules or grammar of the language, and produce an infinite number of original and appropriate utterances and written sentences.
- Modern grammars describe three major levels of language: phonology, syntax and semantics.
- Language is to some extent re-created by every infant, working on the above principles, and in interaction with more experienced language users.

Systems

According to most estimates, there are between 4,000 and 5,000 languages in use in the world – the wide margin of variability reflects the many complicated overlaps between discrete languages and dialects. But this amazing variety of spoken languages should not be allowed to obscure what they have in common. A language is a system for communicating meanings using the human vocal-auditory tract and verbal grammatical symbols. Rather than trying to define language in greater detail than this (a notoriously difficult task in any case), most linguists prefer to clarify its distinctive features. This is done by comparing it with other systems of signs.

Human verbal language is a systematic and symbolic means of communication and, as such, it shares some similarities with clothes, movement, music, graphic art, flowers and even food. All of these can be said to communicate symbolically: they convey messages by using varied means and objects that stand for whole ranges of feelings, meanings and values. Consider the following examples and their possible 'messages': a bunch of red roses; a president of the USA wearing a cowboy hat; and the painting by Picasso entitled 'Guernica'. Are the roses a declaration of love? Is the president linking himself and his office with the frontier spirit of the American dream? And was Picasso making an anti-war statement? The roses, the hat and the painting are not simply objects, they are more than they seem: they are cultural signs only fully understood within particular societies.

Semiotics and Signs

What of the more mundane objects and events that communicate – for example, international road signs, traffic lights, musical notation, the game of chess, mathematical signs, fish and chips, wrestling matches and horse racing? They too are signs and can be said to communicate messages just as subtly and precisely as the more obvious and well-known systems, such as the signing and touching used by the deaf and the blind. Signing is not merely a compensation of major sensory handicap – visual signing is relied on by people in many occupations. The daily work of auctioneers, television and radio producers, bookmakers, airport runway controllers, dancers and actors is based on elaborate and systematic gestures and body movements. The study of these cultural sign systems is called semiotics, or sometimes semiology. It studies a vast area of human activities including advertising and food, literature and fashion. In fact, any cultural phenomenon that has a systematic code whose meanings and relationships can be identified and analysed is grist to the semiotic mill! Some sign systems are fairly cross-cultural, for example, diagrams, pictures, chemical formulae, mathematical symbols, the movements of chess pieces on the board and musical notation. But other systems, such as gestures, clothes and food, are very specific to a culture and rely on intimate involvement and early socialization.

Even in a relatively small area such as Europe, the cultural differences in sign systems can lead to insults and misunderstandings about such apparently minor details as facial grimaces, hand gestures and the distance between speakers in face-to-face conversations. It is an interesting fact that the beaches of southern Europe are excellent places for observing and testing 'in the field' the cultural differences surrounding the business of personal body space. If you try the beach towel test you will become skilled at identifying some distinctive non-British characteristics, including an apparent lack of embarrassment at being immediately adjacent to, and even on, the towel of a complete stranger! On the other hand, how do British people cope with the enforced intimacy and body contacts of crowded rush-hour trains and buses? These cultural differences, particularly as they concern the systematic patterns for organizing proximity, relationships, food, clothes and pastimes, are the special concern of anthropologists and sociologists. But these studies are also related to linguistics, partly because of their common foundations in the structuralist theories established by Saussure. Structuralism is not the concern of this book, but its emphasis on studying the rules of the underlying systems of beliefs and communications that hold together groups and societies is – because language is one of those systems.

Human language has unique properties that linguistics aims to describe. Linguists study a range of nonverbal systems of communication (sounds, gestures, facial expressions, etc.) in order to clarify the unique characteristics of verbal language. In particular, they analyse the paralinguistic features that accompany the production of all verbal language: the prelinguistic communications between infants and their care-givers and the characteristics of animal communication systems (see below).

Nonverbal Communication
It is understandably easy to become fascinated by the communication systems of such social insects as bees and ants, or to become drawn into the controversies that regularly break out over the 'language' skills of chimpanzees or the intelligent messages exchanged by dolphins. So often the result is that one knows a great number of disconnected 'facts' about bees wagging their abdomens, dolphins clicking and chimps signing requests for drinks from the fridge, but one does not know why, or even if, this is relevant to language study.

Perhaps what is useful in these studies and of relevance to the non-specialist student of linguistics is their clarification of the differences between animal and human systems of communication. These differences actually highlight the unique features of human language.

Most modern commentators on language and animal communications rely on the comparative approach used by an American linguist, Charles Hockett. He based his analysis on thirteen design features, or characteristics, which he identified in spoken language (Hockett, 1960). Any system of communication under investigation can be compared with this checklist: a high score of positive similarities is taken to be indicative of a communication system that is like language. Disagreements and difficulties arise when individual design features are said to be present in various animal systems. While few of us would wish to claim that there is anything unique about the human use of sounds, even those created by the vocal-auditory channel, there really is something very dubious about the suggestion that bee dancing is productive or (as it is usually described) creative. Productivity in language is used to refer to the highly creative ability of humans to produce endlessly novel utterances and written sentences: the bee dance will always and only be about the source of nectar.

Some of us have similar problems with other items on the design-features list that are not considered unique to human language. An example would be 'arbitrariness', which refers to the total independence of the form of a signal from the reality or meaning it communicates. In other words, there is nothing horse-like about the word 'horse' and it could just as effectively be '*cheval*' or '*Pferd*'. Yet students of animal communication claim arbitrariness for the song of the lark and the calls of the gibbon. If there is some degree of arbitrariness in these examples, it is at a fairly low level, consisting of the genetically inherited pattern of a song or sets of calls for specific dangers and social contacts. This is hardly comparable to the 2-year-old child's vocabulary of words about animals, ideas, people and feelings, many of which the child has never encountered in reality.

With these comments on the power of human linguistic creativity and arbitrariness in mind, we can note that animal studies confirm other unique features of human language, notably cultural transmission and duality of patterning. Duality of patterning refers to the double layering of human language – the way in which our language sounds (which have no intrinsic meanings) are combined to create meaningful sets of sounds we recognize as words. Cultural transmission is a reminder that we are not born with a completely preprogrammed language system sufficient for a specific range of needs but that we have to learn our particular language or languages over a lengthy period of time in a language community.

Displacement is another very significant feature of human language and refers to our probably unique ability to communicate about events and things remote in space and time: the 'not here' and the 'not now'.

Finally, the unique nature of our grammatical competence should be emphasized again in this context. Our understanding of the internal structure of utterances and sentences – not at the surface level of numbers or words, but at the level of meaningfully linked components – cannot be found in any animal system. We understand, even if we cannot easily explain, the interrelationships of actors, actions and consequences in utterances and sentences. This complexity is true of all human languages: there are no primitive human languages.

Paralinguistics

Human verbal language is also closely linked to another range of communicative systems that exploit subtle and flexible uses of the voice and the body. Paralinguistics is the term for the great variety of phonetic features available to every speaker, features such as intonation, speed and quality of voice tone and the richly varied characteristics of accents. This system includes a range of noises, such as 'mm', 'uhu' and 'ah' that oil the wheels of conversation and assure speakers that they are being listened to and understood. In fact, these features form a special system known as phatic communication. This has particular importance in sustaining telephone communications: the phatic 'noises' used vary from culture to culture because they reflect the particular ranges of sounds that dominate or are favoured by specific languages.

We all know that the meanings conveyed by a particular utterance can be changed and varied by the skilled use of voice tone, speed and even accent switching. Thus a fairly bland statement can be laden with overtones of threat, irony, frivolity, gloom or erotic innuendo. Very few educators and carers need to be reminded of the power and subtlety of the human voice in group or classroom interactions and management. Similarly, most people who care for babies are aware of the great sensitivity with which infants respond to changes in emotional tone and pitch in adult voices.

Kinesics

We can also add another support system of nonverbal communicative signals to our use of the linguistic and paralinguistic: the huge range of body 'language'. This idiom is known as kinesics and includes facial expressions and head gestures, the use of the hands and arms when communicating, whole-body movements including walking and sitting and, of course, subtle judgements about distances between speakers and the rules for touching others. It would be difficult to over-estimate the importance for interpreting meanings, moods and responses of our reliance on the body messages we receive from our conversational partners, or large groups and audiences.

Again, educators are experts at reading the silent language of dropped eye contact, smiles and frowns, head nods, slouched bodies and fidgety hands and feet (Hall, 1973). However, it is equally certain that infants and children of school age are also experts at reading the kinesic messages given out, quite involuntarily, by their parents, minders and teachers. These systems are very much a matter of culture and, although they exist in all language communities, they vary enormously. The potential for offence is great, and our spontaneous responses may sometimes need a little conscious thought and modification in multicultural communities, group settings and schools. In fact, it is quite difficult to bring these subtle systems to conscious awareness, as we are often only aware of them when they are disrupted by infringements of particular cultural norms.

Clearly, these human nonverbal communication systems have some relevance for educators because they are major ways of conveying messages in group settings and classrooms, from children to adults and from adults to children. But these systems are also of great significance for students of first language acquisition in infancy. It now seems fairly clear that the paralinguistic and kinesic idioms are established in earliest infancy, long before speech. The significant features of this preverbal communication in most British and American cultures are the establishment of eye contact as a preliminary to interactive talk and play; the placing of gaps or pauses in the adult's talk so that the child can potentially be drawn in; the use by the adult of rather exaggerated intonation and stress patterns; and the adult use of body tickling, bouncing, bold gestures and rather dramatic facial expressions.

It is clear that much of this elaborate use of paralinguistic and kinesic behaviour by the adult partner is natural and unselfconscious, and that it tends to break down in embarrassment if commented on by observers. Something of this very heightened used of nonverbal systems is also noticeable in the interactions of professional carers and educators with very young children.

- Human language is a system for communicating meanings using the vocal-auditory tract and verbal grammatical symbols.
- Language can be compared with other cultural, communicative systems of symbols, such as music, clothes, road signs, mathematics and food.
- The general study of all these cultural systems of signs and symbolic communications is known as semiotics.
- Human language is developed on an earlier foundation of nonverbal signs and communicative strategies: the paralinguistic, involving voice tone, pitch and emphasis, and the kinesic, which includes the whole area of body language.

Teaching and Learning Suggestions

* Collect examples of signs and logos to bring into the classroom/setting (use photographs where appropriate and include different languages and dialect forms).

* Take the children on sign and print hunting walks. Follow up with displays and plenty of talk and language play and experiments (such as creating their own names, signs, logos, notices and banners).

* Share published nonsense verse with the children and help them create and record their own versions (on tape, written down, bound into books). Let everyone (adults and children) become familiar with the 'almost meaningful' nonsense language structures of verses such as ''Twas brillig, and the slithy toves/Did gyre and gimble in the wabe;' or terms like 'Reeling and Writhing' (Carroll, 1872; 1865). How does this work? How can we make up our own versions?

*Read *The BFG* (Dahl, 1982) and work out the language system of the giants. Use it for extending the story or creating a class/group BFG dictionary.

* How do dictionaries work and why do we use them? Create flexible loose-leaf dictionaries with index cards or postcards (based on the children's queries and interests).
* Use the spell check on a computer wordprocessing program. How has it been organized and what must you know to be able to use it?
* How could we begin to help a space alien understand our language/ languages?

Notes

1. For part of this summary, I have drawn on Jonathan Culler's introduction to *Course in General Linguistics* (Saussure, 1974).
2. This comment is attributed to Lord Beloff in *The Daily Telegraph*, 15 February 1988, p. 14.

Further Reading

Aitchison, J. (1996) *The Seeds of Speech. Language origin and evolution*, Cambridge University Press.

Aitchison, J. (1997) *The Language Web. The power and problem of words*, Cambridge University Press.

Crystal, D. (1987; 1997) *The Cambridge Encyclopedia of Language*, Cambridge University Press.

Crystal, D. (1995) *The Cambridge Encyclopedia of the English Language*, Cambridge University Press.

Pinker, S. (1994) *The Language Instinct. The new science of language and mind*, Penguin Press, Harmondsworth.

Yule, G. (1985; 1996) *The Study of Language*, Cambridge University Press.

2

Sociolinguistics: language and cultures

Language is not an abstract construction of the learned, or of dictionary makers, but is something arising out of the work, needs, ties, joys, affections, tastes, of long generations of humanity, and has its bases broad and low, close to the ground.

Walt Whitman[1]

Although the scientific and detached studies of the descriptive linguists generate many models of language, they carefully exclude most 'close-to-the-ground' considerations. In contrast, those sociolinguists who study the language worlds of communities, homes, factories and schools reveal the indisputably chameleon-like characteristics of human languages. Remarkable variety and continuous change are the norms, not just between languages but within language communities. This fact alone adds further layers of linguistic subtlety and complexity to any discussion of language. Sociolinguists have always countered the more abstract constructions of the 'pure' linguists with their own richly diverse accounts of the relationships between languages and cultures. This chapter is a professional educator's summary of the ways in which language variety and change are usually described, but even this limited approach must include some consideration of the social and personal value systems involved. Any account of the human contexts in which language occurs must try to reflect as vividly as possible the complex interweaving of values, prestige, power and individual identity.

Language Variety

The topic of language variety can be discussed in two ways: first, in terms of the practices of distinct language communities and, second, in terms of personal and idiosyncratic usage. We might call these the macro- and the micro-dimensions of linguistic variation. The macro-linguistic dimension reveals the huge number of human languages that exist as well as the immense variation found within any one apparently uniform language community. The micro-linguistic dimension emphasizes the highly individual nature of language use, including the operation of different styles and linguistic choices. At the macro-linguistic level, in any speech community variety comes from two sources: the 'broad' and 'low' bases of accent and dialect.

Accents and Dialects

Accents

Accent refers simply to matters of pronunciation: the sound qualities of the language as it is shaped and articulated by a speaker. Discussions and mild disagreements about English phonology tend to focus on such differences as the sounded length of the vowel '*a*' in '*bath*', '*path*' and '*class*'. This well-known variant is associated with a north–south geographical divide, the short '*a*' sound being commonly used from the Midlands northwards and the long '*a*' being a typically southern form.

However, geography is not the only explanation for accent variation in Britain: social class and notions of educated speech complicate the picture. Our voices are the immediate and most obvious indicators of our origins because in infancy we begin by speaking and sounding like those around us. However, regional accents are subjected to the most extraordinary non-linguistic judgements: basically, personal likes and dislikes.

We are all aware of, or have even been the victims of, the many guardians of linguistic standards who express strong disapproval of such characteristics as the dropping of sounds at the ends of words in casual rapid speech. Similarly, the glottal-stop feature found in London dialects that replaces the sound '*t*' in such words as '*butter*' and '*bottle*', is regularly condemned. And the dilemma about when and when not to sound the initial 'h' in many words can make fools of us all!

A cool and unemotional appraisal of these kinds of issues reveals some interesting facts. For example, the pedantic sounding of all terminal sounds would make many English utterances slow, cumbersome and stilted. Indeed, many other languages feature regularly unsounded terminal letters. The juxtaposition of words in English utterances affects phonetic patterns and ease of articulation, frequently resulting in the dropping of terminal sounds. Try listening for the final '*t*' sound in '*last*' when it is part of an everyday expression such as 'that's the *last* straw!' The relative pleasantness, ease or even feasibility involved in the physical production of the sounds of a language are significant factors in the spoken form.

However, ease is only one among many elements: some apparently very difficult sounds, such as clicks, glottal stops and the English '*th*', are standard features of particular languages and dialects and 'natural' to their speakers. The glottal stop is much maligned by some speakers of standard British English, yet it is a distinctive standard feature of the German language. As for the dropping of the initial aspirated 'h' in English, it can be a sign of aristocratic birth as well as of working-class origins.

All these strange contradictions indicate that careless pronunciation or even phonological limitations are *not* the major issues in discussing accents. Social judgements and cultural myths are usually being aired. Undoubtedly we hear the voices of the people we meet – children and adults – through a heavy curtain of cultural beliefs, personal experiences and social values. It is not surprising that in the course of their lives many individuals effect a blurring or weakening of their localized accents until they approximate to a more standard and prestigious variety. These changes are influenced and facilitated by such life experiences as extended education, membership of the professions, social-class mobility and personal ambition.

The most prestigious accent in the UK is Received Pronunciation (RP), and it is also associated with the most influential dialect, Standard English (SE). These two special cases of variety will be discussed in the context of power and influence in language issues, as well as in the following discussion of dialect. Before moving on to consider dialect, it is important to re-emphasize the emotionally charged and value-laden nature of our responses to the sounds of voices. All kinds of feelings and prejudices may be aroused simply by the sounds of vowels and consonants. The accents of our childhood can evoke powerful memories of warmth or community, but their reception by others at a later stage may have caused us either to exaggerate or to modify them. We may even have changed and rejected them completely.

Dialects

Dialects are usually associated with specific geographical regions and, therefore, involve the use of regional accents. The concept of dialect regions is complex and variable (see Trudgill, 1994). We may find that sociolinguists are referring to areas as vast as the USA, or as specific as the city of Norwich or the Harlem district of New York. However, the notion of dialect is clear and is not restricted to the sounds of a phonological system. A dialect is a true variety of a language and it includes distinctive vocabulary and syntax systems.

We are usually first aware of a dialect because of the lexical choices speakers, and sometimes writers, make, for example, 'bairn' and 'greetin'', 'mither' and 'flit', 'faucet' and 'pocketbook'. The regular use of the previous examples would identify speakers of Scottish English, Lancashire dialect and American English, respectively. The differences in syntax, such as the order of words in utterances and sentences and different ways of marking plurals, tenses and agreements are not always so obvious. However, some very distinctive forms of syntax are widely recognized: 'I kinda gotten used to' from the USA or the British variants, 'I dinna ken' and 'Tha's a reet proper good un'.

Dialects are regular, rule-governed systems of language and, just as it is impossible to speak at all without an accent, so it is impossible to speak without using a dialect. We are all dialect speakers and we all have accents. Judgements, preferences and views about these dialects and accents are social and cultural features of language in use, but not purely linguistic facts.

The issues become even more complicated when we take account of the influence on British English of two high-status language variants. In the matter of accent there is Received Pronunciation (RP). Outside linguistic circles it has been known variously as Queen's English, a public-school accent and even BBC English. Most of my own young pupils neatly summarized it as 'talking posh'. The RP accent no longer reflects any geographical origins but it still has considerable social and political power and, in combination with Standard English (SE), has been called a 'class dialect' (Edwards, 1976, p. 47).

The really posh or affected form of RP appears to have lost favour in recent years and been abandoned by the BBC. It can only be heard amongst the older generation of royalty, certain politicians and senior military and public-school 'types'. Contemporary RP is still an establishment accent, suggesting a decent education while retaining some slight traces of regional affiliations. The accents of those who have experienced lengthy post-secondary-level education, entered the professions or the higher managerial levels of business and industry tend to be modified in the direction of RP by neutralizing any strongly localized sounds.

RP is the accent usually associated with the prestigious dialect of SE, but it is very important to understand that this dialect may be spoken with a range of accents. This fact is demonstrated by radio and television broadcasting: programmes of news, current affairs and the arts are now presented by speakers using SE dialect in a wide variety of regional accents. Apparently, many presenters are able to enhance their own personal popularity, as well as the programme ratings, because of their appealing accents, be they east London, southern Irish or Cumbrian. The appeal or otherwise of accents is an issue that will be returned to in the next section, but the dialect of SE dominates broadcast media, the printed forms of the language and education, where it is a statutory requirement in the National Curriculum. It is also the dialect taught to foreigners and to British children and their families who have a different first language. These important uses of SE indicate that the prestige of the variety springs from its significant social and cultural functions rather than from any inherent linguistic superiority.

It is not difficult to see that in a complex democratic society, command of one fairly standard form of the language is important for unambiguous national communications, access to information and education and full individual independence and participation in the community. This does not mean that SE is the best dialect for all of us, for all purposes and all personal needs, although for some groups and individuals it may well be their first dialect. Nor should any discussion of the National Curriculum requirements for SE be confused with a notion that it is feasible or desirable to teach children to speak with RP accents.

Idiolects and Registers

Idiolects

If variety is the norm at the macro-level of world languages and the diverse forms within them, it is certainly the case at the micro-level of individual language use. Just as there is a multitude of world languages, so there are as many different ways of using language personally as there are individuals in a language community. This may seem a wild claim but we each have a unique way or ways with our language or languages. This individual linguistic style is called 'idiolect' and is made up of the very slight differences in phonology, syntax and vocabulary that are normal in individuals and give us our instant linguistic identity among family, friends and acquaintances. Ironically, these different personal language styles are what the professional linguists must observe and collect in order to produce their objective summaries of a language. Dialect descriptions are generalized hypotheses about a collection of idiolects – but the situation becomes even more complicated than this!

Within our own idiolect range we all switch language styles and this again includes changes in phonology, vocabulary and syntax. Many people use at least two distinct dialects and many are operating two or more distinctive languages. This bilingual feature will be looked at separately but the regular use of more than one dialect has already been implied in the comments on SE dialect. Children and adults whose home or regional dialect differs from SE still hear it on the media, they read it and see it in books, newspapers and other written materials. Children also see, hear and read SE in group settings and schools and become expert at negotiating the dialect switches involved in moving between nurseries, playgroups, classrooms, playgrounds, streets and homes. But such complex and yet effortless switches are not restricted to those whose schools and homes are culturally and linguistically different worlds. Our daily lives and language contacts involve a great variety of thoughts, actions and responses that are handled in appropriately different ways and linguistic styles.

Registers

There are no single-style speakers in any dialect and we all have a wide repertoire of sociolinguistic responses. These ideas are usually described in terms of 'communicative competence' (Hymes, 1971) which is one of the central concepts in modern sociolinguistics. The theory states that grammatical competence alone is not an adequate way of explaining the linguistically appropriate ways in which we respond to a total social and cultural situation, as we perceive and categorize it. We differentiate our ways of speaking according to the who, where, when and how. This kind of communicative competence is specific to cultures and societies and their differing value systems, but the end result is that competent communicators anywhere employ a wide range of linguistic styles.

These styles, which are tied to certain situations and activities, are usually called 'registers' and can range from the very formal to the very casual. For example, a meal can be announced in a range of registers and the possible settings may be easily guessed. 'Dinner is served.' 'Would you like to sit down now?' 'We can eat now.' 'You must be starving!' 'Grub up!' 'Come and get it!' 'Get stuck in!' 'Eat!' In this array of registers there are subtle indications of differing power relationships between the speakers and their audiences. Registers are usually indicators of interpersonal relationships, status and power. Thus we find that there are different but appropriate registers operating in talk between teachers and pupils, and doctors and patients, etc. Social settings call for varied registers and people switch styles as they move between homes, schools, factories, etc.

Amongst our repertoires of registers all of us will be able to call on some elements of that extremely informal style known as slang. On the whole slang tends to rely on a special range of vocabulary, for example, 'cool', 'laid back' and 'bread' taken from the world of jazz. Similarly, a few set phrases can be typical of a slang, as in the 'OK, yah?' of the Sloane Ranger social set. The world of jazz and the world of the Sloane are a reminder that slang is usually closely tied to a place and a life-style, and has also been at times synonymous with racy street language.

Slang can be ephemeral and easily dates over-enthusiastic users who fail to move with the times. We probably cringe now at a 'gosh' or a 'wizard prang' but some slang does enter the fairly permanent stock of the language. Perhaps this status has been achieved by such terms as 'super', 'OK', 'sleaze' and 'wally'. Slang is not a modern deviation from some golden age of language – it has always been used and recorded by historians, diarists, novelists and amateur and professional linguists. Furthermore, it is ordinary evidence of the vitality and creativity of language in daily use. Just as we delight in the linguistic inventiveness of very young children, we can savour in slang the language play of adults, particularly young adults. Slang is often richest and most diverse in youthful subcultures. It is exemplified by the following creative and witty comments arising from a fast-living, car-based life-style: 'Let's have a little glass action, man, squeeze the breeze' (close the car window, USA).

However, there is a darker side to slang: it has always been used to mask activities involving crime and violence. When slang is a secret criminal language it is called 'argot', and many claim that one of the most famous slang dialects, Cockney, began as an argot used by London's criminal underworld. The traditional use of rhyming slang requires reference to just the non-rhyming half of the word pair. Thus, only those in the know would understand the intended meaning of 'Wash your boat and put your titfer on. We'll 'ave a butchers at me old China'. Cockney is now more accurately described as a social-class dialect rather than an argot or a slang.

One other language register frequently confused with slang is jargon. Again, most of us have some jargon in our repertoires and we use it appropriately. There are hints of criticism and disapproval in most references to jargon but it can be a useful linguistic tool. Jargon tends to come into a language as new technologies, occupations and pastimes enter and permeate the society. Some of the vocabulary and phrases are ephemeral but others achieve wide currency. Like slang, jargon is a source of enrichment and creative usage, and we would all be linguistically diminished by the loss of some contributions from space exploration, information technology, science, medicine and the media, to name but a few sources.

The jargon of occupations and professions also fulfils a very positive role. 'Talking shop' enables us to communicate efficiently and accurately with our colleagues and can be absolutely vital in the context of hospital operating theatres, airport control towers and the factory floor. It is just as important, if a little less dramatic, in educational settings when we talk of 'fours in Reception', 'special needs childen', 'concrete experiences', 'emergent writing' and 'KS ones'. There is, however, a negative side to jargon and this probably gives it a bad name. When jargon is persistently used, often outside the appropriate setting in which it makes good sense, it functions as a barrier to exclude outsiders. 'Talking shop' then becomes a way of intentionally limiting communication to a chosen few. Although it certainly enhances their sense of group solidarity, it tends to infuriate outsiders.

- Language variety is reflected in the different languages of the world but it is also a feature within apparently uniform language communities.

- Two major aspects of variety within a language are accent and dialect. Accent refers solely to differences in pronunciation – the sounds of a spoken language. Dialect is a variety of a language with distinctive variations in syntax and vocabulary, as well as pronunciation.
- Standard English is the high-status dialect of English that is used in the written form of the language. It is also used widely in business and professional circles, the media, education and the teaching of English as a foreign language. Standard English dialect may be spoken with any accent.
- Received Pronunciation is a prestigious non-regional accent associated with prolonged education and, traditionally, the public-school system, Oxbridge and the BBC.
- Variety is also found in every individual's linguistic repertoire because we all switch registers, changing the degrees of formality in our language, according to the perceived social context. Individuals use a variety of other forms, including other dialects, slang and jargon. We all develop a unique idiolect that makes our voices and language styles instantly recognizable.

Power and Influence

The old advertising slogan, 'how to win friends and influence people', is still a useful tool in the hands of those who take advantage of the networks of power and influence that permeate language use in Britain. Think of the so-called language teachers who promote their services on the front pages of many daily newspapers, for example, 'Why Are You Shamed By Your Mistakes In English?' Or those who run elocution classes in aspiring middle-class areas, often in association with dance and drama instruction. The private speech teachers and the steady output of magazine articles, books and audio-tapes that claim to be able to increase our word power, our influence over others and our business and social success are evidence of the power of social judgements about language.

With respect to children and education, it is clear that one of the 'good things' families buy when they pay for their children's education in private schools is fluency in 'good English'. Evaluative judgements of this kind about English have little place in purely linguistic descriptions of the many varieties of English. However, British people do understand and use such phrases as 'good English' or 'talking properly' and they know that these expressions refer to SE spoken with an RP accent, although not necessarily a posh or affected form. The decent education suggested by the consistent use of RP and spoken SE is often synonymous with private schooling or a State schooling topped off with an Oxbridge degree. These comments run the risk of being dismissed as unfounded generalizations, but there is something to be said for accepting the existence of linguistic prejudices and distortions (see Andersson and Trudgill, 1990), noting their operations and their power and evolving clear and principled responses to their influence.

There is some irony in the fact that, as the prescriptive tradition in linguistics has been weakened (if not fully replaced) by a more scientific descriptive approach (see Chapter 1), its influence in the social and cultural spheres has not diminished. Yet it is in the daily use of spoken and written language throughout society and in many influential institutions that people's life chances may be deeply affected: 'Although public discrimination on the grounds of race, religion and social class is not now publicly acceptable, it appears that discrimination on linguistic grounds *is* publicly acceptable, even though linguistic differences may themselves be associated with ethnic, religious and class differences' (Milroy and Milroy, 1985, p. 3).

It is the case that people still fail to obtain jobs, accommodation or even places in higher education because the sounds of their accents and the dialects they use trigger in others immediate reactions that equate some voices with stupidity, dishonesty, lawlessness, poverty and the general condemnation expressed as 'common'. The fact that these judgements are direct reflections of power and status, and not inherent in accents and dialects as such, is obvious because they occur when the weaker partner, the applicant, speaks a low-status language variety. If you have become a successful employer, property owner or college principal you can be as broadly Cockney or Glaswegian as you choose, within the limits of intelligibility. This now happens in the broadcast media where the whole irrationality of it becomes obvious. A very popular and highly paid chat-show host, or disc jockey, can use a low-status, east-London accent and dialect but a female newsreader with a Scottish accent speaking SE is subjected to a torrent of abusive and complaining letters!

Most people cope with these types of situations by becoming bi-dialectal in their professional and personal lives and making the necessary switches according to the current state of the particular power game in which they find themselves. This means that if we are not native speakers of SE dialect, we may choose to add it to our spoken repertoire and use it in those situations where our home dialect may put us at some social, political or cultural disadvantage. In practice this is what many of us do, but some sociolinguists would deplore this on ideological grounds and urge us to set about changing the attitudes of society. In the long term this may well be the aim of all informed and concerned linguists, academics, lawyers, politicians, employers, and so forth. But educators have a professional commitment in the present to the children and young people who are in schools and group settings now. The professional educator not only works towards the futures of all our children but must also have a response and a policy for next Monday morning. It is for this reason that the role of the SE dialect in education must be clarified.

Standard English

In 1988 the National Curriculum English Working Group set out some perceptive general principles for educational policies on Standard English (DES, 1988b, pp. 13–16), emphasizing the sensitive nature of the issues. In 1995 the relation between language and social or national identity was again at the centre of the controversial decision to require the teaching of SE at all four Key Stages of the revised National Curriculum. However, in these requirements there is a linguistically unsound emphasis on the social 'importance' of SE and on the implication that it alone uses distinctive vocabulary and rules of grammar. The richness of dialects and other languages are only remarked on in terms of the contribution they can make to pupils' knowledge and understanding of SE. There are more significant principles to consider, as the original

1988 paper indicated. First, there is the issue of access to SE: children have an undoubted entitlement to learn to use the standard form. This argument rests on the role of the standard variety as the common and shared communicative and cultural basis of British society, particularly in its public, commercial, industrial, professional and educational spheres. The role of SE extends beyond the UK and its competent users have automatic access to a world language.

This reasonable claim for access to SE for all children raises the question of how this is to be organized and taught in educational settings. The dilemma can only be successfully resolved by the establishment of a second principle, one well grounded in linguistic knowledge about dialects. SE must be learnt and taught in ways that do not denigrate the non-standard dialects spoken by many children and adults. Educators need to be aware of the powerful symbolic and emotional charge non-standard dialects carry. They also need to recognize the damaging impact on children, their families and their communities of a too-premature or forceful imposition of SE in group settings and schools. Early-childhood educators need to be particularly sensitive to the confusion, distress and lack of progress an excessive zeal for standard forms in talking and writing may produce. Much older children can choose if, when, and how they will use SE in their lives, because they are able to judge its limitations and its power and set it alongside their home dialects as yet another option. Very young children are emotionally and socially vulnerable and experience language forms as intimately bound up with the people who use them. At its most positive, this is revealed when they are playing and dramatizing roles and they slip easily into talking as a posh or pompous person, or even imitate the ways in which their carers and teachers tell stories or deliver reprimands. An amazing command of SE is frequently demonstrated on these occasions!

Teaching SE in schools is most fruitfully and positively focused on the teaching of the written form. This constitutes a third principle: SE is the language of non-regional public communication and children need to be able to communicate and have control over their lives beyond the limits of family and local culture. This aspect of political and democratic power may be years away from small children in playgroups, nurseries and primary schools, but the foundations of literacy are laid in the early years. We all learn a new form of the language when we begin to read and write and this gives a sensible, shared focus for literacy in the early years. The written SE dialect can be taught well without undermining children's pride and involvement in the personal and cultural worlds of family, faith and race. Indeed, families and local communities look to the schools to advance their children's literacy; they also teach them many things about reading and writing themselves and they take a pride in their children's early mastery of literacy.

If insisting on the use of spoken SE at all times can be a dangerous game, how much more so is rash interference with accents. Regional and class accents are intimately bound up with early infancy, personal identity and community. Furthermore, the complexities of phonology are such that any artifically imposed changes may be totally negative in their effects. We choose to vary our accents, we choose to sound like the people we admire or wish to be associated with and, conversely, we can use our accents as clear markers of resistance or dissent. It has already been noted that accents are often the focus for extraordinary and instant sets of prejudices, assumptions and aesthetic judgements. Nowhere is this more so than when the accent indicates foreign origins or non-British varieties of English. The totally unpleasant nature of these discriminations can be appreciated if we contrast the generally positive status accorded to some European accents, for example, French or Spanish, with responses to Asian or Chinese accents. Racism and prejudice are often linked with ignorance, fear and competition for limited resources such as wealth, good housing and education. In the USA, a Spanish accent is frequently linked with deprivation of all these good things and provokes some very negative responses. This is in marked contrast to positive British feelings about Spanish accents: they can evoke the passionate Latin temperament, images of cities like Seville and Granada, as well as the glorious Iberian climate! We have come a long way from pronunciation to Spanish holidays but the implications are clear. People's initial responses to each other are strongly influenced by the feelings, assumptions, experiences and ideas they attach to certain dialects and accents.

Language and Gender

The complicated issues of discrimination and bias have also been linked with language and gender studies in recent years. It has long been known that in many cultures there are differences in the language forms used by women and men. In English language cultures and in the West generally, these differences are stylistic tendencies rather than clear language varieties. However, they can still be identified by ordinary native speakers. The spoken language of women has tended to be closer to prestige dialects and women's accents may also move closer to high-status accents in public situations. The impression is that women speak 'nicely' in their social contacts, even if they are not speakers of high-status varieties by regional or social-class origin. This is further reinforced by the general absence of swear words and taboo references in women's habitual talk.

Some observations of women's talk have also suggested a greater use of tentative and deferential forms: 'If you don't mind . . . ?' 'Would you like to . . . ?' 'Is it alright if . . . ?' But these tendencies are fairly general and they can be true of the weak, the insecure and the dominated of either sex. The language forms mainly associated with women can be seen as the appropriate deferential responses of any powerless group. Until recently it appeared that women regularly used these subservient forms rather than resisting by exaggerating their non-standard and low-status varieties, or choosing positive and even aggressive language. The reasons for this are not linguistic but reflect social training and habitual roles. Women appear to be very status conscious: they tend to 'set a good example' to the children they are raising. Furthermore, their own earlier socialization may have emphasized that low-status, aggressive or rude language is masculine and tough. Feminine language must be nice and docile.

However, this state of linguistic affairs is changing and the tendencies mentioned here are lessening rapidly, particularly among women who are employed and in the younger generations of women and girls generally. This points to the really important factor: language reflects and also emerges out of social practices and situations, not genetic sex differences.

Gender issues are also very obvious in the linguistic area of word choices in texts and the conventional and unthinking use of the written language system. These issues have particular significance in education and the teaching of literacy, and should be the focus of a continuous, sensible and sensitive consciousness-raising approach. This applies to apparently unintentional bias as well as to specifically sexist usage. The matters to be addressed have received considerable attention in recent years but should still be in the forefront of the concerns of thoughtful language users and educators. Careless and frequent references to 'mankind' or 'the history of man' may not be as sex neutral as is traditionally claimed, particularly for young and unsophisticated early readers, viewers and listeners. Also, do we need to be made a little uncomfortable about always automatically writing 'men and women' rather than 'women and men'? Some real changes in awareness are beginning to affect the use of such terms as chairman, postman and paperboy, but spoken and written references to barristers, consultants and professors often assume the appropriateness of the male pronoun, without first verifying the gender of the individual.

The use of the allegedly neutral male personal pronoun in the written forms has now been questioned so much that authors have to provide a gender disclaimer. But is this good enough? Sensitive usage adopts the plural 'they' whenever possible, or carefully specifies her or him, she or he, hers or his.

The books schools and group settings use carry considerable status and approval, so great care needs to be exercised over the messages texts and images carry about all forms of discrimination. With respect to gender, educators are now very much aware of the attitudes conveyed by narratives, photographs and illustrations. There has been a long tradition of reading primers that featured boys helping fathers service the car while girls helped mothers to wash dishes and make beds. Such obvious stereotypes are easily identified in readers, but other textbooks and teaching materials that use drawings, photographs and apparatus need to be examined carefully. We must always ask, 'Where are the women and girls? What are they doing and saying?'

Schools and individual teachers also have to deal with attitudes that mainly associate art, literacy, books and sensitive or caring responses with girls and women, while such areas as mathematics, science, technology, physical courage and boisterousness are the prerogative of men and boys. These attitudes or prejudices are often deeply rooted in certain social classes and ethnic groups and will only be modified by a long process of reasoned challenges, caring attitudes and continuous talk between schools, families and their communities. Policies and provision in early years settings should continue to emphasize male/female cooperation, raise gender awareness and challenge stereotypes (Minns, 1991), while also seeking imaginative alternatives to practices and deeply-held beliefs which devalue girls and restrict the literacy achievements of boys. These brief comments can only indicate once again that gender bias, like many other prejudices, is not primarily a language problem: language only reflects and perpetuates existing social attitudes.

- The topic of language variety is bound up with sociocultural values and judgements about people as much as about identifiable linguistic features.

Language variety reflects individual and group identity and loyalties, because it originates in geographical regions and close-knit communities.

- The SE dialect and the RP accent are high-status because of their links with education, wealth and power in British society.
- Children have an entitlement to learn to use SE, particularly in the formal written mode, because it gives them access to national and international culture, education, democratic autonomy and employment.
- The teaching of SE in schools must respect children's home dialects and be sensitive to the social and developmental needs of young children.
- Language and gender studies highlight the links between power and language use in a community. Typically submissive female language is not genetically ordained – it is the language of the insecure and dominated.
- In educational contexts great care must be given to avoiding written and spoken language forms that appear to marginalize or ignore girls and women.

Language Change

In the light of all the language varieties that have been discussed so far, it is not surprising to find that change as well as difference is the normal state of affairs in any language. Most of us are fairly sensitive to the changes that have occurred in our own first-language lifetimes: we are aware of subtle differences in the language of old films and we may even sense that our grandparents' generation talk and use written language differently. In the case of English literature, we see and hear remarkable changes in Chaucer's, Shakespeare's and Pinter's language. Historical linguistics has always studied languages as they change over generations and centuries, but this perspective has now been somewhat superseded by an interest in studying the subtle, ongoing processes of change in progress in contemporary language communities. The disciplines of psychology, sociology and media studies are used in modern linguistics to support the claim that human languages are in a constant state of change.

Change in language is mainly associated with the vocabulary and pronunciation of the spoken form because these features are so easily noticed; however, change affects other aspects of a language, such as semantics and syntax. The following discussion outlines some major sources of change and their effects, mainly concentrating on the nature of changes at national and group level.

However, some linguists would claim that even individual language-learning experiences and histories are a part of language change and modification. The misunderstandings, mishearings and mis-analyses of the beginner in a language group are a source of variations sometimes retained in families and groups. Most of the non-standard sound patterns (past tenses and plurals or misunderstood word meanings) are gradually corrected but, in certain social situations, fluent speakers may switch to a lisped pronunciation, a 'foreign' accent, a babyish word or an ungrammatical plural or word order. Families frequently preserve and use some expressive features of their children's first language experiments, for example, 'mapple' (apple) and 'cufflink' (Catholic). Even academics take over and preserve rather literal non-English translations, such as 'writerly' and 'readerly', because they are so useful and right for their purposes.[2] But these are very minor features of change and more closely related to human linguistic playfulness and social sensitivity than the kinds of changes that affect a whole language community.

Major Sources of Language Change

New technologies

The arrival of new inventions and the influences of new forms of mass communication lead to a sudden increase in the numbers of new words in a language. The effect in terms of vocabulary is particularly noticeable with respect to nouns and verbs. But words are not mere labels and the new terminologies provide ways of thinking about and using the new concepts involved in areas as diverse as psychoanalysis, space exploration, television and environmental issues, etc. Some of these ideologies and technologies seem nearer to our daily concerns than others, but their concepts provide metaphors that pervade our language and our thinking.

It is interesting to note the everyday occurrence of terms that already distance us from our parents' and grandparents' generations, for example, 'inferiority complex', 'countdown', 'lift off', 'close-up', 'panning', 'number crunching', 'on disc', 'zap', 'software', 'media hype', 'cloning', 'test tube baby', 'the greenhouse effect' and the use of 'wicked' as a term of approval. One publication (Ayto, 1989) is attempting to record these additions on an annual basis and its compilers highlight the current political and social influences language change reflects. The compilers indicate that the late 1980s will come to be 'dated' by such usages as 'big bang', 'yuppy', 'dependency culture', 'mergerites' and 'lager louts'. All these additions to English are not fully established and we can still argue and disagree about their exact meanings, their origins and even their unsettled spellings. The new edition of Fowler's *Modern English Usage* (Burchfield, 1996) indicates the constant state of flux which is the normal state of the living language. This is a salutary reminder to us all that languages are living, changing and partly provisional: they are not as rigid, sacred or immemorially true and perfect as is sometimes suggested by a few teachers and many policy-makers and textbooks.

Group loyalties

The idea that languages are responsive to and shaped by the needs of their speakers brings us to a consideration of group identity as a source of language change. Within a single language community (although the concept of 'single' will have to be greatly modified in the next section), the various social, economic and regional groups or classes use varieties of the main language. These varieties are the dialects discussed earlier and their distinctive grammatical forms and vocabularies are the means by which their speakers assert and maintain their group loyalties and identities. Group dialects also include such specialized registers as argots and slang and some of their variations in syntax and lexis also enter the general usage of the greater language community. Clearly, it does not do to become too solemn about careless slang ruining the language: after all, 'pram', 'buggy' and 'car' are today's standard words but they were slang only a few generations ago.

Group solidarity also provides us with good evidence for the changes in phonology that occur in a language. The subtle changes and value judgements associated with accents are very interesting in that they reveal two different and opposed tendencies. Furthermore, this aspect of sociolinguistics has been well researched and the evidence is substantial (Trudgill, 1974, 1978; Milroy and Milroy, 1985; Aitchison, 1991). Accent change in a language community can be said, in a social-class sense, to pull two ways. First, there is the more generally known tendency for speakers with a low-status accent to shift closer to standard or high-status features of pronunciation when talking to speakers with a 'superior' accent. This has been observed among female sales staff in New York department stores (Labov, 1966) and it was confirmed in street interviews with members of the public in Norwich (Trudgill, 1974). This suggests that it is a rather conscious decision and such examples may reflect a bid for prestige in certain social contexts, or even a general admiration and envy of the life-style and affluence of those who habitually use high-status pronunciation patterns. When we are involved in the one-sided social situation of a formal telephone call, many of us tend to make a bid for instant prestige by greatly exaggerating, and even introducing, RP features in our voices. Over time, many of these changes in accent cease to be careful shifts and become subconscious matters of fine tuning in appropriate social settings.

However, in careful and planned speaking there are instances when the process is reversed and the change is from the high-prestige to the low-prestige accent. The paradox here is that, for certain social and cultural reasons, a low-status accent can become so admired and indicative of success that people want to imitate it. There was a time when the influence of the Beatles elevated the scouse dialect and accent to a status they have never quite lost. Every university common room and college hall of residence seemed to be full of people trying to replace their RP vowels and consonants with the Mersey sound. Now, highly-educated and middle-class youngsters are integrating Cockney-style expressions into their speech, saying such things as, 'get it sorted', 'I was gutted'. The point of the paradox is that high and low status, as used to refer to accents and dialects, are sociocultural value judgements and subject to change, as are all tastes and values.

There is further evidence that this type of change can occur in far more subtle and unconscious ways. One linguistically analysed change of this kind originated in the speech of a group of indigenous American fishermen and their families living off the coast of Massachusetts, on Martha's Vineyard (Labov, 1972). They reacted in various ways against the annual invasion of their island by hordes of wealthy summer visitors, but their subconscious resistance was expressed in a considerable exaggeration of the very distinctive vowel sounds in their speech. These sounds are not found in the standard New England pronunciation that was the accent of the summer visitors. However, the non-standard vowel change was rapidly taken up by many of the visitors themselves and spread through the island. Was this a subconscious gesture of admiration for the life-style and traditional integrity of the original islanders? If solidarity works in this way amongst a small threatened group on a holiday island, what happens in national communities?

Historical and political developments

Generally, language changes caused by large-scale historical and political developments are greater and more dramatic than vowel shifts and accent switching. Imperial conquest and trade have been the major sources of changes and of enrichment in the English language. It is important to note that this is not just a matter of a few new words or borrowings, although much of Britain's national past is richly preserved in such everyday words as 'tomato' and 'cocoa' (Aztec), 'pundit' and 'verandah' (Hindi), 'sofa' (Arabic), 'caravan' (Persian) and 'khaki' (Urdu). Borrowed words for particular items are easily and conveniently assimilated into a language and sometimes a whole area of cultural experience becomes dominated by a foreign tongue. Thus French is the traditional language of much European cooking and Italian is still used in musical notation.

The earlier history of the English language can also be traced in the words used and seen daily. Thus Latin, the language of the Church, the Court and the Law in the distant past, is still with us in such modern forms as 'solarium', 'exit', 'discipline' and 'language'. However, the accidents of history and politics have produced changes in language that go beyond the borrowing or retention of isolated words and phrases. New and distinctive varieties of English have evolved under the pressures of conquest, trade and basic survival. These varieties are known as pidgins and creoles and their significance has been linked with the embryonic and new-born stages of language (Aitchison, 1991).

Many naïve misunderstandings surround pidgin or creole language forms: they are frequently condemned as broken, primitive or bad language. Once again, these pejorative terms are really social judgements and prejudices about the status and lives of the people who use them. The linguistic facts are more interesting and more complex. Pidgins are the first, or foetal, stage in the development of a new language and arise under the special conditions of conquest and foreign domination. When two language communities and cultures are thrown together some form of basic language for trade and daily survival must be evolved. The simplified language that emerges is usually based on an existing language in use and dominant in the region; this has sometimes been English, Spanish or French. A simple grammar of rules for combining words is provided, but often the lexis is borrowed from indigenous languages in use in the area.

Once a pidgin of this kind is used extensively, groups of speakers begin to elaborate its simple grammar and vocabulary because they are using it to meet needs and circumstances more complex than simple trading and survival. At this stage the pidgin is on its way to becoming a creole. A creole has a crucial definition: it is a pidgin that has become a genuine first language. It has developed the potential to meet the full range of human language needs, including children's early socialization.

The desire to stop, or control, language change is found at national and at individual level. It seems that the idea of change in languages is deeply unsettling and provokes reactions whose strength and irrationality confirm that our sense of identity and personal worth is partly rooted in our language. Many complainants about language change appear to be middle-aged or older, suggesting a general anxiety about change often associated with growing old.

The desire to freeze language at a precise point in time remains and is even tackled nationally in some countries by establishing academies and committees to regulate the language. This has very little effect, particularly on the spoken forms, because language is constantly evolving to meet the needs of its speakers. In Britain, 'the complaint tradition' (Milroy and Milroy, 1985, p. 31) functions as a kind of informal academy and, although it is forceful and persistent, it does not affect the living, changing language. What it does do, however, is uphold and promote unjustifiable views about the absolute perfection of a very narrow conception of language. Language change is never random and chaotic – basic patterns of syntax and phonology are very stable and only certain features alter in predictable ways. The addition of new words and new phrases is not a recipe for confusion: change is balanced by powerful and influential pressures for maintenance and stability. Among these stabilizing influences are the serious media, the formal education system, group pride, loyalty and identity. Fear of language change frequently masquerades as an attempt to protect and preserve the linguistic inheritance, but the fact remains that a language can only die with its last speaker. Language change is evidence of growth and vitality.

- Human languages are in a constant state of change. Change can affect the areas of syntax, phonology, semantics and lexis.
- The major sources of change are: individual language learning and development; new inventions and technologies; historical and political changes; and group identity and loyalty.
- The areas of vocabulary and the related conceptual ways of thinking are particularly enriched by new inventions and discoveries and by historical and political changes.
- Historical and political changes and notions of groups identity have led to the creation of new languages through the evolution of pidgins and creoles.
- Language change, like many other changes in life, can arouse deep feelings of anxiety and danger. But change may be seen as evidence of the vitality and growth of a language.

Multilingualism

Any discussion of language variety and change in communities and nations must take account of the fact that many individuals living in supposedly homogeneous monolingual societies use more than one discrete language. Patterns of individual movement and settlement between different countries, as well as larger-scale group emigration caused by economic, political, religious and racial pressures mean that, in reality, true monolingual communities are exceptional. This fact comes as a surprise to many monolinguals in Britain, particularly because they speak what is fast becoming the acknowledged world language. But many British citizens are bilingual, using English and a different first language of their family's origin. The latter is sometimes called a 'heritage language' and it may be Urdu, Welsh, Hindi, Greek, Turkish, Cantonese, Italian or Arabic. The list could be extended but it is representative of the languages used by children in schools in and around the larger British cities.

The term 'heritage language' was probably intended to have positive connotations, but the implied associations with ancient heirlooms and museum preservation need to be questioned. This does not seem an entirely appropriate or useful way of designating a living and culturally significant language. Many individuals and families operate more than two languages and can themselves be considered multilingual. It is not uncommon for children to grow up in families where three languages are in active use, including a variety of written forms, and a fourth may be latent but surfaces in songs, rhymes, old tales and memories. This is not just a hypothetical example but a summary of the linguistic home environment of my own grandchildren, who are also learning Welsh in their primary school (Whitehead, 1990; Engel and Whitehead, 1993).

Aspects of Bilingualism

Given these facts of multilingualism in the world, it is not surprising that the definitions of bilingualism for any individual or group are inherently complex and need to be expressed with great flexibility. Definitions should attempt to reflect something of the degrees of competence in the two languages, the manner and situations in which they are acquired and used and also whether competence is in the spoken forms only or includes degrees of literacy. Because of these dimensions of complexity, it is now usual for linguists to describe the bilingualism of individuals in terms of points on a continuum. One speaker's range of bilingual skills can be plotted with reference to oracy and literacy and the fluctuations attributable to age and circumstances. Thus it is possible for individuals to be anywhere between an abstract ideal of complete fluency and literacy in both languages, and simply possessing dormant or very limited understanding of a second language.

These degrees of interchangeability and fluency in thinking, speaking, reading and writing with two languages are partly reflected in the 'language switching' and 'language mixing' typical of many bilinguals, particularly when they are speaking. 'Mixing' tends to be used to describe the combining of words and phrases from both languages in a single utterance, often by young bilingual children who are in the process of learning to separate their two languages (Arnberg, 1987, pp. 26–7). This should not, however, be equated with random muddle or inadequacy. Some very young infants appear to be associating one language with a particular person, activity or situation on a very regular and systematic basis. In the first two or three years of life, the use of particular words from a second language might on occasions be preferred because of their ease of articulation, particularly if the equivalents in the dominant language are phonologically more complex.

'Language switching' is frequent and usual among older and more fluent bilinguals and can occur at many points in utterances, readings, conversations and monologues. Sometimes words are switched, sometimes sentences and sometimes phrases within sentences – the permutations are probably infinite. Linguists explain these switches in terms of several possibilities: simple tiredness and distraction, the lack of a word or concept in one language, a sign of group solidarity and identity, a device to exclude outsiders, a means of emphasis and clarification or an association of certain activities and concepts with one language and culture only. The possibilities are many and complex and emphasize that language switching by bilinguals can be a powerful and subtle tool. There is no linguistic support for the misinformed assumption that this phenomenon is a symptom of inadequate and confused understanding of either or both languages.

Amongst monolinguals there are considerable misunderstandings about the nature of bilingualism and a readiness to associate it with problems and difficulties in personal, national and educational life. The most pervasive belief (and one that tends to be a covert assumption rather than a specific and stated claim) is that the mind is like a bucket, with a limited capacity for only so much language.[3] To have it full of one language, that is, to be monolingual, is the natural and ideal linguistic state. To have a second language involves an automatic reduction of the available brain capacity for either language. These naïve misconceptions are mainly based on ignorance of how language develops in response to the experiences and the needs of individuals in communities. Such beliefs can, however, permeate and undermine educational policies and strategies for bilingualism and expose children to the damaging effects of institutionalized low expectations.

Despite all the myths and popular misgivings about the brain's limited language capacity and its propensity for linguistic muddle, many children acquire two languages from birth and are bilinguals on entry to early years group settings and schools. Three distinct stages of development can be identified in this process of simultaneous acquisition (Crystal, 1987, p. 363). Initially, the infant acquires a list of words, as in monolingual first language learning, but the words are from both languages. Sentences of two or more grammatical elements, when they appear, contain a mixture of words from both languages. This only lasts a short period of time and the child's increasing vocabulary in each language leads to a growing capacity for translation between the languages. Finally, around the fourth year, the different sets of grammatical rules are separated out (before this happens, one set of grammatical rules seems to be used for both languages). Young bilinguals reveal their awareness that their languages are different in the choices they make about whom to use a particular language with, as well as where and when each language is appropriate. Such subtle social and linguistic competencies are a far cry from muddle and confusion and they are also demonstrated by children who acquire their two or more languages successively.

Successive bilingualism is usually defined as occurring after the age of 3 and, therefore, tends to be developed among linguistic-minority children when they first attend primary schools, nursery schools, crèches and other care centres. It is also one of the results of being old enough to play outside the home and, of course, it occurs among children whose families happen to move between countries and linguistic communities. One positive advantage of successive bilingualism is the fact that the child has already learnt one language and has some general skill in handling people, the environment and linguistic concepts. Young successive bilinguals are also readily engaged in play activities and playful language behaviours that support second language learning linked with meaningful activities. When bilinguals are acquiring other languages they may use a strategy of 'bridge-building' to get from a known language to a new language. This often involves using words from the new language, but organized by the grammatical patterns of the securely known language. This is a highly-skilled temporary solution called 'inter-language' (Selinker, 1992).

Very young bilinguals are also less likely to be self-conscious or upset about trying other language forms and pronunciations. Thus, they rapidly approximate to native-speaker sound patterns.

The dangers of accepting the general view that bilingualism is a problem or an abnormality are bad enough, but they are also compounded by unthinking prejudices about certain languages. To be bilingual in French/English, German/English or Swedish/English can be considered a social and cultural gain in some circles. It even appears to overcome the bucket problem! Furthermore, private schooling or 'finishing' in a French *lycée* or exclusive Swiss school can be purchased in order to gain this extra social cachet. In Britain there is one nationally established precedent for bilingualism in State schools: the provision of a full education service through the medium of a language other than English. This is, of course, the use of Welsh as a first or second language in schools in Wales. These positive images of bilingualism do not, it seems, always extend to speakers of Bengali/English, Urdu/English or Turkish/English. This should force us to think about the social attitudes that so sharply differentiate some European languages from languages associated with old empires and present, third-world poverty.

Another strand in the web of irrational fears and attitudes surrounding these specific examples of bilingualism is a deep anxiety about all things foreign and strange. This dormant xenophobia about other races, religions and traditions sometimes emerges as a pseudo-linguistic fear for the survival of English language and traditional culture, particularly in areas of the country with noticeable minority groups and communities. This can have an immediate and damaging impact on local group settings and schools. Fear of a loss of linguistic and cultural dominance is frequently expressed in terms of objections to educational policies concerned with anti-racism, equal opportunties and bilingual instruction in schools.

Educational Policies

Educational policies for multilingualism and the issue of first language support teaching in schools for young bilinguals highlight a dilemma that may not be peculiar to Britain, but is certainly aggravated by its traditional insularity, monolingual assumptions and linguistic status as the source of a major world language. Most children, whatever their degrees of bi- and multilingualism, will be taught for most of their educational careers by monolingual practitioners. The temptation to pressure very young children into being English speakers first and foremost is strong, but this may act against the children's best interests, both as learners and as English speakers. There is a general agreement among many linguists, as well as experienced and successful bilinguals, that some considerable element of first language support in early years settings is highly desirable.

The reasons for this are, first, children's learning and cognitive development increasingly depend on the confident use of human language that satisfies their personal needs for thinking and planning, as well as structuring their social and cultural interactions with others. Second, children's self-esteem and confidence, as well as their linguistic and cultural identity, may be undermined if they do not encounter their first language in some significant areas of early years educational provision. Third, if young children's languages are not respected and used in early years settings and school contexts, there is a danger that monolingual practitioners may unconsciously retain damaging lowered expectations and attitudes towards the development and achievements of young potential bilinguals.

Important as these justifications for first language support are, we do have to recognize that they are complicated by the nature of urban multilingualism. In many inner-city schools, playgroups and nurseries there are often several minority languages and the clear identification of one or two dominant tongues is not easy. However, modern approaches to multicultural education emphasize the richness of the contributions linguistic and cultural diversity can make to the ethos and the curriculum of a group setting. There is also much to be said in cognitive and affective terms for putting children into the roles of language teachers and researchers for part of their day. That is to say, we can encourage them to share, investigate and demonstrate their knowledge of other languages. And, by extension, we can invite children's families into our schools, groups and classes to share with us their daily experiences of moving between the language worlds of the wider community and their homes. A consistent determination to bring the children's languages and cultural lives into educational settings may eventually help to combat the racism that afflicts many of our communities. Such an approach might also counter the misguided belief that there is something deficient or inadequate in languages and writing systems from distant countries.

- Multilingualism is the norm in many language communities: patterns of migration caused by economic and political pressures mean that truly monolingual communities are rare.
- Individuals are often bilingual although they, too, can be multilingual. Definitions of bilingualism need to reflect a range of degrees of competence in both spoken and written forms.
- Young bilingual children may use two languages from birth. This is simultaneous bilingualism. Alternatively, they may acquire their second languages after the age of 3 in a process known as successive bilingualism.
- The mixing of languages and the switching of languages are powerful linguistic tools for the bilingual. These skills should not be misguidedly attributed to inadequate and partial language learning.
- Educational policies for a multicultural society need to include provision for first language support for very young bilinguals in schools and early years group settings.
- Policies also need to avoid implicit notions of compensating for, or lessening the significant use of, children's non-English languages as soon as possible in schools and group settings.

Teaching and Learning Suggestions

* Create a group/class/school language inventory by listing all the languages known by children and adults (include examples where only one or two words are known). As appropriate, explore the use of these languages outside the group setting and any knowledge of their societies or countries of origin. Also explore any ability to write various languages and scripts. Display, discuss and update the inventory regularly.
* Just as above, create group/class/school dialect inventories. Begin to explore the nature of accents (draw on children's television viewing for a wide range of accent experiences!).
* Involve parents, extended family members and other carers and minders in adding to the language and dialect inventories.
* Choose a range of stories, poems, rhymes and songs which use languages and dialects (known in the setting and also new to the children). Listen to nursery rhymes, poetry and stories on audio tape spoken in a variety of dialects and accents.
* Organize regular 'teach ourselves another language' days. Make it a self-help effort with tutoring from child and adult speakers of different languages. This may be limited to greetings, counting and songs and rhymes, but it can be enriched by cooking and eating food from the appropriate language communities.
* Invite speakers of different languages and dialects to visit the setting and share something of their language and culture (many potential language visitors may be found among the parents and families of the children and early years practitioners in the setting).
* Organize visits to any distinctive language community areas (shops, markets, clubs and places of worship). These experiences can be recorded in class/group books and they can also enrich drama and role-play areas by suggesting new settings and scenarios.

Notes

1. Walt Whitman (1885) *Slang in America.* Quoted in Howard (1984), p. vii.
2. These terms derive from the works of Roland Barthes, particularly *S/Z* (1974).
3. These comments have been influenced by the work of Martin-Jones and Romaine (1986), but the 'bucket' is my own terminology!

Further Reading

Aitchison, J. (1981; 1991) *Language Change: Progress or Decay?* Fontana, London; Cambridge University Press.
Arnberg, L. (1987) *Raising Children Bilingually: the pre-school years,* Multilingual Matters, Clevedon.
Baker, C. (1993; 1996) *Foundations of Bilingual Education and Bilingualism,* Multilingual Matters, Clevedon.
Cameron, D. (1995) *Verbal Hygiene,* Routledge, London.

Engel, D.M. and Whitehead, M.R. (1996) Which English? Standard English and language variety: some educational perspectives, *English in Education*, Vol. 30, no. 1, pp. 36–49.

Hoffmann, C. (1991) *An Introduction to Bilingualism*, Longman, London.

Milroy, J. and Milroy, L. (1985) *Authority in Language*, Routledge & Kegan Paul, London.

3

Psycholinguistics: the big questions

Wally: *When you're little you try to think of what the name of something is and people tell you.*
Eddie: *Oh, yeah. Your mother tells you. You come out of her stomach and she talks English to you and she tells you the name for everything.*
Paley, 1981, p. 116

The story of psycholinguistics is a record of attempts by psychologists and linguists to answer some of the most puzzling questions about language: questions which are many faceted and complex (Conti-Ramsden and Snow, 1990). For example, how can we possibly account for the breathtaking speed and efficiency of the journey from the first cry at birth to the profound conversations about the nature of language and living of these not particularly advantaged pre-schoolers, Eddie and Wally? This has to be a kind of quest story: a saga of painstaking searches, exciting discoveries, difficult problems, some confusions and a few disagreements. And the quest is not over, we are telling the story 'so far'; the following version offers only partial answers and tentative suggestions.

Psycholinguistics has already been defined as the shared area of study of psychologists and linguists. This indicates that issues of speech and language (the concerns of the linguists) and of mental processes and learning (the concerns of the psychologists) will be involved in any introduction to psycholinguistics. 'Psycholinguists are interested in the underlying knowledge and abilities which people must have in order to use language and to learn to use language in childhood' (Slobin, 1979, p. 2). This interest might be rephrased as the big questions of the chapter title: how do we learn to understand and produce our first language or languages? What is the nature of the relationship between language and thought?

The first half of the chapter is concerned with early language acquisition, while the second reviews the complex relationship between language, thought and culture, and the nature of concepts and words. If these seem to be rather grandiose and theoretical aims for an account that should simply concern itself with explaining how we come to produce speech, understand other speakers and think with words, the reason is that language learning and development are not so simple and straightforward. One important idea that must be grasped and understood is that we are concerned with two things – not simply speech but a language system. This relates back to the earlier references to 'langue' and 'parole', or language and speech, as discussed in Chapter 2. This being so, it is not surprising that studies in psycholinguistics frequently refer to the mind, the nature of thinking and ways of understanding the world.

There remains one other possible confusion: should we call the process language acquisition, language development, early language learning or first language learning? These terms have all been used and preferred at various times by researchers and writers. Perhaps there is a tendency for 'acquisition' to be used by linguists because of their greater interest in the language system being taken over by the learner. Conversely, some psychologists prefer the terms 'language learning' or 'language development' because of their focus on individual learning processes and the development of understanding. Primarily for the sake of clarity, the phrase 'early language acquisition' will be used in most of the discussion. This usage has the advantage of retaining a focus both on the language system to be acquired and the individual developmental processes of the early years.

Early Language Acquisition

Changing Views
Explanations of early language acquisition have changed dramatically this century, particularly in the decades since the 1950s (see Perera *et al.*, 1994). The differing views and theoretical positions are best thought of as useful pieces added to a still incomplete puzzle. All have in their time answered some questions about processes in early language acquisition and revealed some developmental characteristics. In very general terms, the different views about language acquisition are the products of different schools of psychology, and we can usefully distinguish between behaviourist, nativist, cognitive developmental and social-interactionist views of early language.

Behaviourist approaches
Behaviourist approaches dominated nineteenth- and even twentieth-century psychology and produced theories of learning often based on studies of animal behaviour and laboratory experiments. There is a tendency for such work to explain learning as the imitation of models and small segments of behaviour. The process of learning (whether it be of language or of anything else) is seen as being shaped and controlled from outside the learner by a process of reinforcement; that is, the correct responses are rewarded and the wrong ones are ignored or penalized in other ways. On the surface it would seem that behaviourist accounts of early language learning explain the useful social phrases and instructions very young infants are apparently imitating when they first start saying such things as 'bye-bye', 'ta' or 'up'. It is also obvious that very positive reinforcement is significant in early language acquisition. Adults and older children are immensely enthusiastic and supportive of babies as they begin to produce speech-like sounds and words. However, closer observations

and reflections on the behaviour of infants and adults indicate that there are serious limitations to the traditional behaviourist view.

Apart from a few obviously imitated words and expressions, infants do not speak and use language in the same ways as older children and adults. Their first combinations of two or more words are very unusual and could not have been imitated. The child-language literature is full of such examples: 'No Mommy read' (de Villiers and de Villiers, 1979, p. 56); 'Är det ducks?' ('Is it ducks?') Arnberg, 1987, p. 69); 'He's keying the door' (Clark, 1982, p. 402). We should, of course, bear in mind that imitation may be significant at different stages in acquisition: it may have some part to play in extending vocabulary in the pre-school and early school years, as well as helping considerably with the control and practising of the sound system, or phonology, of a language. The issue of reinforcement is also complicated because at first adults enthusiastically reward and support a child's every attempt to speak – even if the utterance is grossly mispronounced, socially inappropriate or an untrue proposition. Indeed, it often seems that the adults are the ones who delight in imitating the child in these early stages. The rule adults appear to be following is, respond with excessive enthusiasm and delight to anything the child tries to say and take it up and keep it going jointly as long as possible.

Perhaps an actual observation best captures the unbehaviourist behaviour of parents with their children. The setting is a seaside café on a wet and blustery morning where a young couple with a small girl of about 18–24 months are waiting to be served. The mother leaves the child sitting on the father's lap while she goes to find the toilets. The little girl watches her mother intently as she crosses the long room, then she raises her arm and clenches and unclenches her fingers and shouts, 'bah, bah'. The mother laughs, turns round and calls, 'Not goodbye, I'm not going, I'll be back in a minute'. But she does go out of sight and the child repeats her 'bah, bah'. The father now sits the child up on the edge of the table, positioning her closely face to face with him. He says, 'Not goodbye, she's coming back, I promise you'. The little child appears very contented, nods her head enthusiastically and starts repeating her 'bah, bah', for sheer delight, along with rhythmic head nodding and leg swinging. The father now joins in this head nodding and chanting of 'bah, bah', and they play this musical game until the mother returns.

It is obvious that at some point this little girl has learnt to imitate 'bye, bye', along with the conventional arm and hand wave, although her articulation of the speech sounds is still an approximation. But she is rewarded with warm approval, as well as sensible explanations about the inappropriateness of the response in this particular social context. The child then proceeds to take full control of the misjudged situation by turning it into a game with her father in which she 'calls the tune'.

It is this kind of child-initiated behaviour and inventiveness, going well beyond basic linguistic responses, that makes traditional behaviourist explanations thin and inadequate. The sort of positive reinforcement that does occur in early language acquisition is a subtle concern for establishing and maintaining joint attention and conversations. The actual truth of a child's statements is more likely to be monitored and corrected by adults than are grammatical or phonological accuracy. What seems very clear to the most casual observer as well as the psycholinguist is that parents and other adult care-givers do not settle down at any point to teach young infants to speak, let alone to understand the language system. The task would be beyond the capabilities of most, if not all, of us!

Nativist approaches

This is the dilemma of early language acquisition: how is it that infants manage it when they are not obviously taught, and are not able to comprehend so complex a learning task? The nativist approach attempted to resolve these questions by returning to some seventeenth- and eighteenth-century theories that proposed the existence of innate and therefore universal features of human mind. In the 1950s these ideas were revitalized by the American linguist and philosopher, Noam Chomsky, in what he likes to call the second cognitive revolution. This revolution recently gained a new lease of life as 'the language instinct' (Pinker, 1994). The old order overthrown by Chomsky's revolution was the simple behaviourist explanations of language learning, and the new era he introduced has probably made possible all the developments and achievements in child-language study since then. Even those who dispute Chomsky's emphasis on studying the abstract rules of grammar would probably agree that at least he revealed what remarkable things children can do with language at a very early stage.

After Chomsky's attacks on behaviourism (1957, 1965), researchers really listened to young children and began to note their innovative and unusual production of words and utterances, as well as their amazing sensitivity to rules, regularities and patterns in language. For example, children's grammatical mistakes are highly systematic and rather admirable: in English they overgeneralize the rules for making plurals and past tenses once they have deduced the add an '-s' or add '-ed' rules respectively. Around the years 2–5, children talk of 'mouses' and tell us that they 'rided' a bike. Clearly they are demonstrating some degree of sensitivity to regular patterns and a possibly innate ability to make analogies with the regular forms, such as 'houses' and 'walked'. One thing is certain, they do not imitate invented forms from adult speech, and they are not taught explicitly that a grammar is a system of rules.

The nativist view is that children are pre-programmed to learn a language and are highly sensitive to the linguistic features of their environment. Chomsky emphasizes both the process of maturation in children's linguistic development and the generative, or essentially creative, nature of all human language use. We are all continually involved in recreating and generating new and appropriate utterances. But Chomsky's central concern is with the human mind: he sees linguistics as the study of mind and of the mental structures that make language possible. His suggestion that there must be some internal Language Acquisition Device (LAD), or propensity that enables the young infant somehow to process all the language it hears and generate its own meaningful utterances, led to considerable research into grammatical systems in the 1960s and 1970s. But the approach has been criticized for its tendency to look at language and the mind in a vacuum, divorced somewhat from significant human relationships and social settings, and from all the other kinds of learning with which babies are actively involved.

Cognitive approaches

Cognitive psychologists in the 1970s criticized the Chomskyan preoccupation with the structures of language and its comparative neglect of the personal intentions and uses to which infants put their developing linguistic knowledge, along with all their knowledge of people and the environment. Language development was seen from this perspective to be part of general cognitive development. This view could be linked with Piaget's descriptions of the important mental structures, or schemas, created by the infant's interactions and explorations in the environment in the first 18 or so months of life. To some extent it could be claimed that early language acquisition must wait for these sensorimotor thinking developments and build on them.

This cognition hypothesis does not necessarily deny the existence of an independent linguistic system in human development (Cromer, 1974), but it does reassert the significance of other cognitive abilities that must also mature and create a framework for early language learning. Furthermore, this approach allows for the eventual dominance of human thinking by language and by mental processes derived from language (Vygotsky, 1986). Studies of child language that were inclined towards this cognitive focus tended to highlight the complex meanings carried by children's early one- and two-word utterances. Full understanding of children's words was seen to require detailed knowledge of the social context and possible intentions of the children (Brown, 1973). Much of the research described learning a first language as a kind of mapping problem – young infants had to map their meanings onto the structures of the adult language (Macnamara, 1977).

Social-interactionist approaches

At this point the task of early language acquisition is again beginning to sound almost impossible and highly abstract, but there is another viewpoint to be considered. In the late 1970s and 1980s, developmental psychologists with a deep interest in the nature and effects of human social interactions began to reassert the importance of the role played by adult and child relationships in learning. They also focused on the functions language fulfils for individuals and for groups. We learn a language because of the things it can do for us and the part it plays in making us social beings.

An emphasis on using language to get things done and to make sense of the world of persons and situations is generally associated with the linguistic theory of pragmatics. This view of early language was also supported by a body of research evidence that demonstrated the remarkable competence and social sensitivity of infants, including the newborn. Interlocking with these abilities was the finely judged and supportive tutoring in two-way communication adult care-givers provided for their infants. Bruner (1983) has summarized these discoveries in a memorable way: the infant's language-learning capacities, akin to Chomsky's Language Acquisition Device (LAD), could not function without the aid given by an adult, who provides a Language Acquisition Support System and scaffolds the child's entry into a language (*ibid.* p. 19). The great importance of these research findings may well be the descriptions they provide of the preverbal foundations for communication on which all later language and speech will build. This modifies the traditional cognitive view that language must simply wait for the prior establishment of essential general thinking skills and indicates that language has its own prior skills of preverbal communication to establish.

There is general agreement that early language acquisition has both a cognitive and a linguistic component, but one area of challenge and mystery still exists: how do infants move from pre-linguistic to linguistic communications? Part of the answer must be that infants do not wait around passively and are not left to go it alone, so the 'impossibly difficult to learn' dilemma of early language acquisition is less intractable. Children learn to be social beings and language users in close partnerships and collaborations with caring adults and other children who participate eagerly with them in the adventure of reconstructing a language for getting things done.

Research into language acquisition is not a saga of competing beliefs and warring factions but the record of a variety of investigations into the many factors that must affect the learning of a first language. What is now very obvious is that psycholinguistics has moved from its traditional concern with the origins and development of strictly linguistic and cognitive structures to a complementary interest in the processes of language and learning in a social world. The disciplines of sociolinguistics and psycholinguistics have come together in order to answer the old question, how do we do it?

- Changing views of early language acquisition are the products of different approaches in psychology but none of them can claim to have answered all the complex questions surrounding the subject.
- Behaviourist perspectives placed great emphasis on the child's imitation of the language of others, supported by adult reinforcement. Later research has tended to discredit this view.
- Nativist approaches emphasize the existence of innate and therefore universal abilities in the human mind and claim that the child is pre-programmed in some way to learn a rule-governed language system.
- The view of cognitive psychologists is that language development is an aspect of general cognitive growth and depends on the maturing of these general structures of thinking for its development. This approach also stresses the intentions and meanings of children and the uses to which they put their developing language ability.
- Social-interactionist approaches view the total social and cultural setting in which language is learned as just as necessary for its emergence as individual grammatical competence. This work emphasizes the social skills of newborns, the tutoring role of the adult carer, and the importance of the establishment of a preverbal communication system from which language emerges.

How Do we Do it? Stages in Speech and Language Development

If we return to Wally and Eddie in the kindergarten (Paley, 1981), it seems that between them they have summarized the problems of learning a first language as well as having evolved some promising ideas for overcoming them. Apparently, small children have thoughts and intentions they wish to communicate:

they need the names of things. Parents are also eager to talk to their infants and they begin to tell them the names for everything. Of course, names are import-ant but they are not enough. Language is not a collection of labels, as the first chapter has indicated. What else must be understood and produced by the child in the early months and years of life? The simple answer is those complex interdependent elements of language described in Chapter 1, namely, phonol-ogy, syntax, semantics and lexis. Modern research would add to this list the important and all-pervasive aspect of language known as pragmatics – that understanding of the functions language is performing in many situations.

The first year of life is particularly significant for the development of phonol-ogy, or sound production, and for the establishment of a range of interpersonal communication skills. The first words and grammatical utterances are built up on these foundations in the ensuing months and years. There is a vast amount of research evidence that records the stages all children go through in their early development of speech and language, and the process is remarkably similar for any language (Brown, 1973; Nelson, 1989; Harris, 1992). In the brief review that follows, I have chosen to highlight those stages and aspects of early speech and language that reflect the child's need to master the produc-tion, understanding and functions of language. These three dimensions and the manner of their emergence in infancy may have significant implications for continued language learning in the early years of education.

Listening, Watching and Sharing

It is now clear that a lengthy period of listening, watching and playful social interactions precedes the first production of recognizable words by young children. Babies are born with exceptionally sensitive hearing and are able, within hours of birth, to discriminate human speech from all the sounds that bombard them. Furthermore, there is evidence that they find human speech so noticeable and pleasing that they will attempt to prolong its occurrence, even in preference to musical sounds.

Even more remarkable than this, babies appear to be sensitive to the actual sound differences that will eventually distinguish the words of many lan-guages, for example, '*b*' and '*p*' and '*d*' and '*t*' (de Villiers and de Villiers, 1979, pp. 22–3). In phonological terms the differences between these kinds of sounds are complicated matters of very slight time differences in the start of the vibration of the vocal cords. These facts are interesting examples of infants' pre-programming or readiness for speech, long before it can possibly be pro-duced and understood by them. Such research findings are also reminders that the production of speech sounds and the understanding of language emerge after many months of finely selective listening to human voices, particularly the voices of familiar and caring adults.

Listening to people is very important for babies but it is also accompanied by equally discriminating and intense observations by babies of those adults who consistently care for them. Studies of newborns indicate that not only are they highly sensitive to patterned sounds, but they are also as highly attuned to certain visual patterns. In particular, the configurations of faces and eyes at-tract the most attention and babies gaze at the eyes of their carers. This normally elicits warm and responsive behaviour from the adults singled out for such rapt attention! Clearly this is most important in establishing the sort of human social interactions that will involve the infant and adult couple in lots of language, joint attention and playful sound production.

However, patterns of eye contact are also essential to the ways in which all verbalized conversations are started, maintained and ended. Eye contact is the major regulator of the turn-taking so typical of face-to-face conversations. We rely on such techniques as catching someone's eye and holding their gaze, as well as periodically dropping eye contact, to manage the to and fro of social talk. Mutual eye contact is an important method of gaining and maintaining joint attention – an essential prerequisite for most social exchanges and conversations.

The significance of young infants' observations of faces and their active seeking of eye contact is confirmed by evidence that they are deeply upset by any failures of sensitivity and responsiveness in their adult partners. An alert infant who is showing by eye gazing a readiness for play and talk will be deeply distressed and even grief stricken should the care-giver present a blank and unanimated face (Schaffer, 1977). Conversely, infants can and do signal their own wish to stop socializing and playing by dropping eye contact, lowering the head and even turning away. They also become fretful and restless if these important signals are ignored by an over-enthusiastic adult. The social and cultural significance of turning the face away from someone persists into adult life, conversations and metaphors, but it begins here in the first few weeks of life, as do some other surprising skills.

It appears that infants can mimic closely the facial tricks and grimaces of their carers, such as tongue poking and lip pursing, as well as following an adult's line of gaze (Stern, 1977; Trevarthen, 1993). Although it might be thought that making funny faces is a silly thing to do with babies, it is well worth remembering that complex mouth, tongue and lip movements are essential to the production of speech and may be rehearsed in face mimicry and games. Following the focus of another's eyes is also an ability crucial to picking up clues about whom or what they are thinking about, concentrating on and likely to talk about. What we are able to say about all these surprisingly early watching and listening skills is that they combine to make the baby a potential conversational partner.

Mutual communication between babies and care-givers (sometimes called intersubjectivity) starts at birth when the newborn infant is welcomed into a community. Within minutes of the delivery the child is frequently addressed directly and its grimaces, movements and splutters are commented on, interpreted and even imitated by the adults present. The adult community does not appear to regard the newly born as immature organisms only capable of random physical responses, but attributes sociability and communicative intentions to them.

In the very early stages of an adult's relationship with an infant, the priority seems to be to establish turn-taking behaviours and conversational exchanges: a strange suggestion when the child partner is just a few hours, days or weeks old! Granted that these rituals begin with a minimal contribution from the infant, the adult still maximizes any of the child's burps, yawns or eye contacts by accepting them with courteous greetings, pauses and thanks, or with little invented story explanations of them.

The recorded commentaries of mothers seem to reflect a general belief that tiny babies have motives and intentions and are capable of contributing to gossip and conversations (Snow, 1977). It really looks as if adults are not constrained by a realistic sense of the infant's limited powers of attention and comprehension. Mothers may even try to avoid putting questions to a preverbal child when it has its mouth full of food and could not be expected to answer! Just as extraordinary is the evidence that adult talk in these early one-sided conversations is timed to leave spaces for the preverbal child's reply, and these pauses are the same length as normal adult-to-adult dialogue pauses (Stern, 1977). After such pauses, adults speaking to babies carry on as if they had received a reasonable response and by the end of their first year, many infants are actually slotting their own contributions into these dialogue spaces created for them. Gradually, adults tend to 'up the demand' for more frequent, longer and more language-like contributions to these conversations and games.

Bruner (1975, 1983) has described in some detail the game-like formats and rituals that prepare babies for language and social exchanges. Games (such as 'peep-bo'; naming parts of the body, toys, pets and objects; playful requests for information; and 'please' and 'thank-you' routines with objects) establish the uses of language in meaningful contexts. In the preverbal period, as well as during the emergence of words and utterances, the young infant is continually encouraged to communicate in familiar and predictable settings with familiar and supportive people. Babies and adults do important things together in very predictable ways – routines such as feeding, dressing, bathing, playing and going on outings are marked by distinctive language. Recent research with newborns from several cultures is now demonstrating the playfulness of these first communications, particularly the teasing and mucking about initiated by the babies (Reddy, 1991; Trevarthen, 1993).

The important lesson for students of language, as well as for preverbal infants, is that learning to do things with other people is the basis of learning to 'do things with words' (Austin, 1962). The early acquisition of language would be incredibly difficult, if not miraculous, were babies faced with a learning progression that moved from achieving sound production first, then learning word meanings and finally understanding the complex functions of words and utterances in context. But all the research on the preverbal months suggests that babies from the start (supported by their adult partners) learn what words do in their world, understand what people are like, and what speakers mean or intend, in particular social contexts.

Such learning is an essential part of what it means to be involved in human social interactions – the best metaphor we have for early language acquisition is that of a human conversation. We should take seriously the full force of the metaphor and not attribute all the intentions and activities to the adult partner.

To summarize all this by saying that infants are social is rather inadequate or, in Bruner's word, 'banal'. Infants are 'geared to respond to the human voice, to the human face, to human action and gesture' (Bruner, 1983, p. 26). These behaviours, in synchronization with those of adult care-givers, create the essential conditions for the language acquisition process to build on. The preverbal foundations of language are also the source of that communicative competence (Hymes, 1971) discussed in Chapter 2, which ensures that our linguistic responses and interactions are not only grammatically meaningful but also socially and culturally appropriate. However, it is undoubtedly young children's first attempts at producing the sounds of their languages that really impress adults and convince them that learning to talk has started.

- A lengthy period of very sensitive listening precedes the production of speech in infancy: infants appear to be tuned to human voices and behaviour at birth.
- A similarly sensitive and significant fascination with eyes and faces starts from birth. Newborn infants have a range of varied facial expressions and arm movements that attract and motivate adult interactions.
- Mutual eye gazing and patterns of inviting and ending eye contact are soon established by infants and carers. These sequences may have significance for the later turn-taking patterns of conversations when eye signals still remain important.
- Mutual communication, or intersubjectivity, is established between infants and carers in the first weeks of life and is part of a process of regarding the infant as an intelligent, playful and intentional human communicator from the start.
- The games, teasing and rituals played by infants and their carers establish a basis for a wide range of linguistic interactions.

Sounds and Meanings

All children begin by learning the sounds of their language. These stages in sound production are comparatively easy to summarize but it is important to bear in mind that such vocal experiments and achievements are part of the interpersonal communications discussed above. This meaningful (or semantic) aspect of early sounds has been demonstrated by long-term studies of some individual children who have clearly learnt how to mean by using a repertoire of sounds before recognizable words emerge (Halliday, 1975).

In the first 2 months of life (bearing in mind that any of these age markers are highly variable), noises that are mainly of the discomfort or physical-reflexes type predominate. However, they may have some influence on phonological developments in that they exercise the organs of speech production. Between 2 and 4 months the pleasure sounds develop (these are the rather musical and lower-pitched cooing and laughing responses that so delight caring adults). The child's growing ability to exploit the tongue and lips results in the 'ga-ga' and 'goo-goo' noises typical of this stage.

By about 6 months of age the infant will have started to produce a greater variety of playful sounds consistently rather than accidentally. This may include many 'fun' noises, such as blowing bubbles or exploding air and moisture through the pursed lips in a 'raspberry'. At this point we should note the effect that all this playful experimentation with sounds is having on the adults around the child. Cooing, laughing and other vocal play is highly emotive for the adult carers: suddenly the baby seems to be a real personality with a potential for fun and humour. This often leads to a great upsurge in the number of games played between adult and child, including games that involve focusing joint attention on objects and toys. The hiding, seeking and slightly scary tactics of peekaboo, or of suddenly putting the adult face very close to the baby's face, may now occur. These strange practices can be thought of as ways of establishing patterns of expectations, co-ordinating mutual gaze and attention and generally stimulating and getting in touch with another mind and personality.

Somewhere around 6 months the distinctive development of babbling emerges. Babbling is the regular and rhythmic repetition of a small set of sounds, such as 'babababa'. It is at this stage that we can identify the input and effects of the dominant language surrounding the child because both the rhythms and the sounds of babbling reflect those used most frequently in the language. This stimulates a very special kind of response from the adults around because, in the case of a potentially English-speaking baby, such pleasing sequences as 'mamamama' and 'dadadada' are recognized as real and important words. These sounds are often taken up and repeated by adults and older children so that, again, we have mature speakers imitating babies. Such pleasurable and playful reinforcement will certainly be a factor in the young infant's earliest collection of rhythmic words, such as 'baba', 'mama', 'dada', 'wow wow', 'nana'.

Around this period there are also signs that the infant is actually bringing about changes in the ways in which caring adults talk. As well as copying the child's word-like babbles, care-givers often exaggerate their own intonation patterns, facial expressions and gestures. The actual speech style of carers talking to babies usually includes lots of repetition and questions, as well as simplified clauses and vocabulary, including some baby-talk words. At the risk of parody we might think of it as the 'what's a matter then, has it got a nasty pain in its tumtum, never mind, there, there, soon be all better, kiss it all better then', school of early language! But in all seriousness, what does seem to be going on here is a useful amount of lexical repetition – a rich demonstration of nonverbal communicative skills, examples of the different intonation patterns used in questions and statements and a modelling of the highly expressive style of affectionate talk within a close human relationship. Studies of this register summarize it as a communicative technique for ensuring mutual understanding or keeping two minds focused on the same topic (Brown, 1977, p. 12).

Between 9 and 18 months the development of sounds is rapid, and a great variety of tone and rhythm – as well as the tunes of the particular languages around the child – are noticeable. But most importantly, the signs of real language development are emerging because it seems clear at this stage that the infant means things and intends to communicate when uttering sounds. It is not just a matter of the child repeating the sounds and words adults appear to like – the child begins to use certain personal sounds systematically to express greetings, needs, requests, observations, pleasure and dislike. Some linguists would describe these as proto-words (Crystal, 1997) because they are consistent, systematic and meaningful.

Halliday (1975) noted that his son, Nigel, at the age of 9 months, had his own special sounds for a range of purposes. For example, 'nananana' always meant 'I want that thing now' and 'ber' was a demand for a favourite toy bird. At this stage, Nigel appeared to have a system of twelve distinct meanings and most of them were expressed in unique and spontaneous vocal symbols, having little relationship to the meanings and sound symbols of adult language *(ibid.* p. 24).

Most babies can also accompany their own system of meaningful sounds with hand and finger pointing. They also demonstrate their sensitivity to the turn-taking patterns of conversations by looking at speakers who happen to be holding the floor. They can respond to simple verbal instructions and gestures, such as waving 'bye-bye', clapping their hands and attempting to say family names and basic family words.

Single words begin to appear at around 12–18 months and are often inaccurately described as 'lisping' or 'babyish' in pronunciation. This simplified pronunciation is a reflection of the child's difficulties in using and controlling the very precise movements of tongue, lips and palate required in speech. But these simplifications are well-focused strategies for coping with sound combinations in words, and they appear to be highly systematic. For example, infants may reduplicate an initial consonant so that the articulation of all the consonants is restricted to one area of the mouth – as in 'bubber' (butter), 'goggy' or 'doddy' (doggy). The beginning sounds of new words seem to be very clear to the infant and result in such versions as, 'du' (duck) and 'be' (bed). Similarly, distinctive final parts of words may be pronounced first, as in 'ren' (Karen) and 'tali' (Natalie). Complicated clusters of initial consonants are often reduced to simplify their articulation, as in 'poon' (spoon) or 'mack' (smack). Some children find words that start with an open vowel difficult and appear to need an extra consonant at the beginning in order to ease the production of the word, for instance, 'mapple' (apple).

The emergence of first words also raises the crucial issue of grammaticality (or syntax) in early language, but before moving from sound production to early words and grammatical combinations we can summarize the achievements of the first year.

- The very first sounds, cries and babbles exercise and develop the capacities of the speech organs, and the child's control over them.
- In their first months infants practise and perfect the habitual and significant sounds of the particular languages to which they are exposed.
- The roots of pleasurable games with persons and objects, and of language play for its own sake, are located in these early months. The production of sounds is rhythmic and musical and also involves whole-body movements such as bouncing, as well as hand and arm waving, leg kicking and head nodding.
- From the start infants begin to use their voices to control others and to get them to do things.
- Many infants appear to use a set of personally evolved sounds to express their needs and meanings systematically.

First Words

The first words are usually one- and two-syllabled attempts at some meaningful names and items frequently encountered by the child in the daily routines of home. Personal gestures and intonation patterns, as well as the actual situation, are important guides to a full understanding of the child's meaning when using single words. Some of these single words appear to have the import of full sentences, and linguists usually refer to them as holophrases. These particular single-word utterances are not being used by the child simply as labels and naming devices – they actually function as commentaries and instructions. For example, 'cup' may mean

> Where is my cup?
> I've dropped my cup.
> I want a drink.
> There's a cup in that picture like mine.

Similarly, 'down' may be said to indicate

> I want to go downstairs.
> I want to get out of the high-chair.
> You've dropped something on the floor.

Only the total and unique context in which the child uses these words can fully explain the intended meanings.

This fact highlights the particular social and cultural setting early language encodes for the child. The above examples are invented and therefore rather bland and impersonal, but in an authentic family setting the single-word utterance 'down' has been used by a baby girl to comment on the family cat's dramatic leap down from the top of the tall refrigerator to the kitchen floor. Behind this child's simple observation is a rich background of talk and shared experiences in the family, some of it centred on the cat's preference for sitting on top of the very high refrigerator and jumping straight down to the floor when his supper bowl is put out! The real value of records of children's first words is not in the counting or scoring aspect, but in the remarkable insights they provide into the children's perceptions of their families and communities (Whitehead, 1990).

Linguists, as well as parents and other caring adults, become very excited about young children's first two-word utterances or word combinations. Again, in terms of exact meanings, they are open to many complex interpretations that can only be clarified by knowledge of the child and knowledge of the situation. The research literature contains many examples, such as 'allgone milk', 'no bed', 'more book', that are significant demonstrations of young children's originality as they set about learning languages. In fact, these examples are evidence of early grammars: they are combinations of words that express relationships and actions. For the first time the world is being organized by the child in terms of linguistic categories, such as actors, actions, objects, negation, possession, absence, and so forth. A grammar of early utterances could be described as one that enables young speakers to do at least two very important things with words and simple word combinations: first, early grammatical utterances can be used to interact with others and get things done; and, second, they are a means of commenting on the world or a particular state of affairs. These two major functions should not be under-estimated, as they cover most of our adult uses of language. They are also the basis of a specific view of language and learning that emphasizes the significant interplay of an individual's active participation in the world with a more distanced and spectator-like stance (Britton, 1992).

The work of Halliday (1975) suggests very similar conclusions in that his division of early language into two major functions also focuses on interaction and observation. Halliday calls these two broad uses mathetic and pragmatic: mathetic being concerned with experiences and ideas, the observer role, and pragmatic with personal interactions and negotiations. This dual stance that early language use begins to make possible is pithily summarized by Halliday as the possibility of being both an observer and an intruder *(ibid.* pp. 29–30). The child starts by being in only one role at any one time, through the use of simple utterances, but the gradual development of an adult grammar enables both functions to exist together. We can see and hear this possibility when the 5-year-old remarks, 'That's a nice red bike, I want one like that'.

The acquisition of an adult grammar and wider ranges of vocabulary makes rapid progress in the years from 2 to 4. Children's three- and four-word sentences produce a great variety of highly creative and unusual combinations. Names, questions and commentaries simply flow from the young speaker, as do all the what, why, how, where and who queries. The rather cryptic or 'telegraphic' style of speech lessens as young children begin to express connections, such as cause and effect and narrative sequence, with the linguistic items 'and', 'because', 'so', 'if' and 'when'. The years from 2 to 4 seem to be a peak period for young children's original and obviously unimitated language learning strategies. All the famous errors of over-generalization of irregular plurals and past tenses belong to this stage in language development and indicate that young children are certainly not copying adults.

However, creativity in early language acquisition is not just a matter of 'wented', 'feets' and 'mouses'. Many children learning a range of world languages invent new usages by turning nouns into verbs, producing such forms as 'lawning' (mowing the lawn) and 'I seat belted myself' (Clark, 1982, p. 390; p. 402). These creations from 3- and 4-year-olds indicate considerable sensitivity to the existence of nouns that function as verbs in the standard adult language, as in 'brush' and the regular verb 'to brush'. Once again it is clear that 'lawning' and 'seat belting' are unlikely to have been copied from adult usage. Some children also invent complex new lexical items which are personal constructions based on known words and familiar contexts. At the age of 3, my younger daughter produced the memorable 'bednight sweeties' which has remained in family parlance ever since! It seems to have evolved out of our general practice of attempting to keep the eating of sweets limited to the period between the end of the evening meal and bedtime, but it had obviously become part of the whole range of 'goodnight' rituals and associations.

This personal example illustrates the areas of significant private connections and family and cultural practices that children's early words and utterances encode. These are known as semantic fields because they indicate the major groups of meanings around which children's first language developments and experiments cluster. Much of this language is about the 'here-and-now' world of significant people, actions, food, the body, clothes, animals, vehicles, toys, games, household objects and social conventions. Other important categories are location, the 'up', 'down' and 'under' of toddlers' talk, adjectives and those terms that point things out, known to linguists as deictics. These lists of semantic themes are of great social and cultural significance because they function as commentaries on the traditions, attitudes, rituals and beliefs of the community in which the young speaker is developing.

- First words can only be fully understood within the contexts in which they are uttered. Some of them are not just labels but stand for sentence-like commentaries or instructions.
- Two-word combinations are examples of early grammatical language: the words are put together in order to express the child's perceptions of actions and relationships.
- Early grammatical combinations enable young children to do two important things: to interact with other people and to get things done, and to comment on a state of affairs in the environment.
- In the years from 2 to 4 there is ample evidence of children's unique and unimitated language-learning strategies. Children evolve grammatical rules that produce some errors of over-generalization in plurals and tenses. They also invent verbs and nouns by analogy with conventional forms.

Language and Thinking

The Relationship Debate
The preceding discussion of early language acquisition indicated a considerable degree of interconnectedness between the child's developing language and thinking. But there has always been some debate about which develops first – thought or language – and the exact nature and degree of interdependence between them. The following review attempts to outline four major approaches to these difficult questions. However, the relationship debate should not be viewed as another potential conflict between opposing ideologies, nor is it possible to say that correct and undisputed answers to the questions raised exist somewhere. As with the language acquisition debate, differing perspectives on language and thought have provided useful insights and added to the state of knowledge about them.

These differing views on the probable relationships between language and thinking have also had a direct bearing on their exponents' preferred explanations of early language acquisition. Therefore, the following discussion will be as much concerned with early language as with cognitive theories. Any account of language and thinking must offer possible theories about their beginnings and developments in infancy and early childhood. Some psycholinguistic literature uses the term 'cognition' in place of 'thought' but this does not appear to have any significant effect on the issues discussed. The view that 'thinking' is what the mind does has a respected place in psycholinguistic tradition; therefore, 'thinking' and 'thought' will be used in this discussion.

Linguistic Determinism
Work in language and anthropology in the early decades of this century tended to emphasize the differences between languages, particularly the linguistic gulfs that apparently separated European and non-European languages. This resulted in a very influential approach to the language and thinking problem, which identified language as the source and the determinant of habitual

thought and behaviour. An American linguist, Benjamin Lee Whorf (1956), was mainly responsible for this claim, although it is also associated with aspects of the work of Whorf's mentor, Edward Sapir. Their theory, the Sapir–Whorf hypothesis, suggests that a particular language will dominate and shape its users' perceptions of reality, providing a total world view. Whorf's field-work among the declining South and North American Indian communities revealed the inextricable links between a culture and its language, as well as the ways in which the vocabulary of a language charted the significant and habit-ual features of the life of the language community.

These semantic fields, which are basically groups of words about related areas of meaning, were not the only determining features. The actual gram-matical patterns, or syntax, for referring to time or to actions were very dif-ferent from European forms. These unusual features of some remote languages led Whorf to conclude that language must structure thought – it determines the ways of thinking and responding of which members of a language community are capable. This view is usually called linguistic determinism and it has a further extension, or implication, known as linguistic relativity. This asserts that for a variety of geographical, climatic, social and cultural reasons, the categories of each language are unique to it.

The major problem with this kind of hypothesis is that it views infancy and early childhood as being subject to a process of socialization into a tightly defined world-picture, a closed system of restricted thinking. We are then left with a set of difficulties and alternatives this approach does not address. What of the possibility of independent thought existing before language, or of types of thought without language? What of the influence on thought of our experiences with the world of natural phenomena, and of experiences with objects and people? What of the successful efforts people make to communicate and see the points of view of people from other cultural and linguistic traditions? What of cross-cultural understanding and co-operation in communities and schools? What of the position of bilinguals? Their lan-guages may well give them a hold on two cultural worlds but this can be more of an enrichment than a problem. Are they really muddled and inade-quate thinkers and culturally stateless persons? Finally, what of the very real evidence that good translations between languages are possible and do enrich our lives?

In fact, we know that all these ways of escaping the restrictions of one language are possible. They require conscious effort, goodwill and more elabo-rated uses of language. We may well have to resort to several words or phrases when one will do in another language. This is necessary because different languages encode the important and the obvious in the life and experiences of their particular language community. To take a rather popular example, a wide and subtle range of terms for snow is clearly necessary for groups who exist in the arctic regions. But a child in Peckham also recognizes snow and can talk about it in its many manifestations in south London. It may be freshly fallen and powdery-soft to roll in or packed hard and frozen (ideal for building a snowhouse) or slushy, dirty and melting on busy city roads. Specific lexical items for these states of snow are not necessary in a geographical and climatic region where a fall of snow is an infrequent and exciting event.

Of course, babies and young children are initiated into the language uses and the ways of thinking and living of their communities. However, this is more like an open framework, a trellis for supporting their habitual ways of thinking about experiences and the world, than a linguistic blindfold and straitjacket. A weaker version of the Sapir–Whorf hypothesis has been adopted by some sociologists and educators who would suggest that many children's habitual ways of using language may have a limiting effect on their thinking and their progress in formal education. While some children are readily 'at home' with the language habits and usages of teachers and the linguistic demands of the curriculum, many others may be initially confused and disadvantaged. These kinds of issues will be returned to in subsequent chapters.

Piagetian Views

There is a totally opposite position to that of linguistic determinism, one that argues that thought exists before language and provides the mental structures from which language develops. The researcher responsible for this hypothesis, Jean Piaget, was a biologist by training, but his life's work was the study of the origins of thinking processes in young children. A central feature of his approach is the emphasis it places on the learning achieved by infants in the first 18 months or so of life. This is the period before the main onset of verbal language in many children but, from a Piagetian standpoint, it is the cognitive achievements of these early months that make language possible.

The child's behaviour and thinking are characterized as essentially concerned with 'action and self-directed problem-solving' (Wood, 1988, p. 5). Action, or doing things to the environment, is the way in which the child learns. Action of this kind creates mental structures or schemas that can be used again and modified in further encounters with the world of objects. Knowledge is seen as rather like a store of successful encounters with the environment. In the case of the preverbal infant, these are likely to be sets of schemas or internalized mental representations of actions, such as reaching and grasping a toy, putting a range of objects in the mouth, shaking a rattle and opening a container. In all these thinking and solving of problems behaviours, the important features are the active doing (the motor element) and the seeing, touching, tasting and listening (the sensory element) *(ibid.* p. 22). Hence, this first and most significant of Piaget's stages of development is known as the sensori-motor period.

The general theory certainly allows for greater complexities and for new developments in the child's thinking by stressing the constant need for restructuring and modifying schemas in the face of unpredictable and novel experiences in the environment. For instance, some toys will not be easily grasped, some objects will not fit in the mouth or taste tolerable, and even containers will have a variety of lids and fitting devices. The necessary changes and modifications of the infant's previously internalized ways of acting on these things are described as a process of accommodation. The complementary aspect of this learning process is the knowing or recognizing of a toy or object in terms of what can be done with it, and this is generally described as assimilation.

Piaget's approach to knowledge stresses the ways in which child thinking differs significantly from adult thinking. In particular, the Piagetian concept of child ego-centrism reflects his view that all thinking originates in personal actions on the environment. In the early years, thinking is closely shaped by the child's actual perceptions and unique perspectives on events and objects. This appears to be very much a matter of physical perceptions and personal body-centredness – a case of what can be done with and to objects and materials. It is unfortunate that the term ego-centrism is often confused with the psychological and moral interpretations of ego-centric, with the inevitable connotations of self-centred and self-absorbed behaviour. However, there is a grain of truth in this misconception: it lies in the theory's picture of the solitary, problem-solving infant, who only attains adult ways of thinking logically, and social ways of using language, in adolescence and middle childhood respectively.

Early thinking is characterized as being dominated by perception and the child's inability to give consideration to more than one physical feature of a situation at a time, or allow for the differing perspectives, physical as much as mental, that others may have on the same situation. These features of the Piagetian approach have been radically reappraised in recent years and the new formulations deserve detailed study (Donaldson, 1978; Wood, 1988; Siegal 1991).

It is all too easy to caricature the Piagetian child as either stuck in the one-dimension-at-a-time world of physical perceptions, or stuck in the concrete operations of middle childhood, but the approach to early language in this cognitive theory has tendencies that derive directly from the views of thinking outlined. The approach claims that it is early mental activity that structures language and this tends to marginalize the effects and the significance of the language system as such, particularly in early infancy and childhood. Early language is seen as dominated by ego-centric speech, a kind of personal monologue-cum-running commentary on actions and perceptions. Language is not thought to be truly socialized and directed out towards others until about 7 years of age.

Although in this view language may be seen as increasingly useful in classifying and organizing the child's interactions with materials, objects, people and situations in the middle years of childhood, it only develops a truly significant role in the adolescent and adult phases. The onset of formal operations in early adolescence marks the emergence of the characteristically linguistic mode of thinking that can deal with abstract concepts and mental operations and does not require the props of physical actions and sensory perceptions.

The unalterable order and progression of the stages of thinking in the original Piagetian theory reflect a belief in 'readiness' as an important element in development. All new stages (language being just one) must wait for the appropriate mental structures to develop and to mature. Adult verbal instructions to children will have little effect on these developments; after all, early thinking structures must be created by personal actions on the environment. However, the notion of 'environment' is crucial here. If it is just a world of materials, objects and arbitrary events, the theory can be rightly criticized for under-estimating the most significant feature of a child's environment – other human beings.

To some extent, Piaget's theory has ignored the influences of adults and other children on the infant's early language and thinking, particularly the significant part played by the adult–infant dialogues and interactions discussed in the first part of this chapter. Indeed, the full linguistic significance of preverbal developments in the first 18 months of life do not really have a place in this approach. It is also the case that a theory that minimizes the role of adult instructions and guidance in advance of the child's mental readiness could be in danger of making formal education and instruction redundant. This potential weakness has been known to show up in the misguided policies of a few early years settings, schools and individual practitioners, who thought they were putting Piaget into practice by preparing rich environments of materials, objects and experiences for young children, and then stepping back. They thus left the children virtually alone to explore, solve problems and discover concepts for themselves. This is a travesty of the work of a great and original thinker, who was not a professional educator but a scientist who had no intention of setting out programmes for teachers.

Perspectives from Bruner and Vygotsky

Psychologists, linguists and educators whose early work was inspired by Piaget have gone on to integrate his demonstrations of the ways in which child thought appears to be very different from adult thinking, with powerful accounts of the interpersonal, social and cultural foundations of all human thinking, learning and language. Two such researchers in the areas of psychology, linguistics and education, Lev Vygotsky and Jerome Bruner, have made major contributions to the language and thought debate.

Bruner's early work is often closely linked with Piaget's studies of the initial stages of child thought, particularly as Bruner also describes a period in the first 18 months when thinking and learning are the result of physical actions on the environment. But this enactive phase of representing experience is seen as only the first of a series of thinking strategies that, although they evolve and undergo many reformulations, are still the basis of all later thinking, even in adulthood. Enactive, or action-based thinking, is soon enriched by iconic thinking that creates internalized images or 'pictures in the head' of experiences and encounters with the environment. The development of language leads to a capacity for truly symbolic thinking. However, this is not just another stage on in Bruner's approach, it is a radical re-organization and transformation of the child's thinking and behaviour.

The transforming power of language as a tool for thinking is one of two distinctive aspects of Bruner's view of language and thought. The other is the immense significance of the human social and cultural environments into which children are born. The activities of older people who care for children, participate in language-like games and real conversations with them, and organize small and manageable chunks of social and cultural experience for them to engage with, actually create a scaffold for easy access to the language and culture of the community. These may be complex ideas but they are also describable in terms of another everyday metaphor: infants and small children are apprentices to life, language and learning.

Children work alongside experts who already know the craft or business, but they gradually take over more and more parts of the ways and skills they see demonstrated daily. Bruner does not see the thinking processes of adults as fundamentally different from those of infants, mainly because it is the tool of language that distinguishes all human thought and culture. Language and socialization put a range of strategies for coping at the disposal of both children and adults but, of course, adult experience of language and culture is more extensive, varied and complex.

Thinking symbolically would perhaps best characterize Bruner's view of human cognition and it is language, more than any other system of symbols, that provides the richest range of concepts and distinctions for this. Language in its cultural setting frees child and adult thought from the constraints of the physically and temporally present, the here and now. By substituting words and sentences in place of events, we can have a trial run on reality (Bruner *et al.* 1966, p. 58) and also create totally new worlds of the mind and the imagination.

The contribution of Vygotsky to this debate could be summarized as an inspired compromise between the views of Whorf and Piaget, leading to some radically new hypotheses. He recognized that there were powerful and independent mental and linguistic elements in human thinking but he also claimed that social experiences in early development were crucial to the formation of thought. Before tracing the outline of his complex arguments it may be helpful to have a sense of the distinctive themes that structure his work.

It is important to bear in mind that Vygotsky's research and thinking were done in the 1920s and early 1930s, and first published in 1934 – the year of his death. He has been a powerful influence on many later psychologists, linguists and educators and the implications of his theories are still being explored in current research and thinking (Wertsch, 1985; Bruner, 1986; Kozulin, 1986; Meadows, 1993). One aspect of his work that was revolutionary in its day was his methodology. He chose to look at the genetic roots of language and thinking in the human species by first considering these features, or their antecedents, in our nearest anthropoid cousins, the great apes. From these genetic studies he developed daring and perceptive ideas to link with the approaches of traditional developmental psychology, which studied the origins of language and thinking in the individual child.

Another distinctive feature of Vygotsky's work is his claim that the higher mental processes in the individual (for example, thinking with symbols, such as words and concepts) actually originate in social relationships and processes. The idea that language and other symbolic systems, such as mathematics, writing and art, are psychological tools for thinking developed by cultures, pervades Vygotsky's work and has been taken up by other researchers, notably Bruner.

The theme of mediation is also central to this view of language and characteristic of Vygotsky's approach. He claims that mental processes can only be understood through the psychological tools, the linguistic, mathematical or cultural signs, that mediate them. We can only really understand children's thoughts by a process of trying to understand their gestures, pictures and words. In the case of their words and language, this involves trying to appreciate the cultural meanings of their words, the unique contexts in which they are being used, the range of previous experiences and motivations that may lie behind them and even the style of the utterances and all the nonverbal messages that always accompany words. Just as adults mediate between the child and the language and culture, language, as a system, mediates between the individual and the continual impact of sensory stimuli.

There is also a need for mediation between the spontaneous concepts we discover by exploring the physical environment, for example, 'hot' or 'wet', and the scientific or non-spontaneous concepts we must learn with help. The latter concepts are created by cultures in the process of living, coping and thinking and their preservation is too important to be left to chance: they are taught to the next generation by some form of education. We can include in this 'scientific' category, literacy, as well as scientific, mathematical, technical and aesthetic concepts. All of these have some fundamental links with spontaneous perceptual concepts but they must also be taught or mediated.

Vygotsky's argument in *Thought and Language* (1986) starts from a clear understanding that thought and speech are potentially present but separate at birth, and their subsequent progress is not parallel but undergoes many changes. Vygotsky's study of attempts to teach language to apes convinced him that in the species, as well as in the individual child, thought and speech have different roots. However, at about the age of 2 in individual human development, the separate processes combine.

The earliest thinking in apes and human infants is action-based and concerned with purposeful but basic problem-solving: reaching food or toys and opening containers are typical examples. The earliest 'speech' is sounds produced by air leaving the lungs and passing through the throat, nose and mouth. This provides a very powerful emotional release, as in cries, screams and grunts of pleasure. But this 'speech' also has a definite social function – it keeps the individual in close contact with others and attracts attention and help.

We can see the closeness of Vygotsky's pre-speech stage of thought to Piaget's description of the sensori-motor period of cognitive developments. And Vygotsky's view of the social significance of the pre-intellectual roots of speech anticipates current studies of preverbal interactions. Vygotsky was a contemporary of Piaget and well acquainted with his research at that time, but Vygotsky's emphasis on the significance of sociable pre-speech interactions in infancy was distinctive and out of step with his contemporaries.

When a relatively high level of development has been reached in both preverbal thinking and pre-intellectual speech, the two processes begin to join together to create a new kind of mental function, verbal thinking. This spontaneous merging is unique to the human species and its onset is marked by new language activities in the individual child. It is possible for thoughts to become verbalized and for speech to begin to express rational propositions and requests. This is not an overnight achievement: verbalizing our thoughts and organizing rational speech and writing are the demanding preoccupations of a lifetime.

Vygotsky also described the fusion of thought and speech as partial – some areas of thinking and of speech remain unaffected. Thus, we still appear to be capable of outbursts of non-rational speech, whether under emotional stress or in mindless chanting and rote recitations. We also retain some powerful traces of physical, action-based thinking, particularly in skilled tool use, motor habits and perhaps in such body memories as retaining the ability to swim or ride a bicycle after years of not doing so.

The onset of the verbal thinking process in infancy is marked by two un-mistakable symptoms: the child has a sudden curiosity about words and names for everything, and there is a corresponding rapid increase in the child's vocabulary *(ibid.* p. 82). These symptoms have already been demonstrated in the previous section on early speech and language acquisition, but Vygotsky links this dramatic change in the direction of human thought and language with another puzzling aspect of early language. What is the function and the fate of that talking to themselves out loud that typifies much of the language activity of small children from around 2–5 years of age? Piaget had already observed and identified this verbal accompaniment to the child's activities, describing it as egocentric speech (Piaget, 1926). His initial hypothesis was that it simply died away as the child matured and developed the ability to take the perspectives of others into account and produce appropriately socialized speech.

Vygotsky disagreed with this explanation and produced a rather different account of the evolution of ego-centric speech, claiming that as the child's speech was, in any case, social in its origins, ego-centric speech was not likely to be a symptom of immature ego-centrism that disappeared as the child became socialized in speech and behaviour. On the contrary, ego-centric speech is probably the developmental link between overt language and inner speech or verbal thinking. We all use this continually 'in our heads' as a means of planning, organizing and rehearsing our intellectual, linguistic, social and practical endeavours. Vygotsky noted that the young child's ego-centric speech was already well suited to planning and organizing the child's activities and showed a tendency to become incomprehensible to others. The following example of a 3-year-old attempting to count eight items indicates some of these features: 'One, two, three, four, eight, ten, eleben. No try dat again. One, two, three, four, five, ten, eleben. No, try dat again. One! two! three-e-four-five, ten eleben . . . One! two, three, four, five, six, seven, eleben, whew!' (Gardner, 1980, p. 32).

Ego-centric speech is the same as inner speech in its functions and, although it is initially spoken aloud, it soon turns inwards to become the true inner speech of personal planning. The developmental pattern is, first, social speech, then egocentric speech that appears to branch off, turning inward to become inner speech and continuing to develop as a means of verbal thought. Of course, normal overt social speech also continues to develop, becoming even more responsive to others, as well as capable of expressing more and more of the thinking processes of the individual. It is worth noting that Piaget revised his own initial views on childhood ego-centrism and ego-centric speech, as a direct result of studying Vygotsky's analysis of these phenomena and agreeing with his formulation.

Vygotsky's approach puts its main emphasis on the social nature of the patterns of the speech that is gradually internalized to become a means of higher thinking. 'The child's intellectual growth is contingent on his mastering the social means of thought, that is, language' (Vygotsky, 1986, p. 94). Unlike Whorf's hypothesis, this one is not weakened by the limitations of linguistic relativity but highlights the power of the human language system as such, when it is internalized to become the basic structures of a child's thinking. From the educational point of view, this not only stresses the central significance of human language and culture in the processes of thinking, but it also highlights the impact of the shared and co-operative ways in which language is first acquired.

The way in which early language is learnt in partnership with another led Vygotsky to consider some of the implications for learning and teaching. He noted that small children start by being controlled by others but internalize their language along with the quality of the mutual relationships, thus acquiring a means of self-control. In the speech of the 3-year-old quoted above, the repeated phrase, 'No, try dat again' is very likely to have been first learned from a tutoring and caring adult. It appears to act as an attention-focusing device and a warm counsel of encouragement.

Vygotsky pinpoints this cognitive strategy in a way that makes it relevant, not only for early language and thinking, but also for all learning and teaching encounters: 'what the child can do in cooperation today he can do alone tomorrow' *(ibid.* p. 188). This approach highlights the obvious fact that words and concepts give children access to their languages and their cultures and begin to transform their thinking.

Later research, based on Vygotsky's work, clearly demonstrated the role of language as a regulator of children's activities and the source of complex mental processes concerned with planning, organizing, sequencing thought and action, and transcending the immediate situation (Luria and Yudovich, 1971). This work is a classic demonstration of the fact that 'the acquisition of a language system involves a reorganization of all the child's basic mental processes' *(ibid.* p. 23).

- There are differing views about the nature of language and thought and the kind and degree of relationship between them. These various approaches also lead to different accounts of early language acquisition.
- The Sapir–Whorf hypothesis focuses on the differences between languages and claims that particular languages determine their speakers' ways of thinking. The particular categories and concepts of a language are considered to be unique to that language.
- The view of Piaget is that thought develops first from sensori-motor activities and creates the mental structures crucial for language development. The ability to use language in abstract and symbolic ways develops in early adolescence with formal operations.
- Bruner acknowledges the significance of early perverbal thinking but he stresses the role of adults in organizing language and cultural experiences for the child. Language as a system re-organizes and transforms human thinking – it is the tool for symbolic thought.
- Vygotsky claimed that thought and speech have different genetic roots and growth but they join together, at around the age of 2, to create verbal thought. The primary function of speech is social but from this there develops, in infancy, ego-centric speech for planning and self-organization. This turns inward to become inner speech and verbal thinking. Vygotsky stresses the importance for thinking of the child's dialogues and activities with adults: the internalization of these dialogues brings the tool of language to bear on the structures of thought.

Words, Concepts and a Name for Everything

One useful way of summarizing this chapter on early language acquisition and the development of thought is to return to the main concern of Wally and Eddie, getting a name for everything! The nature of words and concepts has been taken for granted throughout this discussion and it is time to pull together the many implicit assumptions about the early emergence of words, the rapid growth in young children's vocabulary and the ways in which children's words reflect their social and cultural experiences and their own thinking.

To understand words and concepts we have to consider some complex ideas about meaning, reference and the mind (Aitchison, 1994). This can involve tackling profoundly difficult issues and questions that baffle linguists and philosophers and often lead to a kind of mental paralysis! It is notoriously difficult to decide what meaning means, or what others mean by their uses of words and names. There is also the problem of deciding what exactly is being referred to when people point to and name objects, actions and events in the world. In the end, if one is not doing philosophy, one just has to take the common-sense view that external reality exists and that meaning and reference are possible. Clearly, this approach must have been taken intuitively by every adult who ever played and talked with an infant, or we would all be trapped in a wordless limbo of not meaning and not daring to communicate.

The common-sense approach begins with the verbal and social receptions given to newborn babies. First, adults appear to believe that individual meanings and social communication are possible and they attribute these same motives to all the early responses of babies and to their later sounds and words. Second, from the start of their relationship, adult and infant commence on mutual question-and-answer behaviours. This is another vote of confidence for meaning: it implies a practical belief that questions are capable of being answered. Third, as Bruner (1983, p. 86) has pointed out, a few philosophers and most carers do work on the assumption that no one is entirely ignorant, not even an infant, and no one is entirely all-knowing either. This highlights the important fact that meaning is far more extensive than individual word referents: areas of meaning have to be constantly sorted out, negotiated and clarified. The fact that at some time we have all had the experience of struggling to put our meanings into words for an important letter, essay or argument indicates this. Such struggles with words and meanings are a daily feature of children's gradual acquisition of words and concepts in infancy and in the early years of schooling. Perhaps we are not too aware of this because the struggle is often shared with an older language user and is a source of pleasure and delight for both partners.

The business of establishing mutual reference, what it is we are both pointing to, referring to or discussing, is started in the infant's earliest weeks and months. At this stage, as in the later labelling-of-the-environment stage, mutual negotiations and feedback are important and effort goes into getting it as right as is humanly possible. Bruner's *(ibid.)* analysis of a possible developmental pattern for establishing early reference focused on carers' games with babies and the progress from simple eye contacts to shared commentaries on interesting objects, people and events. Often a great number of 'where is it' and 'what is it' games and rituals develop around this stage and they further reinforce the infant's ability to communicate, refer to things and share meanings with adults and older children. Similarly, book and picture reading, involving shared pointing and naming, support and strengthen the child's early awareness of words as labels that mark out and refer to areas of meaning.

Labelling probably plays a significant part in early language and thinking (Clark, 1993). One crucial feature of this activity is the picking out and highlighting of a word! Despite all the philosophers' reservations about what pointing means, adults and older children tend to name unerringly a whole object for a baby. They will say, 'it's a horse', rather than 'you appear to be indicating a grey hair on the left fetlock of a Suffolk Punch stallion'. The establishment of such basic generic categories as 'horse' enables beginners to take a grip on the language. Broad classifications are a good start. Subsets and other distinctions can be organized and refined over time, by general experience as well as organized education.

Pairing objects and names in this way demonstrates a fundamental feature of a linguistic system. There is a conventional, or culturally agreed, relationship between the sign, the phonetic pattern 'horse' and the signified, the living creature in front of us, or its pictorial representation. Playing linguistic games with experienced speakers eases children into the ways in which their communities name the world. It also establishes some of the core meanings of linguistic concepts. A great deal of object naming occurs in early infancy, not just when looking at picture books, magazines and photos, but when participating in daily routines, games of I-spy, peekaboo and body labelling ('where's your nose?') and even when focusing on some television images.

The labelling of actions and attributes tends to follow later, as children become more active, mobile and exploratory. Abstract ideas might seem to be impossible to acquire by pointing and naming activities as there is no object or event to single out for attention, but many ideas do appear to be rooted in early experiences. The mystery of how such very young children pick up core meanings and use them appropriately but in different circumstances and after a period of time has elapsed, is not easily answered. Most linguists accept the mystery and some even talk of the achievement as an insight. However, the separate and rapid development of thought in the early months must also be an important factor.

Vygotsky's research into concept formation and Piaget's and Bruner's into the development of early representation indicate that in the first 18 months or so infants move gradually from acting on their environments and solving problems 'with their bodies', to acting and problem-solving 'in their heads'. This progress from perceptions and actions (through images) to language symbols, is a steady accumulation of physical, iconic and linguistic strategies. It is not a process of discarding outgrown ways of thinking as new possibilities develop. The words children acquire are powerful tools that transform their existing strategies for identifying, sorting, classifying and re-organizing information and experience. This is perhaps one way of accounting for Halliday's (1975) evidence that words are used in two major ways almost immediately: to get things done (the active pragmatic mode) and to contemplate and make sense of words themselves and of experiences (the mathetic mode). Words lock onto children's already well-developed thinking structures for making sense and organizing experience.

When language begins to define the world it opens up the possibilities of making finer discriminations and of handling more elaborated classes of experience and information. Words refer to actual things, states and events in the world, but they are the evidence of underlying concepts or classifications in the minds of their users (Bridges, Sinha and Walkerdine, 1981, p. 137). Concepts are general categories and the means of symbolic thinking. This is the kind of thinking freed from dependence on physical perceptions and present actions: all the action and manipulation is in the head. It is these general linguistic categories that become increasingly significant in children's thinking strategies and dominant in mature adult thinking. But this is to consider concepts at their most abstract when, in fact, they have their origins in perceptions, actions and the shared learning of language in communities.

Concepts are built up slowly in individual development. They are collaborative and shared creations of the linguistic community that are taken over by individuals and coloured by personal feelings and associations. That concepts develop over time and by a process of negotiation and modification in individual language learning is demonstrated by small children's many over- and under-extensions of words in use. Examples are given in the earlier section on first words and in the published literature (see further reading).

Thinking with concepts is a flexible and powerful system because it enables us to generalize and group together instances of 'the same'. With this grouping potential we are also able to differentiate and classify those events and things that are 'not' instances. Linguistic concepts reflect an infinite range of possible hierarchies and categories: many of these mirror habitual ways of thinking in particular cultural traditions. However, this does not necessarily restrict thought, despite the Sapir–Whorf hypothesis. Concepts are a flexible range of options that help us to impose some order and pattern on the complexity and diversity of raw experience. This infinitely adaptable tool for thinking and organizing knowledge is created in the process of learning a language. A concept may start its slow growth from a picture-book label, a simple toy or the experience of being held up to look out of the window by an adult. The development of concepts is affected by personal life experiences, cultural traditions and the subtle processes by which any new information, new experiences and new words are matched to and integrated with the already experienced, named and known. The range of language modes – listening and talking, writing and reading – as well as quiet reflection and the shared life of homes and the wider community, are all influences on individual conceptual thinking.

- Meaning and reference are first established in the games and interactions that are the start of joint attention between adults and their infants.
- Labelling objects, actions, events and ideas begins in earliest infancy and helps to isolate words as specific areas of meaning. First labels are usually general names for things but they demonstrate the language community's ways of classifying the world.
- Words refer to actual experiences and things in the world but they also stand for concepts or classifications in the minds of speakers.
- Concepts are generalized categories: they classify similarities, differences and hierarchies (or families) of connected ideas, objects and happenings.

- Concepts are usually thought to have core meanings, perceptual information and linguistic signs. Personal associations also play a part in the complex development of concepts.
- Thinking with concepts develops with language use and is a life-long process of learning to handle new experiences and information by modifying and re-organizing the already known and familiar.

Teaching and Learning Suggestions

* Use group talking times (circle times or review sessions) to raise language issues quite specifically; e.g., ask children how they think they learnt to speak. Or ask them if their parents, carers and siblings remember the interesting things they said when they were babies. Gradually build up a collection of stories about 'How we learnt to talk'.

* Set up baby care provision in the role-play area and try to audiotape (videotape if possible) the children's talk to the 'babies'. Make observation notes on their ability to modify their language: note any evidence of a baby-talk register, or dialect and language switching. Try to observe body language, eye contact and facial expressions. Add any observations to individual records and assessments.

* Set up a telephone in a role-play area and tape record (audio and/or video) the telephone language of the children. How do they 'create' their non-existent language partner and what sort of issues and topics occur in these 'conversations'? (see Hall and Martello, 1996). Add these observations to individual records of developments and progress in speaking and listening.

* Show the children some films of young babies socializing and beginning to communicate and talk (available from many child development courses and educational film makers). Discuss what is happening and what carers and babies do together. Relate these matters to the children's own understanding of what they use language for and what it does for them.

* Use role play and drama to explore other ways of communicating without using talk. Range as widely as possible, from animal communications to flags and smoke signals: from sheepdog whistles (the film *Babe* might come in here) to human signing (as used by the deaf) and touch systems (e.g. Braille); as well as a range of cultural symbols and signals.

Further Reading

Aitchison, J. (1976; 1983; 1989) *The Articulate Mammal. An introduction to psycholinguistics*, Hutchinson, London; Routledge, London.

Aitchison, J. (1987; 1994) *Words in the Mind. An introduction to the mental lexicon*, Blackwell, Oxford.

Bennett, M. (ed.) (1993) *The Child as Psychologist. An introduction to the development of social cognition*, Harvester Wheatsheaf, Hemel Hempstead.

Clark, E. (1993) *The Lexicon in Acquisition*, Cambridge University Press.

Gallaway, C. and Richards, B.J. (eds.) (1994) *Input and Interaction in Language Acquisition*, Cambridge University Press.

Harris, M. (1992) *Language Experience and Early Language Development*, Lawrence Erlbaum, Hove.

Meadows, S. (1993) *The Child as Thinker*, Routledge, London.

Smith, F. (1992) *To Think. In language, learning and education*, Routledge, London.

Vygotsky, L.S. (1986) *Thought and Language*, MIT Press, Cambridge, Mass. (revised and edited by A. Kozulin).

Wells, G. (1987) *The Meaning Makers. Children learning language and using language to learn*, Hodder & Stoughton, Sevenoaks.

Wood, D. (1988) *How Children Think and Learn*, Blackwell, Oxford.

4

Knowledge about language and the early-years educator

From Theory to Practice?

Knowledge about language has become a crucial issue for educators and children since the 1995 revised programmes of study and attainment targets for English in the National Curriculum made Standard English and Language Study general requirements for Speaking and Listening, Reading and Writing at all levels (DFE, 1995). However, decisions about what to do in educational settings do not automatically emerge from official documents or from an explicit knowledge of linguistics, nor do children 'change their use of language merely because teachers say they should' (Sealey, 1996, p. 68). If we can derive from a knowledge of linguistics useful pointers for good practice in early years education, it will be by a subtle and complex process which puts great responsibility on the professional role of the practitioner.

If it is a fallacy to assume that educational practices can be deduced directly from research-based theory, it is also a fallacy to pursue the 'practitioner' equivalent which adopts a one-way-street view of education: in effect, teachers teach and children learn (De Vries and Kohlberg, 1987, p. 14). This belief permeates the National Curriculum documentation and the Desirable Outcomes for Children's Learning on entering compulsory education (SCAA, 1996a), indicating a curriculum model which does not acknowledge studies of pedagogy and child development and their contributions to our understanding of learning and teaching and language development. What works is, apparently, what works for teachers and the responses, contributions, knowledge and misunderstandings of children are irrelevant.

How, in practice, are we to avoid the linguist's fallacy that goes straight from linguistic knowledge to curriculum content and the practitioner's fallacy that goes one way, straight from teacher to pupil? One solution is to reinstate the somewhat eroded professional role of the educator as one who makes informed choices and creates the educational context for knowledge – linguistic or any other. We must place what we know about language in a framework created by our detailed professional knowledge of children, our curriculum expertise and our involvement with the families and communities who use early years settings and schools.

Detailed knowledge of individual children is built up by sustained observations and record-keeping, plus the cumulative experience of being an educator and studying many aspects of child development, as well as social and theoretical perspectives on education. A curriculum is always a selection from all the available knowledge and experiential resources of a culture and even the nationally imposed curriculum only stipulates broad areas of consensus. There are still many choices to be made, from linguistics and myriad other activities and disciplines. Choices and value judgements are unavoidable. At every point in the day educators are saying and implying, 'this rather than that'. It is surely better for these choices to be informed rather than blind, to be explicit rather than hidden, or even irrational. Educators have to contextualize language knowledge, not just for 'these children', but for these children in this place, at this time and in relation to these families and these communities. Professional involvement in children's out-of-school or group-setting lives is not an excuse for offering a watered-down curriculum or third-rate education and care. On the contrary, it is a serious acknowledgement of children's great potential for language and learning, especially when sustained by familiar and important environments and relationships. Early years settings and schools cannot hope to be just like homes and families but they may, as institutions staffed by caring and knowledgeable practitioners, learn how to minimize their drawbacks and develop good human learning practices.

The choices made by educators must be informed and this is where the usefulness of a body of knowledge such as linguistics can be assessed. So, of what use to early childhood educators and young learners is knowledge about modern linguistics? Put as bluntly as this, the question forces a reconsideration of the material in the previous chapters. This task is one we all have to do for ourselves, statutory requirements and lists of easy answers are not really helpful. After all, they lack the crucial contextual knowledge of situations, individuals and pedagogy which only the professional educator can bring together.

The combined knowledge, information, experience and insight that help us to move from 'knowing about' to 'doing something about' is often expressed as a move from theory to practice (Stubbs, 1986). In the context of this book informed choices guiding the move will necessitate some understanding of the development of the modern study of linguistics with its focus on utterances, or 'parole', including an awareness of the theories put forward by linguists to account for how language works as a system, or 'langue' (Chapter 1), and how languages are learned and used in particular social settings (Chapters 2 and 3). These preceding chapters attempt to describe the theories, although the descriptions are highly selective and presented with the concerns of early years educators in mind. Educators also need to know how to activate and nurture young children's conscious knowledge about, and delight in, their own languages. The following sections are pointers towards educationally worthwhile practices that might be developed from some of the things educators, carers and children know about language as a system, language in social contexts and language in thinking and learning.

Language Knowledge and the Educators

The high profile for Language Knowledge, or Language Study, began with the Bullock Report (DES, 1975), was developed by the Kingman and Cox Reports (DES, 1988a, 1988b) and was then worked on by the LINC project (Language in the National Curriculum, 1989–1992, unpublished). It is now re-emerging as the Standard English and Language Study components of the revised orders for English (DFE, 1995), although there is nothing straightforward and uncontroversial about either topic. Perera (1987) identified at least three possible meanings involved in linguistic knowledge: our implicit competence in our first languages; the explicit knowledge gained from any study which heightens our language awareness; and the technical knowledge of the professional linguist (see Chapter 1). Some explicit linguistic knowledge can be an exciting gain from the best kind of language awareness courses for children and adults, but there is always the lurking danger of what Perera calls 'the naming of parts' approach to language study (1987, pp. 37–9). This has the effect of detracting from the richness and variety of language in use and de-skills competent users, children and adults alike, although it is what so many ill-informed commentators take to be 'proper' language study!

One of the great dangers of formalizing in legislation what constitutes knowledge about language is the creation of an orthodoxy, a kind of received view of language. This will tend to under-estimate the inexperienced and very young users of a particular language, as well as any other people who are in the process of learning the language. An established national view of language (or of anything else) is always in danger of becoming petrified and unchangeable. The terrible irony of this is that languages are always changing in subtle and complex ways in order to meet the evolving needs and circumstances of their speakers.

Although the National Curriculum documentation rejects a return to Latin-style notions of grammar, there is a move towards the teaching of parts of speech in the specific focus on Language Study, especially as it is linked with SE. Assumptions about the superiority of English and its associations with order and control in society have permeated the public perception of language teaching for generations and are now reflected in the Desirable Outcomes for Children's Learning on entering compulsory education (SCAA, 1996a) and the draft proposals for Baseline Assessment (SCAA, 1996b). The continued use of the label 'English' for what was once known as 'language in education' is leading to a reduction in the breadth and significance of language teaching in schools. It has, in effect, reduced all the variety and complexity of human language to a territorial definition (Cameron and Bourne, 1989).

The time has come to re-claim some professional and linguistic territory. Language knowledge for early years educators should, at the very least, include familiarity with all the detailed, long-term ethnographic studies that reveal the richness and intellectual power of young children's language development in secure and familiar domestic settings (Heath, 1983; Cochran-Smith, 1984; Tizard and Hughes, 1984; Wells, 1985). The grammatical, cognitive and social perspectives outlined in the first part of this book suggest that educators, carers and families should know that:

- all children are linguists
- all languages are complex grammatical systems
- all natural languages are, or have been, spoken
- language and thinking are inextricably linked.

This knowledge should be an expansion and enrichment of practitioners' insights, not a requirement to narrow our concerns to a tight set of attainment targets in spoken and written English. Language in use for living and learning is still the core of the language curriculum and this broader conception of knowledge about language should inform all the thinking and professional practices of teachers and other practitioners.

Early years educators may be further helped by some important curriculum principles for language planning. First, very young children entering group settings and educational provision have already accomplished their greatest intellectual and social feat of learning: they have, with very rare exceptions, learnt to produce and understand a language. Second, our professional practices depend on making informed choices based on our knowledge and experience of children, society and the curriculum. But these choices are themselves provisional and always subject to criticism and reappraisal. Third, worthwhile education in the early years should be dominated by the children's needs to discover, organize, make sense of and enquire about their worlds. These essential cognitive activities will be developed through and by the processes of symbolic representation which enable us all to hold on to and contemplate ideas, feelings and events. This 'holding' is possible because symbols that stand for ideas and experiences of all kinds are created through playing, gesturing, drawing, building, labelling, naming, story-telling and writing. Symbols reflect not just the personal life events and interests of individuals, but the social and cultural practices of communities. Perhaps the most significant aspect of knowledge about language for the early years educator is the understanding that language is about human potential.

Language Study in Early Years Settings

The study of language may seem to be far too abstract and remote from the concerns of small children in early years settings and not likely to touch their lives. But this view does not stand up to serious examination. First, very young children are, as I have claimed above, linguists. They are born communicators, language learners, speakers and listeners; many are bilingual and they are all somewhere on the way to becoming writers and readers. There is nothing remote about their degree of involvement in language matters: much of what researchers know about linguistics is based on studies of child language acquisition and development.

Second, the professionals who work with young children are actually making linguistic decisions throughout the day and these need to be educationally as well as linguistically 'good' reasons for intervention. The educational practitioner should judge 'worthwhile' activities and decisions as being of value primarily for the children. These judgements should lead to choosing, resourcing and supporting activities and areas of knowledge (including language) that are believed to be intrinsically valuable and interesting to the children, that extend what they know and can do already, that enrich their thinking and imagining and that increase their self-control, esteem and independence.

Third, potential, if not very explicit, language study has gone on in early years settings and homes for a long while. We have just described it differently, using such terms as:

talking; listening; interacting; playing and role play; mime; action songs and rhymes; singing; poetry; nursery and nonsense rhymes; mark-making; drawing; emergent writing; story-telling; story reading; shared reading; looking at books; making labels, lists, books, notices, greetings, directions and instructions; using letter magnets, computers and printing sets; shared writing.

This rich panorama of language study can be brought into sharper focus if we concentrate on four significant aspects of the language curriculum:

- playing with language
- telling stories and sharing books
- writing
- using 'words about language'.

Playing with language starts with sound and it starts in the cradle. Sound is the very stuff of language and it is exploited and mucked about whenever and wherever babies (and carers) blow 'raspberries', gurgle, squeal and babble for the sheer delight of doing it. Infants continue to play this kind of language game when they are alone at night, well into the second and third year of life (Weir, 1962; Nelson, 1989). Researchers have recorded highly patterned rhyming and alliterative sequences by young children which indicate a very early delight in practising and playing with langugage:

> bink
> let bobo bink
> bink ben bink
> blue kink
>
> (Weir, 1962, p. 105)

This recording of Anthony at 2 years 6 months was made in the 1950s but modern research studies now highlight the significance of alliteration and rhyme for children's early success in learning to read and understand the writing system (Bryant and Bradley, 1985; Goswami and Bryant, 1990). These issues will be explored further in Chapter 6 but the implications for the educator are already becoming clear. We should avoid reliance on such oddities as 'sound tables' and phonic lists with young children, because people talking and playing with language are the real source of phonological knowledge – not tables! Children in early years settings deserve 'poetry tables' and collections of verse, a rich diet of songs, rhymes and nonsense, word games and commercial and home-made alphabets.

Play with language can be mildly naughty when rude noises and silly words emerge from phonological and alphabetical experiments, but this subversive aspect of language play is not only motivating for the young linguist, it is intellectually stimulating. For it is not only sounds and words that are mucked about with; right from the start ideas are turned upside down. In the 1920s

Chukovsky wrote of the 'topsy-turvies' (1963, p. 94) which constitute children's first jokes and the humour of ancient folk tales and nursery rhymes. This is the world of cottages running away on chicken legs, adults going to sea in a sieve, cold porridge burning the mouth and cows jumping over the moon! The examples spring to mind endlessly, but it is worth thinking of them as test cases of reality in a culture, and as soon as little children get to know what is what they exploit it relentlessly. It is as if knowing something means knowing its opposite and its 'non-instances'. The following example from my 5-year-old grandson indicated his awareness of the cultural assumption that children must learn to count:

> I can count up to one hundred. One, two, miss a few, ninety-nine, a hundred.

The power of such subversion is that it not only gets round the problem, it amuses adults and deflects criticism, but it also snatches back some self-esteem. This is crucial for the young and vulnerable who are never quite old enough, big enough or knowledgeable enough, hence the significance of all those characters in stories and rhymes who are sillier and dumber than any living child.

Early encounters with stories and books support language study by introducing children to distinctive language and narrative patterns, such as beginnings, threats, challenges, solutions and endings. These kinds of events are marked by ritual openings, as in 'once upon a time', stylized descriptions such as 'rose red', and formal endings where all issues are resolved by the language of 'happy ever afters'. This is not a bit like the everyday spoken English heard and used on buses and in supermarkets, schools, playgroups and clinics, because this is the language of literary genres. However, it is far from unimportant because it provides a first bridge to written SE: just hearing all kinds of stories and poetry read aloud enables children to become familiar with the distinctive patterns of written language. This implication holds good for the language of non-fiction information texts and we should give much more time to reading these texts aloud with children than we generally do. Many picture books also teach aspects of language study and although Chapter 6 will be concerned with the value of books in the early years it is worth noting this very specific function here. Some books are focused on alliteration (*Who's A Clever Baby Then?* McKee, 1988), some depend on the clues given by rhymes (*Each Peach Pear Plum* Ahlberg, 1977, *The Jolly Postman* Ahlberg, 1986), and some explore dialects of English and the delights of rare and beautiful words (*The Mousehole Cat* Barber and Bayley, 1990, *Flossie and the Fox* McKissack, 1986). There is even a deceptively simple picture book which plays with the nature and functions of adjectives and nouns, as well as colours – so why do we need 'colour tables' (*Mr. Rabbit and the Lovely Present* Zolotow and Sendak, 1962)?

If we add to these experiences with books, games with print sets, magnetic letters, computer keyboards and important words and sentences written on strips of paper, we are helping children to explore the creative, or combinatorial, power of language. We are also teaching the first lesson of literacy: speech and writing are different. Talk is experienced as a stream of sound, but if it is to become writing it must be broken down into words and, eventually, smaller sound elements.

For educators and children alike, the fundamental focus of all literacy work must be to establish the understanding that writing conveys meaningful messages: messages that are informative, important and often pleasurable. Very young children use some powerful strategies in order to understand writing and these will be discussed in Chapter 7, but certain elements are worth noting here in the context of language study. First, there is the very effective strategy which we might call 'watch the others' and this includes watching not just adults, older children and peers, but TV, posters, street signs, shops, vehicles, junk mail and public offices.

Then there is the 'use your name' ploy which gives every child a useful tool for breaking into the writing system. Names matter, they place you in the world and are frequently heard and seen in many contexts, but most importantly of all for the beginning writer and reader, they are a known combination of meaningful sounds and symbols. Names give the child a demonstration of how the alphabetic system works and initial letters and sounds are of great significance for this development:

'That's D for Daniel', said Daniel, pointing to a museum dinosaur poster.
'I begin with C', said Cecilia Payton (Payton, 1984, p. 85).

'Exploit what you know' enables very young infants to get started on written communications as they use powerful cultural symbols like 'x' for kisses on letters, or various marks and even letters from their names on messages. The emerging principle seems to be one of 'use what you do know and have a pretend go at the unknown bits'. This can then be developed on to become a full-blown emergent literacy strategy of using alphabetic knowledge, as well as exploiting those letter names which sound like words and syllables in frequent use: RUDF [are you deaf?] (Bissex, 1980, p. 3).

These inventive strategies and processes will take young children further along the road to understanding the alphabetic system than artificial exercises in copying with a high premium put on being correct from the start. Children can be supported by provision which includes writing in role play; collecting advertising copy, newspapers, magazines and leaflets; and opportunities to hear, see, discuss and create play scripts, TV news bulletins, weather forecasts, and so on.

The use of 'words about language' is known to professional linguists as 'metalinguistics' and is an important component of serious language study at any level. For very young children and their educators it is a matter of being confident about understanding and using some special vocabulary for genuine purposes. This does not require the pointless and easily forgotten 'naming of parts' but a frequent recourse to such terms as 'word', 'letter', 'sound', 'capital' and even 'sentence'. Such practices as reading large format books with groups of children, creating pieces of shared writing and making books together, naturally require the use of even more special 'language about language'. For example, 'cover', 'title', 'author', 'illustrator', 'publisher', 'printer', 'page', 'endpaper', 'chapter'.

This approach is not only meaningful and pleasurable for children and adults, it is a sensible way of satisfying the Key Stage 1 Language Study requirements that children should be encouraged to develop an interest in words and the language of particular genres and social settings, and given opportunities to consider the characteristics of different kinds of text, as well as helped to extend their written vocabulary and their interest in words and meanings (DFE, 1995).

Language Study need not be narrow, dull and limiting; it should be about playing with sounds and meanings and loving language. It is going on all the time and the children are keen to show us the way, as I discovered on a recent visit to a Year 1 class when two 6-year-olds set about subverting a particularly dreary science lesson on the naming of the parts of a tree.

'This is the bark', said the teacher.
'Woof, woof', said a little voice.
'And this is the trunk'.
'Elephants have trunks,' piped up another little linguist.

Language in Social Contexts

Children are born into language-using communities and they gradually learn to communicate and share the language or languages of their particular social worlds. Earlier chapters have emphasized the high degree of linguistic variety within and between language communities, as well as the range of language choices individual speakers operate. However, one aspect of variety has been glossed over and this is a direct reflection of the comparative thinness of research on the topic: early language acquisition in non-European and non-Anglo-Saxon cultures. The wealth of research material on infant and care-giver behaviours has been predominantly biased towards American and European cultures, and towards the child-rearing practices of mainstream, school-orientated or middle-class groups. We still have only a partial picture of the early stages of language learning and many children in our schools will have experienced cultural practices that are different and unknown to their teachers.

We must always be cautious in our acceptance of any research in the area of human relationships and child rearing, bearing in mind that the observing of families and groups is an intrusion that changes the patterns of response and interaction in subtle ways. All research reports are broadly generalized and over-simplified in ways that make the actual experiences reported blander and less detailed than real life feels to the participants.

There are other ways of welcoming babies into the world, nurturing them and supporting their learning of the particular languages and communicative traditions of their groups and societies. In recent years attempts to understand and to record these other ways have begun to influence linguists, psychologists and educators. These approaches are generally described as 'ethnographic' and the most widely known studies are those that have investigated how young children experience and respond to forms of literacy and early schooling in cultures not traditionally formal-schooling and book-oriented. Ethnographic studies are a branch of anthropology and focus on all aspects of the social life of a cohesive social group. Ethnographers go to great lengths to make themselves part of the social worlds they study, accepting their norms and styles and avoiding, as far as possible, the use of intrusive and alien technologies and styles of interaction.

Such approaches have begun to influence general work in child language and the result is many long-term studies closely based on daily life in homes, family groups, nurseries and schools (see, for example, Heath, 1983; Cochran-Smith, 1984; Tizard and Hughes, 1984; Wells, 1985; Polanyi, 1985). This work tends to focus on such issues as who the main care-givers of babies are in the early months and years of language acquisition and what the characteristic features of their interactions and relationships are. The answers to these questions are tentative, but some general features may be worth adding to our own cultural assumptions about language learning.

The human infant is usually highly valued and cared for with some degree of affection and, although not always mothered by one adult only, is the special responsibility of certain adults and groups of older children. The main aim of these carers seems to include 'teaching' the infant the ways and the language of the community. This is not necessarily done by looking at picture books or playing games of peekaboo and 'what's this?' Instead, there may be instructions in religious stories, rituals and eating habits, or the involvement of the infant in the games, songs and language play of older children (Heath, 1983). Behind all these teaching activities in many cultures is a strong desire to help young children join the community as full speaking members as soon as possible. To this end, interactions with very young children are generally tolerant of their inadequacies, supportive of lots of language practice, full of praise and pride in the children's progress and, sometimes (but not always), simplified in the range of linguistic forms used:

Mother: I'm going to do this work first, love. I've got washing to do.
Child: Yeah?
Mother: Got ironing to do.
Child: Yeah?
Mother: I got hoovering to do.
Child: Yeah?
Mother: Yeah, well it all takes time, love.
Child: And then you're finished?
Mother: Yeah, and then I'm finished.

(Tizard and Hughes, 1984, p. 166)

Donna, the child, was learning not just some language patterns but the realities of working life and priorities for women and children of a specific social class in inner London. In communities and societies everywhere, children learn their languages as part-and-parcel of their learning about roles and functions individuals perform in the community. They learn when to speak and when to stay silent, they learn when to be deferential and when to assert their rights as speakers. The complexity of these judgements makes them part of the inside knowledge of a group.

Educators who are on the fringes of many communities must, like ethnographers, try to observe, understand and acknowledge without imposing their inappropriate judgements. If teachers can learn to listen to their pupils and their families without prejudice, they too may learn to move more easily and confidently between language worlds and cultures. This is, after all, what schooling demands of many of these young children. Cultural variety also involves diverse kinds of voice intonation and pitch patterns and markedly different ranges of body language. Such differences put considerable responsibility on the professional educator to be knowledgeable, observant and less easily offended than the average person.

So many different 'ways with words' (Heath, 1983) should shake us out of our Western research complacency but not obscure the fact that all children learn to speak in broadly similar stages and rates. Across many different cultures infants begin by gaining control of those major functions Halliday (1975) has called personal and regulatory. Children learn to insert themselves and their needs into the ongoing concerns of the group and they learn to involve other people in doing things for them. Researchers are now aware that this is achieved in secure and intimate first relationships which allow infants to be playful, bold and teasing (Reddy, 1991; Trevarthen, 1993). The role of older and more experienced members of the community remains very significant in all children's learning and language acquisition. This role may be performed differently, according to the values and beliefs of the group, but it is geared to the child's well-being and eventual full participation in the community:

> They gotta know what works and what don't, you sit in a chair, but if you hafta, you can sit on other things too – stool, a trunk, a step, a bucket. Whatcha call it ain't so important as whatcha do with it. That's what things 'n people are for, ain't it?
>
> (Heath, 1983, p. 112)

One other common factor emerges from studies of learning to speak in many cultures: the central role of the oral narrative. Children learn much of their language and their culture by listening to the telling of anecdotes, legends, gossip, stories, jokes, dreams and memories, and they are often encouraged to make their own story contributions, or praised for seizing the story-telling initiative. This is so fascinating and significant a feature of human language behaviour that it is looked at in detail in Chapter 5.

Multilingualism in Early Years Settings

Many children in early years settings are already bilingual or at some stage in the process of acquiring their second language, usually that of the group settings, schools and wider society. The simplicity of this description needs to be treated with caution and set alongside the reality of life in many multilingual families: one language with parents, another for grandparents, another for religious observances and instruction, another for neighbours, shops and schools. Recent research has confirmed that this degree of linguistic variety is quite usual for many young children (Barratt-Pugh, 1994) and leads to situations in which these children become the essential mediators, advisers and links between their families and the mainstream public world (Mills and Mills, 1993).

Bilingualism is not a hindrance, but an asset which will increase children's linguistic awareness, cultural sensitivity and cognitive functioning. Similarly, teaching and caring for young bilinguals can offer practitioners the same benefits, but only if they are open to challenging new ideas. For example, the theory of interlanguage (Selinker, 1992) highlights the creative and complex ways in which the early stages of multi-language learning are marked by 'borrowings' and subtle movements between the languages being processed. This gives us a far more informative picture of language acquisition than approaches coloured by negative assumptions about language 'interference'. Young bilinguals are already operating with at least two potent symbolic systems for handling thought and experience and their language learning in group settings is best supported through a variety of representational forms, such as pictures, stories, puppets, modelling and building, music and visits in the wider community. Educators must hang on to the conviction that 'good practice for monolingual children should also be good practice for bilingual children' (Mills and Mills, 1993, p. 60).

Faced with children's linguistic creativity and diversity, monolingual educators must first acknowledge the greater linguistic skills, experience and potential of their pupils. A start can then be made on using other languages in schools and early years settings for important functions and the prestigious curriculum areas. Dual language signs on cloakrooms and offices may be useful, but restricting some languages to utilitarian functions signals their possible exclusion from education, achievement and success in the wider dominant culture. To exclude a language is to exclude its speakers. Yet even the well-intentioned arrangement of two languages in dual language textbooks and other materials needs careful thought: unacceptable hidden messages about status and values must be anticipated and avoided. A few authors and publishers have begun to change the practice of printing English first, with other languages underneath, and there is a modest amount of worthwhile children's literature and reference texts in several languages. But still not enough.

Early years educators do not have to wait and hope that more quality material will eventually be published. It is essential that we produce it ourselves in our settings and extend book-making projects to include making games and other materials and, most importantly, the contributions and involvement of the children's families. The existence of such technologies as computers and publishing software, ring-binding and laminating machines, photocopiers and fool-proof cameras, etc., supports and extends the basic professional skills of the educator who must still be able to print clearly and mount and display children's work.

Home-grown publishing projects have the added advantage of making us all face up to our own limitations, attitudes and intentions with regard to parental and community involvement in settings and schools. None of us has the linguistic skills and cultural experiences to meet the language needs and strengths of all the bilingual children in our settings. Recruiting some bilingual teachers and other professionals, as well as inviting the participation of parents, grandparents, older siblings and other members of the local linguistic groups, can provide a rich human resource of multilanguage tutors. This open door policy can also teach us a great deal about the home and community-based language and literacy experiences of the children and the expectations their families have of mainstream schools, nurseries and other early years settings. There is well-researched evidence which suggests the existence of some huge mismatches between minority community expectations and mainstream practices, particularly in literacy learning. This is aggravated by the general ignorance of many educators and carers about the out-of school/nursery/playgroup lives and learning of young bilinguals (Gregory, 1996).

If, in essence, learning a new language is about 'making sense of a new world' (*ibid.*), we should all make a start on an effective policy for bilingualism by learning as much as possible about the spoken and written forms and traditions of the languages used in our early years settings and communities. A good range of help and information is now available for those who work in a professional capacity with young bilinguals (Baker, 1993) and some of this material has been prepared in 'question and answer' form for parents, carers, teachers and other professionals (Baker, 1995).

We should always be very positive about the languages of the children in our settings: encouraging play, talk and singing between speakers of languages we do not ourselves understand and use, as well as supporting these children as they take on the roles of interpreters. We can encourage older, or more confident, bilingual children, as well as parents and other family members, to be support tutors for us and the children. This human network will enable us to make a start on teaching and learning the songs, dances, rhymes, legends and stories of other cultures – sometimes in translation and always in the original forms.

Story-telling supported by gestures, dramatic expressions, pictures and other props or guides to meaning, and poetry and song with their rhythmic musical messages, can be accessible human experiences across many languages in the early years setting. Children, parents and professional educators can write and print bilingual texts about the children's lives and learning and collect examples of the different scripts in use in the community. This could be extended to the writing of letters, notes and information about the group setting and/or school, so that genuine and mutually helpful multilanguage material emerges out of real needs and is formulated for real audiences. Such collaborations may help us to understand other languages, appreciate the complexities of bilingual choices and of translations between languages, and even help us to understand other people a little better.

Language Variety and Standard English

One of the biggest problems in communication between people of different languages and cultures is an irrational fear of the incomprehensible and unknown. This is also true, to a slightly lesser degree, of our reactions to the variety of accents and dialects in our own first language. Much has been written about accent and dialect and the main issues are outlined in Chapter 2. Early years educators need to know these facts and fables and relate them to their daily work with children and their families.

Professional educators' responses to certain accents and dialects can be as irrational as anyone else's. These reactions may be rooted in early encounters with long-forgotten people and incidents, or in well-remembered and resented events and humiliations. However, a professional approach to educating and caring requires us to ensure that young children are not subjected to the after-effects of our personal pains and prejudices. Children are closely bound to the accents and dialects of their homes and communities: very young children know no others and they associate the familiar 'voice' and forms with deep affection and their closest relationships. Any outside criticism or rejection goes beyond language to become an attack on the child and the home. The most damaging criticisms of all are the unspoken ones which small children pick up so quickly: raised eyebrows, grins, grimaces, shudders, physical recoil, pursed lips and averted gaze.

The controversies which surround the nature of SE and the feasiblity of teaching it have now entered early years settings and come centre-stage for educators. There is a formal requirement that all pupils in the statutory schooling phase be 'given opportunities to develop their understanding and use of standard English' (DFE, 1995, p. 3). Although few would quarrel with the notion of 'opportunity', the justifications offered are linguistically weak. If SE is distinguished from other forms of English by its vocabulary, rules and conventions of grammar, spelling and punctuation (*ibid.*), so is every other dialect! The problem is, as many linguists have noted, that these kinds of attempts to define SE are circular and simply depend on the social (not linguistic) recognition of SE as the desirable standard, with all the associated prestige such recognition confers (Sealey, 1996).

All practitioners must clarify their own thinking and approach to the SE requirements in the National Curriculum, but there are some particular problems for early years educators. Older children may be helped to understand that all dialects are linguistically equal and those that are very highly regarded are so because of social judgements and historical accidents. Young children are, however, only at the beginning of this language awareness process and the best thing that can happen to them is to spend time with lively, sensitive and caring people who use SE dialect. Such experiences may leave open for most children the possibility of using SE themselves when they need it and judge it to be useful for a range of purposes.

It is all too easy for the use of the standard dialect to become equated with received pronunciation (RP) and it bears repeating that changing our accents is a highly complex matter of phonological adjustments and psychological motivation. Children begin their speaking lives sounding like the people around them and they develop their accents in ways that reflect the various significant groups they attach themselves to, including peer groups in school and care settings, clubs and streets. We all change our accents if we wish to sound like and be accepted by particular groups, so that many of us end up being flexible users of several ranges of English accent. These are adjustments that reflect the patterns, accidents and opportunities of our lives. There is no justification in this to suggest that educators should or could attempt to change the accents of children.

The previous comments on changing accents raise a very positive area for practitioners to consider. Young children's developing skills in using various linguistic registers and switching between them may be supported and extended in educational settings in ways that enrich the curriculum. Registers are socially appropriate forms of language use, varieties all of us can produce as circumstances and audiences change. Sensitivity and appropriateness are the key concepts and young children can switch registers with remarkably few hiccups, particularly in play contexts. Their linguistic and emotional explorations of human values, relationships and dilemmas can be fostered by provision for socio-dramatic play of all kinds. Such simple devices as pretend telephones and answering machines, radios, televisions and video recorders, in the role-play homes, clinics, offices and cafés we set up, can stimulate impressive language switching and playful experiments with standard dialect and even RP. This early work in drama and role-taking is often extended by children's spontaneous and guided re-enactments of favourite books, stories, legends, songs and poems. In Britain there is a tendency to introduce literature and set up the role-play provision and then leave the children to get on with it, but in Sweden there is a developing tradition of early years educators themselves initiating and participating in drama and play (Lindqvist, 1995). We could learn from this if we wish to make the most of the great range of possibilities for language switching, new forms and new vocabulary found in literature. The challenge of drama is, how do you talk, gesture and walk like a queen, a shopkeeper, a fairy godmother, a pop star, a cunning monkey or a hungry monster? Making and using puppets provides another way of changing and exploring all the possibilities of language in use. While a child is hidden behind the persona of a puppet many emotional, cognitive and linguistic risks can be taken: rude challenges to powerful adults and expressions of terrible violence are all safely licensed.

Permission to be bad, or be someone else, in a secure setting is a central feature of early childhood play, literature and art and understood by most early years practitioners. However, the beginnings of sociolinguistic research are not usually associated with the early years curriculum, but young children and their educators can start to collect samples of language variety in use. Mutual benefit and pleasure are generated if elderly people are sometimes invited to visit the group, school or class. Listening to old people reminiscing and telling tales can demonstrate the many subtle changes in local language use over a life-span. Guests from other regions and other countries might spend time working alongside the children and sharing with them something of their different assumptions, languages, voices and thinking. This is a more appropriate use of visitors in the early years than talks and slides in a large hall. Small children need to get close to people in a very personal way, to talk with them and share ideas and anecdotes. Properly managed, such initiatives will not be disruptive but a liberating enrichment that comes from placing the language of educational settings in the wider context of many knowable social and cultural worlds.

Language, Thinking and Learning

These discussions have returned frequently to the significance of some kind of adult–child partnership in early learning in general and in language learning in particular. It has been claimed that early language acquisition can be likened to getting involved in meaningful and mutually satisfying conversations with people we care about and respect. This model of how we are helped to achieve our greatest feat of human learning – the understanding and production of meaningful and appropriate language – might well serve as a model for teaching and learning in the early years setting. Perhaps planning, initiating and developing a curriculum for the early years should be guided by the principle that young children need to be involved in doing things with people and with words.

A major theoretical support for this approach can be found in the work of Vygotsky (1978), who claims that adults make a special contribution to children's learning and development. He describes this (*ibid.* p. 85) as 'a new and exceptionally important concept': the zone of proximal development. The significance of this idea is that instead of gearing teaching and learning to what is apparently a child's present level of development and competence, good teaching always aims for potential by taking learners, with adult support, just beyond their present achievements. The zone of proximal development is the area of the child's maturing and emerging abilities: this is where, with adult assistance, a child's language and thinking are most fruitfully developed. This theory, which focuses on adult assistance and support in child learning, is an explanation of 'how the more competent assist the young and less competent to reach that higher ground from which to reflect more abstractly about the nature of things' (Bruner, 1986, p. 73). It is a description of good educational and child-rearing practices in many cultures, homes, early years settings and schools. It must also be the crucial factor in the remarkable success of projects that encourage families to read, write and do mathematical activities with their children at home.

The studies of language acquisition discussed in the previous chapter reveal other general features that could usefully be taken forward into planning for the early years of language learning and development in group settings and classrooms. One set of factors is the richness and complexity of the social, cultural and linguistic input to which babies and infants are exposed. In the world outside schools and institutions there is little evidence of controlled and restricted language models, of limited access to adults or rather narrow and safe notions of what is sensible and suitable for children to see and do in terms of daily life and work. This may account for the intriguing fact that children often display greater ingenuity and determination in their linguistic and general learning outside classrooms than in them.

In streets, homes and markets small children make choices, switch languages and dialects, argue, build, repair, feed animals, help smaller infants, make messes and mistakes and even clear them up. This is not an argument for unregulated child exploitation and labour, but a reminder that children are people and already on the way to being well versed in the values and preoccupations of their cultures.

Perhaps something of this richness of human experience could be allowed to permeate and make human sense of the curriculum in the early years. At the least, it is a warning about the impoverishment of learning that occurs if we present children with very limited models of language in use and rather artifical examples of written language designed especially for beginning readers and writers. Research and observations suggest that children can only begin to develop their full linguistic and cognitive potential in response to language and situations that make real demands on them and extend some of their own interests and present understandings. This has implications that need to be fully worked out in language, literacy and literature policies in schools and these are developed in Part II.

In our understandable anxiety to get children going on the subjects of the curriculum and to develop their language, now that we have outcomes to teach and baseline assessments to prepare for, we may be in danger of forgetting the very lengthy periods of watching and listening that precede language production in first- and second-language learning in infancy. We should also keep in mind the prior establishment of interpersonal understanding that characterizes the emergence of language, as well as remembering that the earliest utterances are functional (see Chapter 3). Educators can plan for and establish the kinds of environments and interpersonal relationships that sustain and maximize children's chances of watching, listening, interacting, talking, playing and experimenting with language and with people. Young children themselves will be motivated by their desire to be involved in the social life around them, to understand what is going on and, of course, to get the affection, help and good things which language can deliver.

Studies of language and thought give little support to persistent beliefs in the existence of some 'primitive' and inherently limited human languages. Languages may vary enormously in the meanings and concepts they encode but these differences are related directly to the requirements and circumstances of their living speakers. Language may be best thought of, in individual and group terms, as a barely tapped reservoir – a vast potential for meeting all and any of the needs and changing conditions of human beings. Failure to develop children's linguistic potential must always be investigated in terms of the social and cultural relationships that normally stimulate and sustain language. Restricted and limited language use in children suggests, leaving aside sensory and physical impairments, restricted and limited lives that are very low on ordinary talk, care, domestic routines and general involvement with more experienced and competent members of the culture. Good early-years education can compensate for the rare cases of deprivation of these requirements, but the usual need is for early-years education to enrich, expand and continue ordinary human language-learning practices, not curtail them.

'Good enough' language teachers like 'good enough' parents and carers (Winnicott, 1971, p. 13) mediate between young children and the wider world of cultural language use, presenting infants with just enough novelty and challenge in secure and unthreatening situations. What consitutes 'just enough' novelty and challenge must be judged in terms of that zone of proximal development demonstrated daily in children's play, pretence and interests for those who have the concern and motivation to observe children closely and respond to what they are trying to do (Smith, 1983, p. 24).

In the early years of education there must continue to be a particular focus on the role of spoken language for a wide range of functions and situations. The talk children use to sustain play and pretending is crucial, as is the emerging language derived from books and literary forms. But, first and foremost, the early years setting should be organized so as to promote genuinely mutual conversations between children and adults, and between children and children. This may well involve re-organizing the space, the furniture and the routines, or bringing in adults from the community: grabbing grandparents and tempting teenagers to come and talk with (not at) children and share with them activities like cooking, dancing, sewing, building, birdwatching and gardening. The interesting thing about these kinds of projects is that they involve so much essential talking, negotiating, planning, estimating, sorting, ordering, predicting, writing and reading that National Curriculum attainment targets and desirable outcomes for language and literacy are achieved and surpassed in the course of worthwhile co-operative learning.

Further Reading

Britton, J.N. (1970; 1992) *Language and Learning*, Penguin Press, Harmondsworth.

Carter, R. (1990) *Knowledge about Language and the Curriculum: The LINC Reader*, Hodder & Stoughton, London.

Hall, N. and Martello, J. (1996) *Listening to Children Think: exploring talk in the early years*, Hodder & Stoughton, London.

Nutbrown, C. (1994) *Threads of Thinking. Young children learning and the role of early education*, Paul Chapman, London.

Pinsent, P. (ed.) (1992) *Language, Culture and Young Children*, David Fulton/Roehampton Institute, London.

Sealey, A. (1996) *Learning about Language. Issues for primary teachers*, Open University Press, Buckingham.

Whitehead, M. (1996) *The Development of Language and Literacy*, Hodder & Stoughton, London.

Part II

Literacy

5

Narrative and storying

I am trying on stories like clothes.

Max Frisch[1]

Granted the striking and playful quality of Frisch's comment, it may still seem strange to use it as a way into a group of chapters on literacy, but it does introduce the increasingly widespread claim that experiences of stories are highly significant in our lives and in the development of literacy. It is now usual to find that books on language, learning and early literacy include sections on the importance of children's experiences with stories. However, it is worth remembering that caring teachers and parents have always tried to link the pleasures of telling stories and sharing books with their children's first attempts at reading. But understanding why encounters with stories have great significance for early literacy depends on more than good sense and cosy feelings about story-telling and books. The professional educator's knowledge about the nature of stories must go deeper and include some insights into the nature of narrative.

Narrative

Narrative is the backbone of any story:

> I'll tell you a story
> About Jack a Nory
> And now my story's begun
>
> (Opie and Opie, 1951, p. 233)

At its most elemental, narrative begins with the urge to tell about an event, person or feeling. Narrating may even be the oldest and most basic human-language activity. 'Someone telling someone else that something happened' (Smith, 1980, 1981, p. 228) is the beginning of legends, chronicles, history, memoirs, biography and novels. Basic narrative is preoccupied with holding on to occurrences by telling about them, thus creating sequences of events ordered in time:

> Solomon Grundy,
> Born on a Monday,
> Christened on Tuesday,
> Married on Wednesday . . .
>
> (Opie and Opie, 1951, p. 392)

This remembering, retelling and ordering into a sequence hints at the ancient links between telling a tale and 'tallying' or counting and ordering any other sequence of events. Tellers are counters in the mathematical sense as well as in the story sense, giving their 'accounts' of life and events.

Professional students of narrative have speculated on the possible reasons that drive us all to tell endless stories about our daily lives, our families, our holidays, our childhoods and our probable futures. There are no undisputed answers to the speculations but narrating seems to be closely linked to the organization and recall of memory. The suggestion has been made that our narratives constitute a continuing proof of our existence, a sort of notch-cutting that bears witness to our lives (Le Guin, 1980, 1981, p. 194).

Speculations about our very existence are linked with another remarkable feature of narrative: the urge to evaluate or make judgements about persons and events. Narratives that are just concerned with telling a sequence of events in time order can become very tedious: we are only prepared to tolerate a sequence of 'and then . . . and then . . . and then . . . ' for a limited time. We are really waiting for clues to the teller's opinions, feelings and values. Indeed, it seems that this urge to tell a tale is really directed towards explaining, gossiping and speculating about human behaviour and the chances of life.

> Ding, dong, bell,
> Pussy's in the well.
> Who put her in?
> Little Johnny Green.
>
> (Opie and Opie, 1951, p. 149)

All this ordering, explaining and evaluating that goes on in narratives is a way of giving meaning and significance to the endless stream of sensations and events. What is very important and yet easily taken for granted in ordinary everyday narrating is the possibility of holding on to and repeating or re-presenting for consideration what was in actuality a transient happening. Narrative is much concerned with going over sequences of events and giving them shape and pattern and, consequently, some kind of meaning or significance. This 're-presentation' of experiences in order to understand them better is a marked feature of human thinking, occurring in children's play, in art and across cultures. Representation, in this sense, is a central theme of the next two chapters on literature and early literacy. This present discussion introduces the fundamental insight that single fleeting events or feelings can be narrated or told any number of times and modified and shaped by the telling. We all feel the need to go over and over sequences of complex, joyful or terrible events in order to make them comprehensible or bearable. We have to live with our stories and we have to get them right. Everyday narrating is concerned with the extremes of celebrating and mourning, as well as with the middle ground where we sort out and construct our personal attitudes, beliefs and assumptions.

These strong claims for the importance of narrative in human experience, thought and culture are supported by psychologists and literary scholars. Literary scholars claim that narrative may be a primary act of mind, demonstrated in such cognitive activities as dreaming, remembering, planning, day-dreaming and a whole range of language uses (Hardy, 1977, p. 12). We do not learn to be narrators simply by hearing stories and encountering books; on the contrary, we bring our own powerful and spontaneous narrative drive to bear on the stories of our cultures.

This view can be joined to another claim from research psychology, that human beings live more by fiction than by fact (Gregory, 1977, p. 394). The suggestion is that the endless narratives we are inclined to generate in our thinking are 'brain fictions' or hypotheses about the possible outcomes of courses of action and sequences of events – the scientist's hypothesis is a story which has great predictive power and flexibility. Narrative may be a crucial element in human evolution and intelligent adaptability, enabling the species to predict or make up stories about likely outcomes as well as remote possibilities. As we generate these scenarios we are evolving narratives of how we might react and cope.

Narrative form provides a way of holding on to experience and exploiting repetition to create a pattern suggestive of order, regularity and permanence:

> January brings the snow,
> Makes our feet and fingers glow.
>
> February brings the rain,
> Thaws the frozen lake again.
>
> (Sara Coleridge[2])

But narrative also enables us to review the past and contemplate change and revolution: 'When Adam delved and Eve span,/Who was then the gentleman?' (John Ball).[3]

Narrative's traditional concern with implied and explicit values and judgements sharpens our awareness of the human voice or teller behind every story. The narrative invites at least our interest in the systems of values and the assumptions of the narrator, if not our whole-hearted approval. Sometimes we are given a conspiratorial nudge, or directly addressed as 'gentle listener' or 'dear reader' and invited to participate in the creation of the narrative spell. Young children readily join in the charm-like refrains that occur in traditional and modern tales, although they may be quite surprised if addressed directly by the authorial voice. This convention is learnt by exposure to the cultural forms of story-telling.

The issue of familiarity with conventions highlights the culturally diverse traditions of narrative. We need to cultivate greater sensitivity to the variety of narrative forms that have evolved. For instance, not all cultures have perceived time as linear and thrusting forwards into the future, as if carried on a railway track:

> To-morrow, and to-morrow, and to-morrow,
> Creeps in this petty pace from day to day,
> To the last syllable of recorded time;
>
> (Shakespeare, *Macbeth*, V. v. 19)

Accordingly, not all cultural narratives and stories display a progression from a clear beginning, through a middle phase to a satisfactory ending where all the strands are neatly tied up. In fact, this familiar form is the creation of literacy – the pattern of the Western book-oriented tradition young children need to be introduced to as part of their emergence into literacy. However, this book-dominated kind of narrative need not be an alienating shock for children socialized into different traditions. Young children's urge to tell about events, to recall sequences of actions, to indulge in repeated tellings and to speculate about feelings and values must be nurtured as the only sound basis for literacy.

Storying

'Storying' is a useful way to describe our continual creation of the basic and spontaneous narratives discussed in this chapter. The term is sometimes used as a way of distinguishing this personal narrative activity from the published or traditional stories current in a community. However, as all storying and stories originate in a need to make meaningful patterns and interpret experience, a too rigid application of this distinction can be unhelpful. Whole communities, as well as individuals, create explanatory narratives.

Cultures Making Meanings

In the communities most of us know, dominated by print and the published book, it is not immediately obvious that cultures still create their meanings, histories and value systems through the explanatory narratives they generate and share. Modern publication tends to stress literacy as a matter of individual authorship and ownership, but the most formative cultural tales continue to be the anonymous and collective myths, legends and religious stories of the oral tradition. In these narratives, now fixed in print, we can still sense the active creation of cultural meanings as patterns of values and beliefs were thrashed out. The stress on the origins of the universe and human life; the concern with the relationships between the worlds of nature, gods and humanity; the issues of right and wrong behaviour and the ultimate meaning of life, are preserved in the myths and legends of all human groups. The usual narrative concern with values is strongly present in this early literature. Time and sequence are also crucial to communities: early storying was the main way of holding on to the chronicles of shared events, the history of a cultural group. The song-like recitation of events and eras, victories and disasters, was crucial to the creation of a sense of group experience and shared history – the origins of the word 'history' itself are linked as much with narrative as inquiry.

Traditional storying in oral cultures was not confined to mythical or epic events: folktales were also shaped to explore the lives of humble people and to offer them advice, hope and consolation. The harsh facts and conditions of ordinary people's lives are still traceable in the prevalence in the tales of early deaths, restless ghosts, abandoned children, disastrous harvests, dying livestock and other catastrophes. However, comforts such as human love and fidelity, unexpected good luck, second chances and dreams of a better future are offered as solace and encouragement.

It would be a mistake to think that these traditional patterns of storying have now finished. Cultures and groups still need to tally the tales of their successes and failures and make of them a bearable record. Perhaps one can best see this in action in Western cultures when the media shape the public's responses to disasters and celebrations, as well as signalling the official view. There is a pattern of continuous repetition and re-shaping of the 'facts' of the story: members of the general public give their 'on-the-spot' responses and views; 'experts' provide specialist commentaries and analyses; while a steady flow of 'editorial' reflections and assessments constantly re-shape the story. Thus we create 'fairy-tale' royal weddings, Falklands' 'tales', American 'dreams', a shuttle 'disaster', road 'rage' and even 'motorway madness', which eventually become meaningful narratives about the events and symbols of the beliefs, attitudes and history of a society.

The significance of such community narratives is in their becoming symbols. Symbols generally represent something beyond themselves, by convention or association, and this is particularly important when the something else they stand for is as abstract and intangible as beliefs, attitudes, emotions and ideas. Symbols make the abstractions real, pictureable or tangible. Perhaps some obvious examples might be a wedding-ring, the Lascaux cave paintings and a degree-conferment ceremony.

The symbols created by the traditional and contemporary narratives of a culture are a kind of readymade resource for the individual. They are taken over and used in the personal storying of all of us. They become a special shorthand especially in the drawings, paintings and oral narratives of very small children: 'a big bad wolf'; 'the robber is going to shoot you'; or 'they got married and lived happily ever after'.

Complete stories as well as characters work in this symbolic way. Anansi, the spider man, represents for many of us human cunning, optimism and ingenuity. Robin Hood stands for the noble outlaw from a corrupt society, and similar characters are found in many diverse oral traditions. A Cinderella story occurs in numerous cultures and represents the eventual triumphant maturity of the poorest and most undervalued child. Or does it? Arguments about what these stories and characters symbolize only illustrate the power and the flex-ibility of the tales. We take them over and make of them what we will, or what we need.

Individuals Making Meanings

'If it's a story I'm telling, then I have control over the ending. Then there will be an ending, to the story, and real life will come after it. I can pick up where I left off' (Atwood, 1987, p. 49). Patterns of group beliefs and values dominate cultural storying but a concern with controlling our own lives and preserving personal identity permeates individual storying. This is reflected in the con-stant need to go over events in our lives in an effort to make sense of our very existence and historical actuality: 'When I was three and Bailey four, we had arrived in the musty little town, wearing tags on our wrists which instructed – 'To Whom It May Concern' – that we were Marguerite and Bailey Johnson Jr., from Long Beach, California, en route to Stamps, Arkansas, c/o Mrs. Annie Henderson' (Angelou, 1984, p. 6). Much of individual storying is like this –

entries in a mental diary or notches cut as reminders of achievements and struggles. However, telling our own story is never totally concerned with self because it is always the story of becoming a person in a social world. Individual storying is, therefore, full of other people and the difficulties and pleasures of relationships.

Ways of evaluating and musing on the possibilities of life can vary with age and with culture. Lists of inventories of activities, preferences, achievements, people and places occur in records of very young children talking to themselves while alone in bed (Weir, 1962). Lists of known words, letters and numerals are also made by young children who are beginning to explore the nature of writing. This is not surprising as listing is a powerful method of tallying or taking a count of what we have done, seen, acquired, felt or learnt and occurs in many cultures and literatures. The Hebraic tradition, as reflected in the Old Testament, the Greek Homeric narratives and the stories of the American Indian tribes list the achievements, personal qualities and property of their protagonists. A modern novel written in the form of autobiographical narrative can still make dramatic use of listing: 'These are some of the things my dad played during his first two days and nights: Avalon, Mountain Greenery, California Here I Come, Carolina In the Morning, Happy Days and Lonely Nights, Chopin's Nocturne in E Flat, Beethoven's Mignonette in G' (Burgess, 1987, p. 127). In listing we are not merely recording what we remember, we are preserving the world, the events and the passions that have made us what we are.

If we are to some extent what we know about ourselves, we are also a created fiction. As we tell a never-ending story about our life we create a fictional self around whom we weave adventures, feelings and expectations, anxious to improve on our heat-of-the-moment reactions by a continual editing process. This storying may be restricted to Western literate cultures (Scollon and Scollon, 1981) but the ability to place ourselves right in the centre of a story is a valuable start to becoming a reader and writer.

Once the self can be narrated about like a fictional character the possibility of creating fictive families and friends opens up truly liberating and consoling worlds:

> Hence, this diary. In order to enhance in my mind's eye the picture of the friend for whom I have waited so long, I don't want to set down a series of bold facts in a diary like most people do, but I want this diary itself to be my friend and I shall call my friend Kitty. No one will grasp what I'm talking about if I begin my letters to Kitty just out of the blue, so, albeit unwillingly, I will start by sketching in brief the story of my life.
>
> (Frank, 1954, p. 14)

Much of the research indicates that children as young as 2 years may start to fictionalize the self and talk like a book if they are immersed in a book-sharing culture (Payton, 1984; Fox, 1993; Jones, 1996).

Literate and oral cultures enrich the evaluating process of individual storying through the cultural symbols of contemporary literature and traditional myths, legends and folktales. As individuals we take over the patterns and the values of the stories we find and adapt them to our own needs. Young children probably make their earliest moral judgements in terms of the powerful opposites found in stories: weak/strong, good/bad, happy/sad. This mythic framework of values is reflected in children's story-telling and writing throughout the early years of education. This is clearly an influence that will vary in specific details according to the dominant culture of the individual and the shared patterns of community beliefs.

The evaluating typical of all narrating cannot emerge from nothing – it develops from the complex mix of different stories, proverbs, assumptions and social reactions that surround us all from birth, in any community. This means, of course, that any description of the development of individual story-ing must be tentative and related to the unique aspects of every individual's early experiences and to the culture in which the individual lives.

Research studies in the UK and the USA have produced a wealth of material that suggests some possible patterns for narrative development. Scholars who focus on the early years of childhood identify narrative as highly significnt in the development of a sense of self, as well as forming the foundations of literary understanding and literacy skills. This leads Jones (1996) to claim that 'narrative form is a turning-point in a human being's understanding both of the world, and themselves' (p. 141). In similar vein, Engel (1996) works from the premise that 'The stories we tell and listen to shape who we are' (p. vii) and proposes a five phase pattern of narrative development. Crucial to this pattern is the adult–child talk and reminiscing which creates a kind of portrait, or biography, of the infant – what Jones (1996) describes as confronting the infant with herself as an object of contemplation (*ibid*. p. 163).

Similar patterns of development are charted by Fox (1993) in her account of the oral story-telling of five pre-school children. This study highlights the shaping effect of early encounters with stories from literature and the media on the children's own storying. The power of traditional and contemporary sto-ries is a significant feature in the work of Lindqvist (1995) with Swedish kindergarten pupils. Her approach is based on supporting children's play and initiating dramatic enactments of the stories the children have heard.

All these researchers plead for a greater awareness of the significance of imaginative play and narrative development in the early years of education and they suggest ways of fostering this in practice (see Teaching Suggestions).

The stories which follow pick out some milestones along the path of narra-tive development.

Developmental Stories

'But if it's a story, even in my head, I must be telling it to someone. You don't tell a story only to yourself. There's always someone else. Even when there is no one' (Atwood, 1987, p. 49). From birth there is always someone who shares little stories with or about the baby or who conducts their own storying over and around the baby. Adult talk to babies as young as 3 months seems to be establishing conversation-like patterns (see Chapter 3; Whitehead, 1983b). Behind the adults' strings of questions and comments there are many hidden stories: propositions about lost and found, good and bad feelings, consolation and even the promise of happy endings. We might bear in mind that the conversation-like exchanges between carers and infants do not just establish early language learning patterns – they also establish the traditional narrative roles of teller and told.

In the first two years of life it is the people constantly with the baby who tell most of the stories but around the second birthday many infants make a bid for the role of teller. Research identifies examples of first stories at around 2 years of age. One white British child, with support from a parent, developed a pretend account of a shopping expedition to buy some sweets. The stimulus for this fictional narrative was the child's noting and commenting on the absence of a man who had previously been working in the garden (Wells, 1981, p. 107). In similar fashion, a black 2-year-old in the USA developed a narrative commentary based on recalling a memorable first visit to church:

> It a church bell
> Ringin'
> Dey singin'
> Ringin'
> You hear it?
> I hear it
> Far
> Now
>
> (Heath, 1983, p. 170)

Other children weave verse-like incantations about the anxieties and dangers they already anticipate in their young lives (Bill, 2y. 10m.):

> A monkey fell off
> my mommy fell off
> mommy got sick and had to go to the doctor
> and my mommy came home
> my daddy fall off . . .
>
> (Sutton-Smith, 1981, p. 54)

It appears that around 2 years of age many children are already speculating out loud – creating little narratives in which they shape their raw experiences into explanations or propositions about life. The storying is usually embedded in conversations, play or commentaries on events and builds on the patterns of interaction established in early infancy: someone telling someone else that something happened!

Around 4 years of age it is possible to hear and observe a much more conscious story-telling stance. The impact of early encounters with the traditional stories of the culture is increasingly apparent in the form of the stories as well as in the content (Fox, 1993). Children sometimes use ritual openings and standard plots, endings and characters (Ezra, 3y. 6m.): 'It's gonna be long/once upon a time there was a big monster' (*ibid*, p. 88). Some children begin to address their chosen audience very firmly and demand the proper attention due to a story-teller (Adam, 3y. 6m.):

> Hey listen to me . . .
> I'm going to tell a story . . .
> Once upon a time . . .
> there were three little crocodiles . . .
> named Flopsy, Mopsy and Cottontail . . .
>
> (Sheridan, 1979, p. 12)

The sense of threat, of disasters narrowly averted and of powerful desires or wishes permeates many of the collections of children's early storying. It seems as if the content of traditional stories children take over and use in their own storying provides symbols for discussing their own life chances. It is a way of thinking about 'me' in the world.

As children progress from around 3–4 years into the early years of education, the influence of the cultural blueprints (Hughes, 1988) for story forms and content becomes more noticeable. But we should be wary of dismissing this as simple imitation or just retellings of stories heard and seen in schools and early years settings. Children use these story patterns for their own purposes to go over and shape the raw material of their own lives. The complexity of the world, as growing children encounter it, has to be simplified and controlled – perhaps matched, somehow, to the categories of good and bad, love and hate, and so on. This is no easy task, but stories for young children help by concentrating on small segments of experience, on clear categories of behaviour and limited characterization.

Most importantly, stories provide endings in which the possibility of sorting everything out or testing experience to the extreme limits exists. It is not surprising that young children's vocalized storying sometimes reveals a preoccupation with myth-like issues of hatred, abandonment and despair, with everybody dead at the end. But the serious and tragic is not the only mode for making sense of experience, as a crocodile called 'Cottontail' has already indicated. At the age of 2–5, children can be both comical and rude as they sort out the inconsistencies of social life and the complexities of being human.

The early years of childhood are a peak period for indulging in nonsense. Nonsense storying is a traditional and respected way of speculating upon the possibilities of re-organizing the world. There is a great deal to be said for the usefulness of houses that can run around on chicken legs, fully furnished wombs that can be returned to in times of stress (Chukovsky, 1963, p. 38) or even garden brooms that can be turned into horses. Playing with possibilities is a central activity in early childhood and is not just restricted to straightforward storying – it occurs in storying linked to play materials, found objects, energetic physical activity and social play with other children.

The necessity of having another person to share our storying with appears to diminish gradually in the early childhood years. This is not because the need for a listener to tell it to has lessened; on the contrary, we ensure that 'there's always someone else' by taking over the function of listener to our own tales. In psychological terminology, we internalize our language partner. This idea is not strange to any of us: the remarkable two-person dialogue of our earliest language learning experiences is still preserved when infants talk aloud to themselves or adults silently rehearse and debate their thoughts and dilemmas. The original dialogues of early infancy gradually turn inward to shape the inner speech functions of controlling, planning, recalling and predicting, as discussed in Chapter 3. But the voice of storying can also be added to the list. We become the tale, the teller and the told.

Around 8–9 years of age, the cultural models of stories are often used in talk and writing to explore the mysteries and worries that surround beginning to grow up. The expansion of life experiences exposes children to conflicts and threats that must be faced and identified. Conflicts between children 'in the middle years' of childhood lead to musings on the rights and wrongs of settling disputes by violence (Scottish girl, 10y. 0m.): 'She really kicked him and punched him and thumped him and punched him in the nose. She got him crying. I wouldnae like to be in this school cause they really could batter you' (Romaine, 1984, p. 148). There is some evidence that evaluating moral issues (particularly the relationships between people) through storying and story-writing leads some children to question the gender stereotypes and social expectations the culture may impose on them (Steedman, 1982).

The very important issue of the individual's relationship to society or cultural groups becomes central in adolescent and adult storying. The best evidence for this is our own insights into the personal storying and narratives that preoccupy us as private individuals. The unwritten autobiographies we are all composing as we go along consist of a set of well-shaped stories we can live with:

> I was born,
> my childhood,
> I went to school,
> my accident, my illness,
> my love affairs,
> my career . . .

Memory is the dominant form but the process of selective recall allows for a great deal of serious evaluating and the framing of significant moral judgements. An adolescent, for example, faces the facts of bullying and poverty and makes a stand on the grounds of personal integrity – the story of himself he can live with: 'So I says to myself "There's gonna be times my mother won't give me money because [we're] a poor family"' (Labov and Waletzky, 1985, p. 22). In extreme old age an individual may look back on a life of poverty and exploitation and condemn the social attitudes and institutions that denied justice and respect to whole sections of society (George, 95y. 0m.): 'I was angry: "There's no need for them red letters! The pauper kids is distinguished all right! You can spot 'em straight away – they's up against the wall watching the others play! They ain't playing"' (Hewins, 1981, p. 72). These memories were spoken into a tape-recorder and the interweaving of personal feelings, considered responses and judgements, as they are triggered by the recalled sequences of the events, illustrate the central features of narrative storying.

Trying on the Stories

Individuals try on the stories of their cultures, altering them to make a better fit; and stories from foreign cultures can be an inspiration – for young children, these stories are an exciting source of endless new roles, personalities and activities.

The possibility of enriching children's own storying is a significant educational responsibility. Storying affects children's understanding of the learning we organize in the curriculum as it is a powerful way of linking together formal learning in schools and other group settings and informal learning in the community. Young children use narrative as a means of putting the abstract and highly organized knowledge of education into the context of their everyday understandings.

School knowledge is subject-based but young children still take experience as it comes, as a totality. For example, the early-years educator may plan a walk in the local park with a group of children and perceive it as 'environmental studies'. However, this experience will mean many things to individual children. It may be memorable and significant because of the sheer excitement of leaving the building during school hours, or because of the warm sun or the cold wind; or the caterpillar they found by the tennis courts; or the lavatories that were covered with interesting writing; or the big house with slippery floors called a 'museum'. Many stories, speculations and day-dreams will need to evolve and be told and retold, played out and re-enacted, drawn or painted, before these differing ways of knowing can be linked to formal learning and environmental studies.

The children's storying and the adult's role as an essentially supportive partner and storymaker must build the bridges between experience and learning.

This view of individual storying in the context of early education emphasizes not simply the value of having lots of possible stories to try on, but the actual ways in which stories are first told, shared and mediated.

The story-teller is the life-line between the tale and the listener, and oral story-telling is a special kind of experience for children and teachers. Placing the skills of narrating at the centre of the language curriculum highlights this art: schooling can be so exclusively organized around books and literacy that children miss out on the patterns and strengths of oral literary language. Yet the limitations of human memory and concentration have pared down the told story to a clear plot, strong actions and the most essential characterization.

However, the linguistic devices of repetition, alliteration, musical refrains, rhymes and conventional metaphors can be used to support and enrich the memories of tellers and listeners. These features impart a mesmerizing quality to language. Good story-telling sessions are magical because no books or pictures come between the participants and the tale. Imagination has to work on words, emotional tone, vocal changes, eye contacts, facial expressions and gesture. This list should be familiar: it is what the infant has to work on in the earliest days of human contact: it is part of the foundations of language and learning.

The adult story-teller models ways for children to create stories and helps them to tune in to even more narratives and to re-shape their own ongoing storying. To do this well the adult must value and enjoy the chosen story, have a clear sense of its shape and an inner picture or image of its characters and events and, most importantly, a real desire to share it with an audience. These features of story-telling will also be brought to bear on the children's early experiences with books and act as bridges between the story told and the story read. However, the early-years practitioner must not become trapped behind or between the covers of the book – the remembered phrases of a story or a poem well told are an inner possession and go with the children into a future we can never predict or guarantee.

A 'story' is a set of events, real or imaginary, and 'narrative' is the spoken or written account that tells about the story's events. Narrative is thus essentially a 'telling', and this emphasizes its selectivity in interpretation. It seems that the mind is disposed to function narratively; disposed to evaluate and tell about particular sequences of experiences. From this it follows that the process of education, if it is a process concerned with the development of mind, must also be concerned with narrative. It also follows that the early years curriculum must preserve a distinct emphasis on oral story-telling (by adults and children), substantial talk about stories and experiences, and much shared reminiscing.

Narrative is the structure that creates and binds together the stories we find in communities; it is also the best way we have of making sense of the formal, self-contained knowledge typical of school subjects. If a link between the worlds of early years settings and community is to happen and be productive it must involve much more in the way of mutual narrative exchanges between settings, schools and the communities they serve. Exchanging stories is just as crucial in the early years of education as the organized exchanging of books, toys, outgrown clothes and recipes. It should be given at least as much time, space and respect.

- Narratives contain at least one, if not more, propositions, for example, shopping for sweets is good or extortion must be resisted.
- Narratives are commentaries in which someone is telling someone else (increasingly that inner person we all talk to continuously) that something happened.
- Narratives are often autobiographical: explorations of our encounters with the world of social and cultural norms and conventions. How are things done? What are the expectations?
- Narratives are also shaped in form and content by the story traditions or patterns of the culture.
- Narratives develop and probe the extremes of human feelings and possible ranges of values.
- Narratives are continually sorting out the complexities of self-knowledge, the relationship between the self and the social world, the possibilities and the probabilities of life's chances.

Teaching and Learning Suggestions

* Create an environment in which telling and listening to stories have a very high priority; this means planning for group talking and telling times: ample opportunities for individual child/adult confidences and chat; and areas in the setting where children can talk in small informal groups (outdoor gardens, sandpits, climbing apparatus, dens and play-houses; indoor book corners, home-play areas, 'offices', 'clinics', water trays, blockplay, clay tables and cooking activities). Think of how much talk and narrating can go on in the course of a 'listening to a child read' episode, or a tidying up and clearing away session – try to boost the narrative potential of chores like washing out the paintpots!

* Introduce the practice of adult staff and visitors telling the children simple autobiographical anecdotes: 'When I was a little boy/girl not much older than you . . .' Encourage the children in their own personal

and fantasy narrating. Find ways of recording these (on audiotape) and turning them into books, e.g. invite parents, carers and families to come into the setting and make the books with the children (provide support with the writing for adults who are unsure of their own literacy skills and welcome non-English versions, as well as offers of translations).

*Build up a collection of taped oral stories, songs, poetry and reminiscences (use some published material but also ask families and members of the local community to record material for the children).

*Seek out any possible contacts with ederly people, through residential homes and age reminiscence centres, for example, and ask them to tell the children (or write or tape record) tales about their childhoods, schooldays, homes, shops, first employment, etc.

Notes

1. Max Frisch (1964) *Mein Name sei Gantenbein*, quoted in Stanzel (1984), pp. 109–10.
2. Sara Coleridge, 'The Months', in Opie and Opie (eds.) (1973), p. 169.
3. Attributed traditionally to John Ball, from the text of his sermon at the outbreak of the Peasants' Revolt, 1381.

Further Reading

Bruner, J.S. (1990) *Acts of Meaning*, Harvard University Press, Cambridge, Mass.

Engel, S. (1995) *The Stories Children Tell. Making sense of the narratives of childhood*, Freeman, New York.

Fox, C. (1993) *At the Very Edge of the Forest. The influence of literataure on storytelling by children*, Cassell, London.

Hughes, T. (1988) Myth and education, in K. Egan and D. Nadaner (eds.) *Imagination and Education*, Open University Press, Milton Keynes.

Meek, M., Warlow, A. and Barton, G. (eds.) (1977) *The Cool Web. The pattern of children's reading*, Bodley Head, London.

Paley, V.G. (1981) *Wally's Stories*, Harvard University Press, Cambridge, Mass.

Rosen, B. (1991) *Shapers and Polishers. Teachers as storytellers*, Mary Glasgow, London.

Rosen, H. (1984) *Stories and Meanings*, NATE, Sheffield.

Whitehead, M.R. (1996) Narrative, stories and the world of literature, in G.M. Blenkin and A.V. Kelly (eds.) *Early Childhood Education*, Paul Chapman, London.

6

Books and the world of literature

*Literature offers pupils the experience of books and the
extension of their experience through books. Only in literature
will they encounter language at its most highly wrought,
capturing, shaping and combining experience, thought and feeling.*

DES, 1986

The experience of books is personal and unique and perhaps the beginning of literary experiences can only be described accurately for each individual. But we can at least presume that whenever an infant comes into contact with books, magazines, newspapers and comics the potential for involvement with literature and literacy is there.

Families and researchers have documented individual children's early encounters with books; there is also the anecdotal and personal dimension to refer back to – many of us have some memories of our first books and comics, or of listening to story readings. However, many accounts are mainly based on pre-school experiences in private homes but, for many children, play groups and nursery and infant schools or classes are the settings for their first encounters with books. This does not necessarily make the home-based accounts irrelevant: it is a central claim of this chapter that the implications of such informal encounters have relevance for learning about literature and literacy in group settings and schools, and that whenever or wherever children first meet books, relaxed and informal approaches should be nurtured and not rushed through or devalued.

Early Experiences with Books[1]

First Encounters

For many infants and small children, books are objects you may stumble over, clutch possessively or move from place to place like building-blocks. Books can also be tasted, sniffed and stroked and this sensual delight in the texture, taste and smell of books may linger into adulthood. The American artist and author, Maurice Sendak, has traced his own passion for creating books back to his childhood and the first book he owned, sniffed, fondled and chewed (Sendak, 1977, p. 242). This is a reminder of the pleasure to be gained from books as objects, toys and possessions.

Many infants gaze with great interest at the pages of books and scrabble with their fingers at text and illustrations, as if attempting to lift them from the pages. The black outlined images and bold print of Dick Bruna's books are particularly arresting for some infants. There is one outstanding account of an 8-month-old baby focusing her gaze on the bold print and later on the pictures in a Bruna ABC (Butler, 1979). However, it is not necessary to turn to studies of remarkable babies and exceptional parenting in order to support the claim that books as objects and toys fascinate very small children.

Books designed to encourage young children's sensory investigations are among the most popular (interestingly, these special book techniques are regularly appearing further up the age-range). Books as toys for infants may feature holes in their pages, apparently eaten by a very hungry caterpillar. Sometimes they have elaborate pop-up devices and figures and the paper engineering can become extremely complex and even be used to illustrate an introduction to the inventions of Leonardo da Vinci, or to the organs and functions of the human body! Books can feature half-pages, hinged flaps and pages which open out and extend or elaborate the pictorial narrative. Some of the most popular books now contain extra features such as removable notes and letters that extend the playful possibilities of the story beyond the book. This discussion of books, simply as toys and beautiful objects, should be kept in mind when planning book provision for the early years of education. The exciting possibilities mentioned here might also be contrasted with the limited aesthetic and sensory appeal of many sets of school reading primers and information books.

First encounters with books in early childhood are usually mediated or shared with an older person and become associated with warmth, embracecs and total security. This strong emotional feeling becomes part of the total attention and concentration associated with books. The experience of temporary withdrawal from the world of practical and external demands, coupled with feelings of safety and comfort, may stay with us in our later reading careers. For many children and adults the favourite places to read are in bed, or in the bath, and small children can be found reading behind curtains, under tables, or curled into the bottom of cupboards.

An emphasis on rooting early reading and involvement with books in secure emotional contexts is more significant than just a means of ensuring that reading is associated with pleasure, important as that is. The sense of safety and well-being may go some way towards explaining the extraordinary fact that children and adults can tolerate considerable threats and terrors in their encounters with literature. In contrast, some school-based reading experiences and practices are often a long way from a setting of pleasure, security and potential excitement. There is a need to question the restricting of school reading to set times, in sensible places and with instructions to 'sit up straight at your table'. How conducive is it to becoming a reader if your shared reading with a teacher involves standing at an adult size desk, the text held flat on that surface, while other children queue, or jostle for pencils, arbitration of disputes and permission to visit the toilets?

Outside schools and group settings, infants probably become aware of books and reading material as things that take over the time and the attention of otherwise devoted adults and older children. People apparently enjoy this and also take very special notice of babies and toddlers who want to join in. Squeezed between adult lap and the pages of the book, infants also find out that books are special: books receive special treatment.

For young children, sharing the 'looking-at-books' game is one way of participating in the importance of books and for many it is a significant way of being like the people they love and depend on. Furthermore, in the early days with books there is less discernible threat or pressure linked with the cultural prestige of reading, so that time with books and a carer is a matter of choice, pleasure and of becoming a person who participates in valued social activities. In terms of later schooling, this raises such issues as, do young children see teachers and other professionals as admired and respected models of being a reader? Are early years group and school experiences of books, literature and stories unpressured, enjoyable and supportive of children's self-esteem and desire to succeed in activities valued by the culture?

There have always been some families who shared books with very young babies (White, 1954; Butler, 1979; Jones, 1996), but in recent years there have been determined and well-monitored efforts to help many more parents and carers do this. One of these is the *Bookstart* project which was piloted in Birmingham and involved co-operation between the City Library Services, the local Health Authority and the Children's Book Foundation. Free *Bookstart* packs containing a book, a poetry card, a poster, an invitation to join the local library (and other information) were distributed by health visitors to 300 parents/carers of 6- to 9-month-old babies in three inner city areas.

The evidence (Wade and Moore, 1993) from the families indicated that sharing books with a baby spilled over into enthusiastic sharing of books with all the family – including toddlers, older children and adults. In some cases this led to joining the public library and also buying books. The scheme has now been extended to other areas, including Sunderland, West Sussex and Hertfordshire.

A recent follow-up study (Wade and Moore, 1996) of the original families shows that long-term enthusiasm for books has been sustained and the children display greater interaction with texts and parents/carers. This may have considerable significance for literacy learning.

Their very earliest experiences with books may have an incalculable influence on children's attitudes to books and literature and on their development as readers and writers.

- Infants come across books as objects that appeal to their senses and offer opportunities for certain kinds of exploration and playful investigation.
- Early experiences with books are shared with caring adults or older children and associated with emotional security and pleasure.
- Books and reading are clearly of great importance and valued by many adults and by the wider community.
- Learning to read in the early years must be understood in the context of infant development.

Some Speculations on Responses to Books

The whole topic of response to books and stories is complex and can involve several academic disciplines – psychology, philosophy, linguistics and literature are only the beginning. For the purposes of this approach, speculations are linked with a view of early encounters with books that sees them as essentially play-like or playful: aspects of literacy ignored by more traditional literary or psychological approaches.

The playful exploration of pictures and written narratives in books appears to be a major preoccupation with young children who enjoy literary encounters. Pictures and texts are often subjected to rigorous questioning and tentative re-organization. Characters who appear to be lost or alone prompt such questions as, 'Where's her mummy (or daddy or granny)?' Desperately unhappy characters may also be kissed better, gently caressed on the page and reassured. The conventions of illustrations are also sorted out as small children ponder whether the tear-drops on faces are rain (Payton, 1984, p. 49–50) or what has happened to the rest of Peter Rabbit when only his ears are sticking out of the watering-can.

Such questioning is challenging and literally eye-opening for the adult reading partner, but for the young child it also marks the beginnings of encounters with totally new and surprising sets of possibilities. Suppose a tiger came to tea? Suppose you were always given hot-water bottles for presents? Experiences found in literature begin to combine with bits of the child's own daily life in rich and liberating ways. A small child can be comforted by a story or a book when away from home and familiar adults or a threatening situation can be eased by the reassurance that a book or story character coped with this or similar difficulties. Success, joy and humour also migrate from the world of books into the everyday world of the young child who is indulging in a little domestic mayhem 'like Noisy Norah', or singing and discovering the pun in 'Nellie the Elephant packed her trunk'. Bits of books and bits of life combine and interact: 'The experience makes the book richer and the book enriches the personal experience even at this level. I am astonished at the early age this backward and forward flow between books and life takes place' (White, 1954, p. 13). Playful encounters with books and literature allow children to take over and use, in unstructured ways, anything they choose from the events and the values of narrative fictions.

Play is safe or 'protected' because it does not have to satisfy demands from the outside world for truth, excellence or completion – it enjoys some distance from real-world pressures. This concept of being safely distanced from demands to get on and make something happen in the real world of practical affairs, may be an appropriate way of categorizing literary responses. Security and protection have already been linked with response to books in the discussion of First Encounters. The point was made that in shared book and story sessions very young children can tolerate fears and dangers which would be unbearably distressing in reality. Literary threats are not simply tolerated, they are contemplated and mulled over in positive ways. Small children actually begin to evaluate the moral issues in human behaviour, they consider motives, apportion blame and they also face up to the terribly arbitrary and accidental aspects of life: rabbits caught eating lettuces in gardens do sometimes end up in pies. Small children must themselves be brave and resourceful when they are out on the street, and you can't always trust the baby-sitter when you are safe at home (Rayner, 1976).

One reason that young children (and older ones too) thrive on terrible tales is usually expressed as the reader or listener being an onlooker or spectator of literary events.[2] In the case of fiction, we are reading or listening to an account or representation of imagined events in which we are obviously not particip-ants. This non-participation gives us the time and the freedom to evaluate more sharply our feelings and attitudes about the events and characters repres-ented – even very small children pick out the kind and the naughty, the dishon-est and the brave in stories, but our ambiguous real-life motives and complex reactions involve heart-searchings, self-delusions and frequent misunderstand-ings. Because literature and play free us from demands to respond in practical ways they allow distanced but very full evaluations, unblurred by personal confusions and involvement.

Poems and stories tap deep responses. Such processes take time and cannot be readily measured or tested by immediate questioning about the surface features of the poems and stories. However, the cumulative effect of our many experiences as spectators of fictive events, feelings and personalities is an enlargement of our imaginative sensibilities and understandings. It is as if the fictional lives, events and emotions we encounter extend the range of our own responses and increase the resources we have for making sense of our own lives. Perhaps small children are eventually stronger for knowing that John Brown comes to accept the Midnight Cat (Wagner, 1977), and older children develop more insight into complex family relationships after reading *The Way to Sattin Shore* (Pearce, 1983) and *Flour Babies* (Fine, 1992).

The complexities of responses to books and stories underline the familiar claim that literature operates on many levels. This again links literature with play, for play can also be described as functioning on several levels at once. For example, a small child dragging chairs into a line and calling them a train can be enjoying simultaneously the physical pleasure of clambering on and off the chairs; the sense of achievement when the line of chairs is complete; the satis-faction of operating in a totally imaginary world of journeys; and the social negotiations necessary to persuade an adult to make real sandwiches to eat on the chair-train. Vygotsky (1978) captures this complexity in his definition of play as satisfying unrealizable desires for the young child (how can a toddler control a train or travel alone?), but also requiring considerable self-discipline and obedience to the rules of the play.

One approach to the levels of literary experiences identifies a continuum from responses to sounds, events, roles and worlds (Harding, 1977). This is a useful list providing we do not regard the levels as stages to be worked through and discarded chronologically, according to age and maturity.

Initially, very small infants just delight in the sounds of patterned language in songs, poems and stories. They may be observed responding with total bodily excitement to rhythms, rhyming sounds, alliteration and words with onomatopoeic qualities: 'splat', 'croak', 'lippitty-lippitty' (Whitehead, 1995). We all retain the potential ability to respond to language as pure sound in aspects of literature and song. Children also delight in the impact of obscure or difficult words and chant them enthusiastically – as if tasting them on the tongue – long before they understand their meanings and begin to use them appropriately.

Very young children follow a narrative closely and make comments: 'What happened next?' 'Is that the end?' 'You left a bit out.' The effects of this sensitivity to story structures and plots are revealed when children become tellers and writers of their own made-up narratives. Clearly there are implications for early-years settings here. Children will need opportunities for storying aloud in nearly every situation. It is all this energetic storying and discussion that inspires and supports the dictated or independently written story plots of young children as they become writers and authors.

Responses to literature in terms of roles and of worlds bring in complex cultural assumptions and perspectives. Children try on the roles of the story characters they meet, often in such activities as dramatic play, drawing and miniature world play. Trying on the roles of parents, doctors, teachers and naughty children are familiar enough pastimes, but literature provides far more varied and complicated characters and situations for the child or onlooker of any age to savour. Young children delight in going along with the reckless behaviour of Goldilocks when it involves plenty of porridge eating, but they often begin to worry about the baby bear who is the loser in all the story episodes!

Moral issues are at the heart of responses to the total worlds created by authors. This is a level of response that can be traced throughout a life-time of reading and sharing poems and stories, but it has its roots in early encounters with narrative and books. Children seem to puzzle over the global meanings of poems and stories long before they bother about the particular definitions of separate words and phrases (Donaldson, 1978, p. 91). Early experiences with books offer alternative worlds for consideration and reflection, and it is highly likely that the possible levels of response consist of far more than the few discussed here.

- Early responses are playful in so far as they are open-ended and explanatory, linking books, stories and life in creative and uniquely personal combinations.
- Encounters with literature are safely distanced by the book and the reading situation and foster a detached spectator-like evaluation of the imaginary happenings.
- Literature, like play, operates on many levels and can support flexible and personal meaning-making strategies.

Listening to Book Language

Response to stories and book language in terms of pure sound has already been touched on but the significance of this for literacy deserves further consideration. First, the voice of the reader mediates and revitalizes the written text for the child listener. All the subtlety and variety of a familiar voice is brought to the task of re-creating the meanings and intentions of the author behind the text. Story and poetry readings are informal demonstrations of the functions of vocal tone, pitch, rhythm, facial expressions, gestures and body language in human communication. And the good reader, like the good teller, must employ all these skills to bring the language off the page.

However, young listeners must also work hard to pick up and respond to all the cues that tell as much (if not more) of the story as the actual words. Many traditional tales and rhymes depend on the irony, exaggeration and understatement communicated by the manner of the telling. Very young children are able to respond to all this subtle underlying story-line or subtext because it is relayed through the expressive medium of a familiar voice.

Infants are immersed in bits of stories, anecdotes, snatches of songs, rhymes and jingles, in their homes, streets, shops, places of worship and community gatherings. All this basic human language experience sensitizes children to the more consciously shaped patterns of book language as well as incidentally providing considerable snippets of literary and ritual language.

Listening to book language read aloud introduces children to the consciously patterned forms of literature. Language as art has been shaped, altered, chosen and carefully placed to produce the effects of just those words in just that particular order. The syntax of written language is more considered and more formal than in most everyday verbal communications. We might claim that experiences of listening to book language help children to move from being talkers and listeners only to becoming readers and writers.

Children listening to stories and poems also hear complex, unusual, foreign and even archaic words. That these extend and enrich children's taste for language is one of the important but unmeasurable claims of literature teachers. What formal test of reading would dare include such items as 'haycock', 'star-gazy pie' or 'monumental'? Who would invite the child to read 'satiable curtiosity' (Kipling, 1986, pp. 34–42) or 'you're cruising for a bruising' (Wells, 1977)? Young children respond to the poetry of memorable phrases and nonsense by collecting them and making them part of their own linguistic resources. Such word hoards increase the potential of their own eccentric language creations and potent 'underground knowlege' about birth, life, death and sex (Causley, 1988).

Poetry and story introduce young children to the literary device of metaphor, but the language of everyday usage is also saturated with metaphors. Small children take nothing for granted and so-called 'dead' metaphors may have a stunning impact on them. Little children puzzle out the meaning links in flower beds (Payton, 1984, p. 55) and clothes-horses, as well as taking on the delights of 'a diamond in the sky' (Jane Taylor)[3] or a 'snow-cone' (Agard, 1983). Sharing more metaphors with children is not just a literary frill for the curriculum: metaphor is a cognitive tool for increasing the explanatory power of language and thought.

The greater complexity and eccentricity of literary book language introduces young listeners to other human voices. Listsening to stories and poems is also listening to the unique voices of many authors. Young listeners must make some sort of link or relationship with the idiosyncratic style and feelings of the person behind the words. This issue is crucial in early reading and a failure to lock into the voice and created world of the author is one major hindrance to prediction and the setting up of sets of expectations in reading. Authors help their readers by creating predictable worlds and roles and setting out helpful cues in the text. Of course, authors are not boringly predictable and they can sometimes surprise us and upset all our expectations. But particular authors are instantly recognizable, like family and friends, so that children can confidently let themselves go for an outing with Anthony Browne, Janet and Allan Ahlberg, Pat Hutchins or Mike Rosen. Strangely, however, most attempts to produce simple reading books for young children mistakenly start by getting rid of the eccentric human creator behind the text and pictures. This has always been a serious weakness of school reading primers.

- The role of the familiar voice is crucial in linking the language of books to the language of daily social life and communications.
- The role of listening is important in introducing children to the highly patterned language of literature and books.
- Listening to literature plays a major part in introducing children to the unique voices and worlds of many authors.

Pictures and Texts

Young children's first experiences with books will be predominantly centred on picture books. Picture books rely on images to carry the narrative sequence and evaluation, either entirely or in combination with some text. It is still not uncommon for adults to dismiss picture books as too simple and infantile to merit serious study. Apart from ignoring any educational arguments, this reaction fails to acknowledge the existence of sophisticated picture books designed for adults, and the fact that distinguished artists and writers choose to create picture books.

The apparent simplicity of picture books is, paradoxically, the source of the considerable demands they place on the reader. Reading picture books might be likened to 'authoring' or creating a story. The very lack of text means that a picture book is rich in narrative spaces that must be filled in by the reader. Successful creative reading of this kind demands sensitive interpretations of the story possibilities in the pictures as well as the text, if any. *Rosie's Walk* (Hutchins, 1968) is a now famous example of picture story and text story running parallel and depending on the reader to link the two accounts and create the meaning of the narrative. The same pattern occurs in *Come Away From The Water, Shirley* (Burningham, 1977), where a repetitive and rather staid text of predictable adult comments partners a wildly adventurous picture narrative. It is frequently the case that the pictures in these books are the challenging and eccentric element, rather than the written text. Maurice Sendak's night-time world of Wild Things (1967), the domestic threat of *The Bear Under The Stairs* (Cooper, 1993), or Ivor Cutler's *Meal One* (1971), are full of wit, anarchy and humour and demand detailed picture readings. It takes many re-readings and careful examinations of the images to build up these complex narratives. This powerful method of investigating the layers of possibilities in a book has migrated to the older children's (Michaels and Walsh, 1990) and adults' book market. Picture books have been used to discuss such issues as the holocaust, a nuclear disaster, military jingoism, the arms race and a wide range of conservation issues.

In recent years picture books have been the subject of some exciting publications and research. Teachers and scholars from several disciplines have focused on the picture book as a bridge between an infant's developing sense of self and understanding of all that is 'not self' (Jones, 1996); as a crucial tool in the early development of literacy (Marriott, 1991; Watson and Styles, 1996); as a sophisticated literary genre which displays postmodernist features of openness, multiple meanings and excess (Lewis, 1990); as a complex system of images and visual narratives (Graham, 1990; Doonan, 1993; Baddeley and Eddershaw, 1994); and as a carrier and subverter of a society's dominant ideologies (Stephens, 1992).

This sophisticated level of picture book study has been an important factor in the development of children's literature as a legitimate field of study (Hunt, 1991, 1994; Styles, Bearne and Watson, 1992, 1994, 1996). Modern picture books may also be credited with expanding our understanding of the subversive, playful and carnivalesque features to be found in literature. Subversion in play and literature involves unpicking systems and beliefs and standing them on their heads – in order to understand them. Carnival in play and literature is also a subversive element that challenges social control and conventions. The playful and carnivalesque aspects of books enable children and adults to explore the wildest possibilities and defuse the deepest anxieties (Whitehead, 1995).

It follows that picture books put young children into the role of active readers from the start. Any lingering belief that reading is a passively receptive language activity disappears when we share a *Spot* book with a child, discuss the surprising things going on during Handa's walk (Browne, 1994) or read the names of the ingredients going into Meg's cauldron. Many of these books actually invite the reader to hunt for a character, to predict the next event on the basis of prior literary cultural knowledge (*Each Peach Pear Plum*, Ahlberg and Ahlberg, 1977b) or to retell the complete narrative without any textual guidelines apart from that most significant story précis, the title.

Because picture-book readers must do so much to make the stories mean something, young readers usually create connections between the books and their own lives and experiences. Authors often help by picturing actual places and events some children will know, as in *Babylon* (Walsh, 1992) or *The Horse at Hilly Fields* (Thwaite and Mills, 1996). Children delight in pointing and telling with the picture book: 'I don't like bananas.' 'We've got a cat.' 'I've been to that park!' Some authors create characters who straddle the literary and the ordinary world by eating through the pages of the book or by getting shut inside the covers of the book by mistake. Children themselves fill the everyday world with characters and possibilities from their picture books. I was reminded of this vital connection by a young visitor to my home who looked at the large freezer and said, 'If I was the snowman I'd get in there for a nice cold rest'. Links with books extend children's creative 'supposings' and these new sets of possibilities enrich the children's individual storying and ensure that even more expectations and successful predictions are brought to bear on subsequent book encounters.

Experiences with picture books establish such basic story conventions as beginnings or ways in, complications, problems and challenges, resolutions and satisfying endings. The pleasures of literary shape and predictability can be judged by the demands children make for repeated tellings of stories and their gradual incorporation of literary conventions into their own created stories.

The raw material of daily life and childhood mishaps is sensitively shaped in a totally satisfying way by the author and illustrator, Shirley Hughes. In *Alfie Gets in First* (1981) we are hurtled into the book and its central action by the desire of toddler Alfie to 'get in first' after a morning's shopping. The complication or problem is immediately clear when the front door is triumphantly slammed on Mum and baby sister by Alfie! He is certainly in first, but he is also locked in, alone and unable to reach the door catch. Triumph soon turns to tears, while a procession of helpful neighbours and trades-people plan various strategies for rescuing poor Alfie. The resolution is delightful in that it comes about through Alfie's own initiative and re-establishes his confidence and sense of achievement. The total success of this book as an artifact that combines pictures and text in an indivisible whole, is reflected in the way in which the book's spine represents the door that comes between Alfie inside and everybody else outside.

The joy of such books as this is that they work for adults too. As I share *Alfie* with very young children I am also savouring again memories of the emergencies and excitements in my younger daughter's infancy, for she too was a triumphant door-slammer! Time and many family retellings have safely distanced our actual crises but this picture book immediately puts me back in contact with the child that was and the affective quality of our relationship.

- Pictures and texts play a complex and significant part in introducing children to literature and preparing them for literacy.
- Picture books are recreated by readers who must behave like authors.
- Picture books are a sophisticated literary genre and establish complex patterns of active reading and meaning prediction.
- Picture books stimulate the creation of links between book worlds and everyday life, and shape individual storying in the direction of literary conventions.

Literature and Becoming Literate

Literary Texts Teach

Literary texts teach those extra lessons about authors, audiences and the conventions of illustration, metaphor and interpretation that go beyond the information given by print (Meek, 1988). Extended encounters with literature in the first years of schooling reinforce and expand young children's involvement in the human urge to preserve and share feelings, relationships, ideas and places. To take the last item first, many literary texts communicate a strong sense of place and this is certainly not restricted to children's books. Young children's responses to particular story-book streets, viaducts and skylines, or to tales of certain riverbanks, bridges and parks, may enable them to picture for themselves the more remote, archetypal dark forests and great rivers of myth and folktale. A pattern of interaction between the totally imagined worlds of some literary texts and the carefully located real-world settings of others typifies literary experiences from childhood onwards. Authors and readers can picture Narnia, Bloom's Dublin and Hardy's Wessex, because the fictional worlds of literature grow out of the known and shared reality of everyday places.

Children and adults respond to literature's created worlds of people and ideas by drawing on their own sense of self and their own networks of human relationships. For example, sooner or later children may experience the over-whelming grief of being temporarily parted from a parent. In the context of this not-uncommon upset, they share feelingly the desperate howl of *My Brother Sean* (Breinburg, 1973) in his nursery class or the deep fears of aban-donment underlying *Hansel and Gretel* (Browne, 1981). In lighter mood, Mike Rosen's poems, 'Chocolate Cake' or 'Eddie and the Gerbils' (Rosen, 1983) encourage us to celebrate and share our own experiences of childhood tempta-tions, joys and mishaps. The process is reminiscent of the mutual pleasure and conversational form of first language learning: the professional author, like the care-giver, may say it better and with more polish, but the young reader or listener, like the infant conversationalist, is an apprentice who can make mean-ingful contributions to the stories and the poems.

Book Language

Literary texts display for their readers the literary uses of language and are examples of powerful new ways of using words. This aspect of literary encoun-ters is usually referred to as 'book language', particularly in studies of early literacy. Clearly, reading literature and listening to readings of literature pro-vide the best possible introductions to those uses of language typical of written forms: permanence, explicit references and cohesive devices. This means that texts can be returned to again and again and they contain all the necessary allusions and information for making sense of their propositions.

Written texts also employ a range of linguistic devices or grammatical cross-references for building together propositions in order to create a cohesive whole. Perhaps the most important characteristic of literary language is its metaphorical rather than literal function. In contrast, the book language of non-literary discourse aims to make as close a match as it can between the language forms and the real state of affairs being presented. Literal discourse may be concerned with, for example, the life cycle of the ant or the technique for making lino-prints and must aim for unambiguous, precise and foolproof language about ants or lino-printing. But literature purposely exploits the ways in which language may be ambiguous, subtle and evocative.

Literature does not aspire to be foolproof but launches itself into the risky areas of reader responses and individual interpretations. Literary discourse takes risks, using metaphor to link diverse and surprisingly disparate areas of meaning. For example in the created world of Anthony Browne, huge, sham-bling gorillas, stirring fearful folk-memories of aggression, monster tales and horror films, become endearing representations of fun, affection and gentle timidity.

Literature plays with language and exploits all of its potential for innuendo and ambiguity, as well as its rhythm and sounds. Metaphors explain much of the delightful ambiguity of literary language, as when Amelia Bedelia 'dresses' the chicken, or the animals in Mr Gumpy's boat revert to 'typical' behaviour. *Each Peach Pear Plum* (Ahlberg and Ahlberg, 1977b) builds on our sensitivity to rhyming sounds as well as our knowledge of nursery rhyme and fairy-tale characters. Young children's earliest encounters with rhymes and poems teach them that they can join in with the highly predictable rhyming end word: 'Incy Wincy spider climbed up the spout/Down came the rain and washed the spider out.' This early language skill, which has great significance for later literacy, will also be employed to substitute alternative and less respectable ranges of words in familiar songs and rhymes. Literary texts create spaces for readers' and listeners' contributions and stimulate play with the rules of language and culture.

Literary Forms

The language of literary texts also demonstrates the different forms, or genres, narrative and poetry can take. Narratives can be stories in rhyme and metre, as in the traditional ballads or modern picture books: *The Jolly Pocket Postman* (Ahlberg and Ahlberg, 1995); *We're Going On A Bear Hunt*, (Rosen and Oxenbury, 1989). Narratives may preserve the patterns of folktales and fairy-tales with their oral conventions of ritual openings and closures, traditional characters and predictable situations.

They can also tell tales of recognizably contemporary dilemmas and successes in streets, schools and supermarkets. They may hurtle us down rabbit holes, through secret wardrobe doors or bring the forest and the night into our bedrooms. Then, in language still very similar to that with which we buy vegetables and make dental appointments, they tell us of awful dangers and dilemmas that will be resolved at the end of the story.

In contrast, the language of poetry is musical, rich in images and economical in the use of words. Poems literally take up less space on the page and their impact is sharper and intensely concentrated:

> All but blind
> In his chambered hole
> Gropes for worms
> The four-clawed mole.
>
> (De La Mare, 1962, p. 78)

The distinctive shapes made by poems on the page are a reminder of the physical characteristics of literary texts. Actual texts teach their readers the conventions of books and print – how books work and how readers must behave. Children who are beginning to write often pretend to have the speed and flow of the skilled writer; they also experiment with the shaping and orientation of letters and they liberally sprinkle their writing with full stops and other punctuation. Similarly, they may investigate and imitate the lay-out of books, the appearance of covers and title pages and the varied ways of arranging blocks of text and illustrations, pagination, lists of contents and dedications. Clearly the literary text also needs the supportive and mediating human 'teacher' who highlights these conventions and models or demonstrates them in writing activities with children and promotes discussion of their functions.

Making Sense of Text

The literary text teaches us to be readers because it urges us to turn the page and make the meanings the author intended. Young children's questions and comments indicate that they work with great resourcefulness and commitment to make sense of texts and illustrations: 'Why's he crying?' 'Where's the dog?' 'She's not very kind.' 'That's a funny hat.' Good authors support the child's first endeavours to read the text alive, by providing verbal and pictorial clues about the events; rhythmic and enjoyable repetitions of phrases and names; and invitations to make predictions about the possible outcomes. This means creating devices like the large spy-holes in the pages of *Peepo* (Ahlberg and Ahlberg, 1981), which entice the reader into turning the page and finding the whole scene. Or it may be the provision of the picture clues in *Piggybook* (Browne, 1986), which chart the increasingly 'pig-like' changes in people reflected in furniture and artefacts. Constant and joyful repetition of phrases ('But where is the green parrot?') or names ('Skolinkenlot and Skohottentot') provide not only the means to drive the narrative forward, but also small and memorable chunks of text and easily recognized combinations of letters.

Good readers are good predictors of what will be the likely outcome of the initial events and possibilities in the poem or story: once a stranger interrupts a cosy domestic setting, we expect problems; once a wolf or a fox appears, we predict danger and possibly death; and once a character hides, we foretell a finding.

Success in predicting outcomes and amazed delight when the author lulls us into a false hypothesis and 'turns the tables' on our predictions is one of the most potent rewards of reading. Real readers of any age find their rewards in the actual encounter with the text. They read to please themselves. Readers who only read to please others run into difficulties if the external reward and motivation is withdrawn. Reading for pleasure, or for a personally felt need for information, is its own reward. This is not necessarily a solitary pursuit. We may be so moved by the pleasures of the text that we want to share them with others.

Good literary texts allow for endless re-runs or repetitions of the experience. Children's delight in hearing a story again and again or poring over favourite books does not just indicate the power of simple pleasurable repetition, although that is important. Literature is only fully understood as a complete entity. We grasp it in retrospect, and in the light of the ending we go back and make sense of the whole pattern. Written texts are ideally suited for going back over, again and again: they are not a succession of fleeting sounds or rapidly changing visual images. Books exist as unchanged objects, playthings that can be returned to at will. Children's requests for 'that book', 'that poem' or 'that story' are testimony to their willingness and need to go over again the experiences they encounter in literature.

Writers and Texts

Children bring their literary experiences and knowledge about authors to the task of learning to be a writer. If this knowledge is based on rewarding meetings with authors, children will have some internal models or patterns of what is involved in writing. Literary texts teach that writing is centrally concerned with the sharing of messages. Literature also demonstrates the ways in which authors use language. We find in literature new words for new worlds and new words for old experiences, as well as meeting old words used in startlingly bright and fresh ways and in new contexts.

The most valuable lesson texts teach children about authors is the quality of 'voice' in authentic writing. Authors communicate their message in language that is shaped and polished to achieve the required precision and clarity. In the hands of good educators, texts invite children to become authors themselves, and children who enjoy literature are usually eager to make their own books and compile anthologies of favourite poems and stories.

- Literary texts teach children that literature is an aspect of human communication. Texts build links between imaginary worlds and daily realities.
- Literary texts display the literary uses of language and support children's explorations of the possibilities of the written forms of language.
- Literary texts show and teach the conventions of books and print and the strategies readers must use in order to read for meaning.
- Literary texts teach children about the roles and preoccupations of authors.

Teaching Reading and Supporting Readers

The Reading Debate

Since the first edition of this book (1990) there has been a swing away from focusing on the role of literature and quality books in the teaching and learning of reading. This is reflected in the revised National Curriculum requirements that, within a balanced and coherent programme, pupils at Key Stage 1 should be taught to use phonic, graphic and grammatical knowledge and word recognition skills, as well as contextual understanding (DFE, 1995, p. 7). However, the changing terms of the 'reading debate' in the USA and the UK predate the revised National Curriculum Orders for English (*ibid.*). They are also more complex than the simplistic 'back to basics' campaign which often passes for educational debate about reading.

The debate about reading and literacy is endless and it is not surprising that issues of such psychological complexity and cultural significance do not yield easy answers and quick-fix solutions. A brief review of the 'debate' indicates how sophisticated and tentative are the conclusions of those who actually engage in research and teaching in the fields of early reading instruction and initial literacy.

The work of Adams (1990a) in the USA was government commissioned and intended as an update on Chall's (1967) pro-phonics conclusions, but the Adams' study proposes more than simply sustained phonemic awareness training in classrooms (this means at ages 6/7 in the USA). There is also an emphasis on the crucial role of worthwhile and meaningful reading material in early literacy and clear warnings about the linguistic nonsense which ensues from attempts to teach phonics in a vacuum (Adams, 1990a, p. 421). Adams also goes a long way down the 'phonics alone is not enough' road in a conference paper (1990b) which affirms that young children must be helped to use both global, or top-down, reading strategies and alphabetic and phonic (bottom-up) strategies.

In the UK there has been a research-based transformation in phonic approaches to the early reading debate. Researchers have demonstrated a powerful connection between young pre-school children's phonological awareness and their early success in reading (Bryant and Bradley, 1985) and identified the crucial factors:

- early knowledge of nursery rhymes
- ability to detect rhyme and alliteration
- ability to produce rhyming and alliterative words.

A further refinement (Goswami and Bryant, 1990) of these studies suggests that pre-school children are sensitive to regularities in the sound of words. Particularly, the regular phonological patterns in

- the beginning sounds of words or 'onset' (especially of a consonant preceding a vowel)
- the end units or 'rimes' (which produce rhymes).

Experienced professional teachers of early literacy still have to interpret the many complex findings of research and clarify the issues in discussions with other professionals and young children's families. Factors which need to be considered include children's different developmental stages, learning styles, cultural, social and home literacy experiences. Learning to read is sited within infant development (Jones, 1996); it can be adversely affected by poverty and inequalities of many kinds (Freire and Macedo, 1987; Lake, 1991; Snow *et al.*, 1991); successful reading depends on a rich background of enjoyable and meaningful encounters with literature and print of all kinds (Smith, 1994); reading is complex and children beginning to read require a range of strategies and information about language and print, as well as close individual support in the early days of settling into statutory schooling (Riley, 1996); reading and writing are two sides of the same coin and should be taught together as a whole literacy programme (Fisher, 1992; Jackson, 1993; Smith, B., 1994; Browne, 1996).

Literacy progress must be monitored closely in the early years; it should be the dominant and joyful focus of the early years curriculum and it should be at the centre of the genuine partnership between early years settings, schools and parents (Weinberger, 1996; Wolfendale and Topping, 1996).

One conclusion from all this research is that there is no one single approach or method that will teach reading to all children. Phonics alone is never enough; teaching the single sounds of letters as isolated decoding tricks does not work. Children must build a considerable sight vocabularly in the course of enjoyable reading and writing activities and gradually have their attention drawn to letter–sound relationships, the sounds (phonemes) in words and their letter symbols. They also have to be prepared for exceptions and not be defeated by them. Only significant and rewarding encounters with language and literature can sustain young children through the complexities of literacy.

Problems with Primers

There can be few teachers now or in the past who believed that they were teaching children to read and write in order that the children should go on reading more and more reading-scheme books and writing in the fashion of 'I see the dog./Run, dog run'. Only a poet could turn such language into a message rich in sly innuendo:

> Go Peter! Go Jane! Come, milkman, come!
> The milkman likes Mummy. She likes them all.
> Look Jane, look! Look at the dog! See him run!
>
> (Wendy Cope, 1986, p. 17)

Teachers and parents have always aimed to move children on to reading real literature and information books as soon as possible. But in the struggle with the initial reading material both children and adults often lost their taste for literature and the most important lesson about reading was never taught or learnt: reading is something people do for pleasure.

The answer to the initial reading-material problem is sensible and logical: we must use authentic books and genuine literature for a significant part of our literacy teaching. Many teachers already use literature, or what has been called the 'real-books' approach, for the teaching of reading, but if it is to be successful and sustained it must go deeper than the unthought-out avoidance of reading schemes.

Literature can only change our approach to the reading process and to young readers if we fully understand it as part of our theory of reading and our theory of education. Problems will arise if inappropriate methods and attitudes (derived from profoundly different views of learning and learners) are linked with the provision of quality books. For example, the colour coding or grading of children's literature destroys the free choice involved in reading books, the pleasure of mulling over much-loved 'easy reads' and the excitement of risking a difficult book because it appeals for personal reasons and answers the questions we are currently asking.

Similarly, the imposition of strict times for children to read to a teacher or assistant volunteer and the limitation on the number of pages that may be read at a sitting, make a nonsense of supporting children as real but emerging readers. Literature involves profound changes in our approaches to the teaching of reading.

There continue to be problems with primers: mainly in the treatment of language, illustrations, themes, characterization and 'readerly concerns'. These problems have been articulated in the form of debates about the relative merits of using literature or primers in the teaching of reading. Does the intrinsic value and interest of the texts that beginning readers are asked to read matter? Can children learn to read from the start with literary and informative texts, or must they acquire and practise reading skills first and apply them later? The use of reading schemes reflects to some extent the latter view and it would still appear to be the main approach in British schools.

Until recently a very small group of reading schemes dominated primary classrooms and constituted the major early reading experiences of many children (for example, *One, Two, Three and Away, Story Chest* and *Ginn Reading 360*). But since the reading debate moved on newer schemes have appeared and prospered (*Cambridge Reading, Oxford Reading Tree*).

It is only fair to note that several other schemes are still very widely used and in some cases are much more outdated and more unsatisfactory than the primers identified in this general critique.

The language of primers

With respect to language, the most striking feature of the primers is a bland and rather humourless quality – if humour is used it is often laboured and repetitive. Abrupt and contrived imperatives still dominate the syntax, resulting in an accumulation of orders to stop, come, help, run or see. Some texts described as 'first level' consist entirely of a one-word instruction (such as 'look') on every page. The disturbing feature of this approach is that it produces linguistic nonsense and many non-sentences. Normal written language is patterned by meaningful arrangements of words that reflect sequences of events, causal connections between actions and the relationships of agents or actors to each other and to events.

When we wish to expose young children to very small and controlled snippets of written language we can share delightfully realistic catalogues of identifiable objects and activities with them. In *The Baby's Catalogue* (Ahlberg and Ahlberg, 1982) of 'toys', 'shopping' or 'bedtimes', the listed experiences and sensitive pictures add up to a lively narrative of several families. The extension of vocabulary is best achieved by enjoying the many modern alphabet books available, for example, *What's Inside?* (Kitamura, 1985), which reveals such wonders as octopus and piano, guitar and hippopotamus. Or *F-Freezing ABC* (Simmonds, 1995) which plays with alliteration and tells a story. These books have a clear narrative sequence and humorously support listing, labelling and curiosity. At the very least, such texts stimulate spontaneous naming games and make links with children's own life experiences and fantasies. By contrast, it is almost impossible to sustain much meaningful discussion around a vocabulary consisting of 'can' 'come' 'help' 'here' 'Dad' 'home' 'I' 'in' 'it' 'look' 'my' 'not' 'stop'.

Once the schemes move on to producing longer stretches of meaningful language they come up with reasonable story openings: 'A little old man lived in a house on top of a hill' (*One, Two, Three and Away* 1A). But compare this with Geoffrey Patterson's (1986) retelling of an Aesop fable: 'Henry and Hilda lived in a pink cottage on a sunny hilltop'. The subtle differences point up the set of choices made by a real author in order to develop his central concern with human characters and their development in the story. There is the precise naming of the couple (Henry and Hilda), the more informative nature of the language chosen (pink, sunny) and the richer extended vocabulary (for example, using cottage to specify a very small house). Furthermore, the initial emotional tone of contentment and happiness is suggested by the setting (a sunny hilltop) and the pleasingly alliterative and homely names of the main characters. In contrast to this, the cool anonymity of some structured reading-scheme language may create a barrier to reading and relating to the text for many young children.

The situation does not noticeably improve when some primers introduce direct speech, as in conversations and questions directed at the reader. Indeed, the artificial control and over-simplification of the language produces unrecognizable talk and unhelpful arrangements of the print on the page:

> 'I will hide./You can look/for me, Jill'./
> 'Yes, Tom./You go and hide./Ben and I will/look for you'.
>
> (*Reading 360*, Level 2, Book 3)

Meanwhile, out on the streets or in playgrounds children are using the sort of language exchanges sensitively echoed in many story and picture books: '"Archie, look what I found", Peter shouted through the pipe, "Motorcycle goggles!"' (Keats, 1970).

A major problem with primers is that they frequently break all the social-communicative rules of human conversations. Children's earliest language experiences model for them the ways in which we set about talking to each other. For example, questions are seen to need answers, in literature as in life, and not just echo-like repetitions. Information may be received, rejected or mulled over and developed in tentative ways:

> 'What kind of a bear are you?; asked Ted.
> 'I'm an Idle Bear'.
> 'But don't you have a name like me?'
> 'Yes, but my name is Teddy. All bears like us are called Teddy'.
>
> (Ingpen, 1986)

Conversations in the primers are stilted because information and meanings are not being exchanged. Indeed, set phrases are declaimed and remain totally unmodified by any responses from a genuine conversational partner:

> 'Look, Johnny! Look!' he cried, 'There is a donkey under that tree'.
> 'Mr. Brown said he was going to get a donkey', said Johnny.
>
> (*One, Two, Three and Away*, 3A, p. 3)

If we are tempted to defend the usefulness of this sort of 'easy' introduction to direct speech in books and stories we should recall the quality of conversations in real books for young children:

> 'I don't see any cat', said John Brown.
> 'I'm sure it's a cat. Go and give it some milk.'
> 'There's nobody there', said John Brown.
>
> (Wagner, 1977)

If we wish to ensure that very young children receive plenty of experience of the written conventions of questions and answers, we should share with them the linguistic hide-and-seek of *Spot* books, or search the pictures for answers to *But Where is the Green Parrot?* (Zacharias and Zacharias, 1965). Picture books repeat their crucial questions on nearly every page and the examples noted come from a huge range of children' books that meaningfully demonstrate the role of repetition in literature.

Repeating the same phrases or significant names is a major literary device and is certainly not restricted to children's books. In traditional folktales and in stories for children repetition is used for the creation of a cumulative build-up to a disastrous or comical climax. In *Mr Gumpy's Outing* (Burningham, 1970), we gradually meet all the creatures who wish to join the boat outing and the dramatic and inevitable capsize entails yet another repetitive unpacking or listing of names and characteristic actions, as does the happy ending.

Repetition often highlights the central dilemma as well as the humour of the narration, so that such phrases as 'Not now, Bernard' (McKee, 1980) and 'Come away from the water, Shirley' (Burningham, 1977) are also the story titles. For the young child, repeated phrases, words and lists make participation in the telling of the story and visual recognition of recurring written words and letter clusters a natural bridge to reading. But the material to be repeated must be meaningful and appropriate in the context – it must be funny, poetic and important. This is clearly demonstrated when children cannot resist joining in the 'huffing and puffing' of the wolf, the listing of the very hungry caterpillar's extraordinary meals and pointing to Bernard's name on almost every page of the book. Primers have always exploited the repetition of phrases and words, although with little appreciation of the musical and meaningful functions of repetition in narrative and poetry. There are now some reading schemes available that provide a good diet of rhyme, poetry and song in all their levels or phases (*Cambridge Reading*; *Oxford Reading Tree*; *Story Chest*).

Uninspired and purposeless repetition is not simply boring, it is very confusing and adds to the difficulties experienced by young children. Pointless repetition results in a great accumulation of words on the page to be sorted out and, in attempts to make sense of them, children usually move away from the text, creating their own desperate narrative explanations that are 'wrong'. Sensitivity to the sounds and rhythms of spoken language, playfulness in using and exploiting it and experience of simply mucking about with words and rhymes support early success in learning to read and write (Bryant and Bradley, 1985). Conversely, a marked lack of awareness of sounds and rhymes in daily language use is found among many children who experience difficulty with reading. Sensitivity to the texture and structures of language is more likely to be nurtured by considerable experiences of music, literature, play and talk than by simplistic phonic exercises, sound 'tables' or tasks such as filling in the missing words in sentences and underlining recurring letters.

Primers often make the mistake of simplifying the rich complexity of spoken and written language and by doing so they remove all the most helpful features of book language: not only meaningful narratives but also memorable, frequently repeated phrases. Other helpful features include the use of rhyme, alliteration and the choice of beautiful, archaic or foreign words. These give stories and verse a unique and unforgettable quality. Most children who encounter stories, poetry and picture books can soon identify and use a rhyming pattern as an important aid to reading prediction: 'Each Peach Pear Plum/I spy Tom Thumb' (Ahlberg and Ahlberg, 1977b). These children also learn about 'cicadas' and 'guavas', or learn non-British usages such as 'mailbox', 'snow-cone' and 'trash'. In many schools there are children who can now recognize such genres as solicitors' letters and mail order catalogues (*The Jolly Postman*, Ahlberg and Ahlberg, 1986).

Illustrations in primers

The treatment of illustrations in the traditional primers often turns into a problem rather than being a help for the beginning reader. Pictures in books are, at the very least, expected to support and clarify the narrative line, providing additional help with the process of making sense of the text. In many primers, very little relevant sense-making and much confusion result from wooden pictures of children and adults who are apparently related, if we read the text, because they wear the same colour hats and even live in houses with the same colour-matched roofs and front doors. Asian peoples are indicated by prominent noses and the wearing of sandals, while Caucasian faces are shaded brown to represent the black people in a community.

Illustrations in primers still fail most dismally in terms of their total lack of aesthetic quality or value as art. There is an absence of sensual delight in colour and texture and some very poor drawing skills. If we allow such schemes to be the dominant experience of books for children in the early years of schooling, we deprive them of a world of books that explode with vibrant colours, display delicate line drawings or exploit techniques of engraving and collage. We may also deprive our children of subtly tinted pages, golden eggs, holes, flaps, moving parts and elaborate end-papers. What is lacking in the illustrations in primers cannot be simply remedied by adding a few of these picture-book features as decoration. The central difference between the illustrations in primers and the artwork in picture books and children's literature is the commitment of the artist, who may also be the author. This lesson has now been learnt by some modern schemes with text and illustrations by named professional writers and artists.

Quality books contain not only the possibility of a relationship with an author but also an introduction to a unique artist. Very young children develop a strong sense of the artist if they meet many books. Young book lovers recognize the styles and conventions employed by some artists as easily as they recognize the familiar features of a friend. This is not surprising: the wicked exuberance of Helen Oxenbury contrasts with the formal restraint and sly humour of Holly Keller or the gentle observations of Mick Inkpen. The textured surfaces, patterns and stylized figures of Pat Hutchins' world are a different reality from that of Shirley Hughes' lovingly observed streets, houses, families and boisterous toddlers. Real artists do not just prop up or illuminate the text, as young book readers soon learn. Pictures are also narratives and run in parallel with the text. Sometimes they share a joke or a secret, as when Rosie is pursued by an accident-prone fox, or they tell an alternative story, as when Shirley is living her pirate fantasy. Artists who work on children's books often create and share a sense of place, as well as of persons, with their readers. John Brown and Rose inhabit a remote homestead in the outback of Australia, Dulcie and her friends remember Babylon while exploring the disused railway viaducts of South London.

Themes and characterization in primers

The whimsy and poor draughtsmanship that has dominated many of the reading schemes are paralleled by weak themes and characterization. In primers no one dies, no one hates and no one loves, but children's books do not flinch from greed and jealousy, rage and loneliness, mourning and death. Primers, however, lack powerful issues and they often ignore contemporary life-styles and unthinkingly perpetuate racial and gender stereotypes. Attention has already been directed to the unsatisfactory drawings of black and Asian characters and, in the early stages of some schemes, the occupations of these people are restricted to manual work and cleaning. Schemes sometimes avoid a realistic multi-cultural world by choosing rural fantasy settings. A popular scheme with a rural setting presents boys as 'doers' and explorers, while the only girl character is left to organize such domestic matters as cakes, pets and getting the boys out of scrapes. Mothers are still limited to the domestic role: a recent set of comic-style books for reluctant readers does have mum zooming around on 'wheels' – while she bakes and ices a cake!

Compared to traditional folktales, the rural idyll favoured by some schemes is flat and flavourless. It lacks the threats, dangers and sudden death meted out by predators in farmyards, the existence of stupid and greedy human characters, the trolls under bridges and the lions who suddenly materialize in the meadow. But these elements are essential to traditional folktales and are reflected in a range of quality books and stories for children. The 'jolly' japes in many schemes, such as falling into rivers and flattening haystacks, seem contrived and make few meaningful links with children's or adults' practical and fantasy lives.

Undoubtedly, teachers who feel confident about the reading materials and approaches they use make an enormous contribution to motivating and sustaining their pupils' successful reading development. However, it is essential that a teacher's personal preference for structured reading schemes does not lead to any lessening of the children's experiences of literature. Recent developments are leading to an enormous increase in 'phonic' schemes and materials available, as well as in the 'phonic' content of existing schemes. But the indications are that simple phonics and isolated decoding skills are not sufficient to create readers who can apply their phonological knowledge to a text in the process of reading for meaning (Bielby, 1994).

Texts and Readers

Much that has already been discussed illustrates some reasons for avoiding total reliance on reading schemes. The advantages of reading books of literary and artistic merit in early years settings and schools are improved motivation, increased literary skills and an enhancement of the educators' and carers' role. With regard to motivation, the young child who is invited to read from quality books is being treated as a serious reader from the start. The resulting pride and self-esteem make a positive and sure foundation for successful literary learning. The use of such books also entices the child to move on to more and more texts because of the lure of further delights in store. Improved motivation is not restricted to learners: educators and families who help young readers are also encouraged by the sheer pleasure of sharing good books. Many parents and educators have in the past come to dislike intensely certain schemes and their vapid 'characters'. These negative feelings must have been sensed by generations of struggling readers. In contrast to this response, educators and families are often the first to get hooked on Burglar Bill, Spot, Avocado Baby and Tich!

The complex skills involved in literacy and its development are at the heart of the arguments about the best way to approach reading. Controlled and simplified texts are not, paradoxically, the best way to help young readers. Complex human texts that contain recognizable issues, motives and emotions described in recognizable language are essential for the emergent reader. If young children are to get a toe-hold on a text they need as rich an array of clues about its meanings as possible. The clues must refer to the contextual aspects of the text: is it a letter, a cookery book or a story? The pictorial aspects are significant: are the images telling about the text and/or expanding it? The semantic clues will be those that help to answer such questions as what does it mean and what is likely to happen next?

Orthographic and phonological clues will enable the young reader to recognize frequently recurring and significant words on sight; to begin to notice initial consonants and distinctive clusters of letters; and to hear similar and rhyming phonemes.

Linguistic clues indicate the grammatical category of possible words and their range of functions. When in doubt over a reading we rely on the linguistic context to indicate whether at this point the text is naming referents, indicating actions or describing and enlarging upon a state of affairs. In order to use these clues and possibilities children must be motivated enough and confident enough to question the text, as we have already seen, and bring all their previous experiences to bear on it. To put it another way, the beginning reader must take on the whole package from the start, going for meaning or comprehension before breaking down the text into its component parts of words, letters and sounds. Reading is not like painting by numbers and we do not help children by starting them off as if it were. Real readers need rich and complex reading materials and good quality texts meet this need.

Educators who use literature for teaching reading, as well as for pleasure, need support and guidance. First, they must read every book they plan to put into the hands of the children. They must be able to speak from first-hand experience of the assumptions the book makes, the quality of its presentation, illustrations and language and the opportunities it potentially opens up for its readers. Does it raise important issues for reflection and discussion? Does it lead to other books or activities in early years settings or in the community? Does it extend the reader's language experience with new words and new ways of using words? Does it offer opportunities for focusing on initial clusters, rhymes and groups of letters?

Second, the teacher's choice of books for the classroom must be both varied and ample in quantity. There must be a wide range of poetry, story and information books and a great diversity of presentational styles or formats. Books in the classroom collection should contain pictures only, pictures and captions, toy-like techniques that pop-up or have holes or flaps, as well as increasing amounts of text. Professional guidance for educators and carers is now available in regularly compiled and annotated lists of available books and in journals that specialize in children's literature.[4]

As educators and carers we must be alert to new publications and new developments in the book world. We also need to pursue a personal programme of regularly reading children's books for pleasure and information. Reading with quality texts places the power of behaving like readers literally into the hands of the children. It puts the responsibility for making informed professional judgements and acting as models of what readers do back in the hands of educators, carers and families.

Reading in and out of School

The use of quality books and literature challenges the traditional approach to 'hearing reading'. Literary texts are multi-layered and must be shared, commented on and interrogated in a mutually supportive reading triangle of learner, teacher and text. In the early stages children need time to experience a whole book at a sitting. Initially this may involve the adult in reading the book first and allowing the young apprentice (Waterland, 1988) to follow the performance, before encouraging the child to re-enact the story with the help of the context, the pictures, known letters and words, the teacher and a variety of clues.

Young readers will also require the time and the security in which to discuss and evaluate the story and link it to their own lives and experiences. Such important human interactions take time and 1-to-1 teaching, with all that this implies for large class sizes in early years settings. These readings are also unpredictable and cannot be controlled as tightly as the kind of 'hearing reading' that consists of checking on a child's ability to recognize a few words by sight in a book of regular size and controlled vocabulary and sentence structure. Teachers who use a range of quality books do not aim to 'hear' individual children read every day. They plan to share one, two or even three complete books with each child every week. However, they have other ways of supporting readers on a daily basis.

All the shared anecdotes, discussions, negotiations, poems, songs, rhymes and stories told or read in the group or class support reading. All the contacts with written materials in the school and the community support reading. Children, teachers and families read newspapers, posters, letters, notices, street signs, carrier bags, food packages, greetings cards, invitations, recipes and the labels on clothes, cupboards and furniture. Parents, families and other members of the community also support young beginner readers by sharing the books many group settings and schools now send home on a regular basis. The young readers themselves contribute to this network of support by sharing their emerging skills with other infants and their peers who are just getting into literacy. At home young readers may read to their baby siblings or family pets, and in school they can share their developing competence with any other children who will listen.

Children can be helped to create a reading network or community if they are provided with books, time, pleasant spaces and, most importantly, an ethos that values books and reading for real. The issue of ethos and attitudes is crucial in approaches to sharing reading. Real readers take risks and they must feel that it is safe and rewarding to do so. They take chances, not only with the choice of book (there are no numbers or colours to guide you on your way in a lifetime of real reading) but also with linguistic decisions.

Reading for meaning needs to be fairly rapid so that the thread of the narrative sense is not lost. Clues must be picked up on the run and chances taken – is it 'Mam' or 'Mummy', a 'horse' or a 'house'? This highly skilled predicting can be more finely tuned and corrected in retrospect if the reader is given the opportunity to go back and self-correct. Once the reader knows that the heroine must have escaped by climbing onto a big, black, horse and not a 'house', the correction is sensible and rewarding, and not without some humour. Amusement and delight in self-correction rely on confidence and space and time in which to re-consider. The supportive teacher does not rush in too soon to fill this particular kind of pause. Knowing when to help, and when to hold back and let the text and the child reader do their own work, is a matter of professional judgement, experience and sensitivity: sensitivity to texts and to children is the most significant quality the reading teacher in any setting can develop.

As part of the process of teaching reading and supporting readers, the professional educator makes links between books and children's lives. In the first place this is done whenever incidents and characters in stories or poems are talked about and linked with events, people, and places the children know well. Clearly professional educators can only make a few of these connections because of their limited access to the children's personal lives. However, the children themselves will be willing contributors to the shared and valuable gossip of the classroom, always assuming that such talk is valued and respected.

Yet another way of linking the worlds of children and of books is through the creation of varied 'story props' that bring poems and stories into the play and general activities of the children and also draw the children into the world of the book. These props can be verions of the characters drawn by children, helpers and teachers firmly mounted on card and backed with felt or magnetic tape and used on flannel boards or metal surfaces. Characters and objects from favourite stories can be played with and manipulated on these boards, accompanied by retellings and re-enactments of their adventures. Playful narrative activities of this kind are further enhanced if similarly mounted photographs of the individual children themselves are available. Children in the group are then able to narrate about themselves and place themselves into Mr Gumpy's boat, or in hot pursuit of the elephant and the bad baby.

Children can be further motivated by displayed photographs of other young children enjoying books and storying, or talking and playing with story props. Sometimes the actual objects mentioned in a narrative can be provided and used in playful book re-enactments – for example, a basket of groceries for *The Shopping Basket* (Burningham, 1980); some fruit for Handa (Browne, 1994); a green umbrella for *The Bear Under The Stairs* (Cooper, 1993) and a collection of hot water bottles for Phoebe (Furchgott and Dawson, 1977). Appropriate puppets, dolls and toys (such as sets of graduated bears, spoons, bowls, chairs and beds) can also be used as powerful invitations to become a reader and enter the story-book world. From these props for young readers it is a short step to helping children become the authors of their own books. Young children who enjoy total immersion in literature are able to create books themselves. Becoming authors is the logical outcome for children who approach reading through the medium of quality literature and books of all kinds.

- Reading is something we do for pleasure and for information, and this is learned from satisfying experiences with books.
- Over-dependence on the use of reading schemes in schools exposes children to the problems inherent in most primers. These are problems with their treatment of language; the use and quality of illustrations; their themes and characterization; and their support of the reader.
- Literary approaches to the teaching of reading involve a careful focus on the nature of written texts, different perspectives on hearing young readers read and a broader view of the place of reading in children's lives.

Teaching and Learning Suggestions

* Create an attractive book corner or area – carpeted and curtained if possible – with floor cushions, comfortable chairs, plants, pictures and display space and storage for books, audio tapes and story props (see below).

* Start a collection of story props (see Chapter 8). Use plastic 'zip' bags or sturdy containers to hold a book and sometimes an audio book tape, plus the relevant props (cut-out drawings of characters backed with magnetic tape or velcro, puppets, soft toys and objects from the story).

* Build up an audio-taped collection of stories, rhymes and poetry recorded by familiar adults (teachers, nursery nurses, assistants, parents, regular visitors, school governors). This should be in addition to published books on tape.

* Start or extend a book collection and organize it thematically and in genres, using child-friendly boxes and open shelving. Include big picture books (see Chapter 8); wordless and minimal text picture books; picture and story books; a variety of alphabet books; books based on traditional tales and myths (including modern versions and subversive re-writings); books focused on animal characters, families, and challenging issues (loneliness, death, prejudice, starting school, jealousy). Include books which provide a longer text in chapters for early fluent readers and for sharing with adults (*The Julian Stories*; *The Owl who was Afraid of the Dark*; *Clever Polly and The Stupid Wolf*).

* Create a poetry collection, including nursery rhymes, nonsense verse, tongue twisters, jokes and songs. Use this material in daily language play sessions; exploit the rhymes, alliteration and sounds and invent amusing word families (sun, bun, fun, run) to illustrate and incorporate into stories, chants and raps. Create some home-grown alphabets to add to the traditional 'A was an apple' versions.

* Vary what is available in the book corner; do not overwhelm the area and the children with clutter. Change the books, tapes and materials according to seasonal, festive, developmental and individual and group interests and experiences.

* Regularly set up thematic or genre displays featuring, for example, fairy tales, poems, reference books, a popular author and/or illustrator.

* Provide some carefully chosen reference and information books. Look for high quality photographs, art work and diagrams as well as reliable and accurate facts (use some books intended for older children and adults if necessary). Check that reference and information texts have clear and helpful lists of contents, indexes, diagrams, etc. so that you and the children can begin to practise study skills.

* Prioritize daily 'shared reading' sessions (see Chapter 8).

Notes

1. This chapter contains allusions to the events and characters in many children's books and the full references will be found in the list of 'Literature referred to in the Text'.
2. See, Harding, D.W. (1937), *The role of The Onlooker*, pp. 247–58, and, Britton, J.N. (1970), Participant and Spectator, pp. 97–125.
3. Jane Taylor, 'The Star', in I. Opie & P. Opie (eds.) (1973) p. 122.
4. For example, *Books for Keeps*, 6 Brightfield Road, Lee, London, SE12 8QF, and, *Signal*, The Thimble Press, Lockwood, Station Rd, South Woodchester, Stroud, Glos, GL5 5EQ.

Further Reading

Beard, R. (ed.) (1995) *Rhyme, Reading and Writing*, Hodder & Stoughton, London.
Campbell, R. (1992) *Reading Real Books*, Open University Press, Buckingham.
Holdaway, D. (1979) *The Foundations of Literacy*, Ashton Scholastic, London.
Jones, R. (1996) *Emerging Patterns of Literacy*, Routledge, London.
Meek, M. (1988) *How Texts Teach What Readers Learn*, Thimble Press, Stroud.
Miller, L. (1996) *Towards Reading*, Open University Press, Buckingham.
Riley, J. (1996) *The Teaching of Reading. The development of literacy in the early years of school*, Paul Chapman, London.

7

Early representation and emerging writing

. . . the process of writing: it is not a merely mechanical task, a simple matter of putting speech down on paper. It is an exploration in the use of the graphic potential of a language – a creative process, an act of discovery.
Crystal, 1987, p. 212

This chapter considers writing within the broad context of children's language and literacy development. In order to do this, questions about the sources of young children's understanding of writing must be asked. Where does writing emerge from? What behaviours and insights preceded the ability to write meaningful messages and understand written communications? There are also those questions about the nature of writing that must be tackled by the would-be writer of any age. What is special or distinctive about writing? How is it related to spoken language and even to thinking?

Questions also arise about the nature of writing as a product of a cultural group or society. What is there to be said about the relationships between a writing system and the society in which it has evolved? And, most significantly in the context of this book, what is there to be said about literacy and early schooling? What is the role of the professional educator in young children's development as writers? Some of these questions about literacy will be returned to in Chapter 8, but they emerge from the issues developed in this chapter.

Before looking in some detail at the beginnings of mark making and writing in the individual child's development, and at the nature of conventional writing, as young children perceive it and attempt to use it, we need to consider briefly some general ideas about writing and society.

Process and Product

On reflection it is clear that we use the term 'writing' in two different ways. However, in everyday communications the context of the situation (as well as of the language) ensures unambiguous understanding. We know that 'writing' may be referring to the psychological and physical processes involved in actively creating a meaningful message. This is reflected in such possible classroom exchanges as 'What are you doing, Delroy?' 'Please Miss, I'm writing my Armada story'. 'Writing' is also an end-product of the writing process and so it can be 'Our class writing about the Castle visit', or the collected writings of Susan Isaacs. Although we are rarely confused by the functioning of the term 'writing' (whether as verb or as noun), we may be less aware of some of the hidden assumptions that colour our responses to 'writing', just because it is both process and product.

The very fact that there is always a tangible end-product to the activity of writing concentrates attention on the 'final' or 'finished' piece of writing. Not only has this tended to detract from interest in and knowledge about the psychological process, but it has also placed excessive emphasis on notions of beautiful, tidy, perfect, grammatical or correct writing. This school tradition of concentrating on the correct end-product inevitably undervalued the first attempts at writing made by very young children. Many parents, teachers and children still think of 'writing' as first and foremost 'handwriting' or 'calligraphy', rather than a form of thinking and communicating (see Chapter 8). When the writing process was considered in the early years of education, it was the physical business of forming letters that received most attention, and this manual-skills approach is still dominant in many early-years group settings and classrooms (where tracing, copying and practising 'letters' continue to obscure the nature of young children's early-writing behaviours and insights). It is perpetuated to some extent by recent legislation (SCAA, 1996a; 1996b).

In the world outside schools and early years settings, writing as product is subjected to a whole battery of complex judgements about its aesthetic appearance, legibility, success in communicating meanings, accuracy as a record and quality as art. This daunting array may seem very distant from the early-years but it can unconsciously influence the responses teachers, nursery nurses, assistants, parents and the community are making to young children's pieces of writing. Making judgements is a dominant characteristic of the teaching and acquisition of literacy, and it is bound up with the fact that the written system is a product of a society or a particular cultural way of life.

Historically, the emergence of literacy changes a society so radically that becoming literate is always a personal, political and cultural watershed. Families are acutely aware of this (even if it is not explicitly articulated), and their fears and anxieties for their children, as well as their ambitions for them, are reflected in the pressure they may put on early years educators and schools to make their children read and write. If early years professionals are to respond with sensitive understanding and educative good sense to such inevitable pressures, they need to know something of the relationships between literacy, schooling and societies.[1]

Literacy, Culture and Schooling

The evolution of a written system in a society leads to the writing down of the significant beliefs and life-style of the culture, and a marked lessening of group dependency on memory and word-of-mouth 'tellings'. The inevitable consequences of this over generations include an enormous accumulation of written traditions; an ensuing historical awareness of the past; huge variations in individual and group literacy skills; and the evolution of new ways of thinking, as human cognitive processes are shaped by literacy. All these important consequences are seemingly 'natural' features of our current lives, permeating society at large, local cultural and community groups and our schools.

Taking these consequences separately, first, the sheer volume of written material that relentlessly builds up means that none of us can ever hope to see and read all that is produced. This may lead sophisticated literate adults to reject confidently what they do not wish to read and to accept cheerfully their own areas of ignorance, but older, naïve readers and young beginning readers may still fear that 'everything' has to be read once they acquire the skills. In a similar vein, some families (unfamiliar with the literacy traditions of schooling) may demand to know exactly what their children must read in order to be educated and successful. This link – presumed to exist between success in school literacy and success or achievement in society – is taken for granted by many parents. It is the 'reading between the lines' message in many teacher–parent discussions about literacy.

The sheer proliferation of documents in a literate society leads to the second consequence: a sense of history. Our awareness of the past highlights many inconsistencies, differences, doubts and changes within societies. The facts of a documented past make it possible to question legends, religious beliefs, nationalism, social conditions and political views. But, even today, such radical challenging of assumptions by a return to the written evidence throws up sharp contrasts with the culture-confirming stories and songs of a surviving oral tradition. The document-based reappraisals of many folk heroes, from Sir Francis Drake to Florence Nightingale and Enid Blyton, often disagree with popular stories and beliefs. But the written word is no more honest and reliable than those who use it – history can certainly be rewritten to reflect a particular viewpoint or a more convenient set of facts and assumptions.

As educators we need to bear in mind the third consequence, that literate societies are nowhere near as uniform in their acquisition and use of literacy as we might be tempted to believe: there are huge variations in the literacy skills of individuals and of groups within any society. Teachers work in the midst of marked social stratification according to literacy achievements, and their work may be seen as contributing to and maintaining this kind of division. Literacy can identify, categorize and value people and groups (socially and economically) in terms of the amounts and kinds of reading and writing they use and produce. These literacy differences are also associated with different value systems in schools, families and peer groups.

The literacy highly valued and rewarded by literate societies and inevitably linked with the more-privileged socio-economic classes is the 'schooled literacy' (Cook-Gumperz, 1986, p. 22) of formal education. This is the literacy of books and essays, and it requires mastery of book language and formal written style. Written style is characterized by chains of logical and explicit reasoning, by narratives that have clearly developed central topics (Michaels, 1986) and by formal literary conventions or genres. Many of these characteristics of book-based literacy have been discussed in Chapters 5 and 6, but the main feature to note here is the disembedded or decontextualized nature of the forms: they are self-explanatory, free-standing and explicit, rarely depending on references to events and features outside themselves to convey their meanings. Perhaps the best descriptive metaphor for schooled literacy might be 'library learning' – it can be pursued in solitary fashion by the use of books, documents and other recorded information. The great power of this 'schooled literacy' is its potential for distanced and reflective evaluation and comparison, which are important intellectual gains.

However, the sort of 'literacy events' (Heath, 1983, pp. 200, 386) that all of us participate in for much of the time and that may be the dominant or total literacy experiences of some groups are the shared interpretations and productions of writing rooted in social and cultural life (for example, the joint letter from a group of residents to a local council asking them to install a light in a dark walkway or the shared attempts by a family to make sense of the instructions for assembling an electric lawn-mower). Such group literacy is typically embedded in the talk, the shared experiences and the cultural assumptions of the participants. However, its closeness to the contributors' common-sense understandings and real-world concerns does not limit it to negotiating public notices and letters from government and welfare agencies. On the contrary, literacy events can be a sort of shared commenting and meditating that ranges over the most sublime and harrowing of human experiences – newspapers, magazines and books are explored in this way.

Group and community literacy is the source of 'schooled literacy', and the only reasonable means of access to it for young children. Where else can our 'library learning' about fictions, official reports or history, for example, have originated but in human lives, communities and language? It may be possible to ignore the shared literacy events children have already known and continue to impose some elements of formal literacy on them, but this often results in superficial levels of reading and writing and an alienating gulf between schools and communities – as well as serious under-estimations of young children's abilities and potential.

The important intellectual gains that arise from the development of literacy are forms of reflective and 'disembedded' thinking. Literacy is not just a performance skill with the written system of the language but a cognitive tool that transforms our capacity for self-reflection, mental re-organization and evaluation. In the histories of cultures such cognitive gains are indicated by the development of the reflective and analytical studies of philosophy, logic, linguistics and literary criticism. At the personal and professional levels we use the cognitive tools of literacy daily when we write our 'reflections' or evaluations of our own classroom practices, or set down on paper our priorities and policies for specific curriculum areas, or educational issues. Children are performing this same sort of reflective and self-evaluating thinking when they write with genuine interest about their new baby, or the television news film they saw. Writing is not just for conveying information and instructions, nor is it just for sharing pleasure and messages – writing is for thinking.

- The term writing can refer to both physical and psychological processes as well as to the end-product.
- The final product we call writing is always assessed and evaluated and this may tend to detract from a deeper knowledge about the process, particularly the cognitive process.

- The writing system of a society has, in its gradual evolution, changed the nature of the culture and provided a new tool for individual thinking.
- The consequences of these literacy changes have an impact on our approaches to, and judgements about, schooled literacy and community literacy.

Early Representation and Symbolizing

In order to understand the complex process of writing, we need to know something about the cognitive developments and strategies that precede it. Initially, thinking develops from the internalizing of actions, movement and images. This is known as sensori-motor and iconic representation, and is well established in the first two years of life. The appearance of gesture, language and make-believe play indicate the developing ability to represent thought symbolically. This is increasingly accompanied by mark making, drawing, the pretend writing of messages and, eventually, recognizable conventional writing However, this list could be misleading and its significance over-simplified if the apparently linear progression were to be taken literally. All the developments, once established, continue to exist and interact, affecting and supporting each other. For example, early mark making is highly dynamic and shaped by bodily exploration of space and the possibilities of materials. This can be seen when we observe 18-month-old children excitedly daubing paint, crayon or food over a flat or vertical surface, as well as their own bodies. This total bodily involvement is often accompanied by vocal sounds, single words or a brief explanatory narrative.

Early representation probably originates in the first weeks of life when feeding, sleeping and waking routines form regular and predictable patterns, but the speed of the ensuing developments will be hugely varied. We know, for instance, that some 3-year-olds begin to establish graphic signs and create emerging writing while other children only achieve this around 8 or 9 years of age. These differences are likely to occur in a complex process that is both personal and cultural and constructed out of interactions between individuals and their unique life experiences. Young children develop the necessary structures for thinking and understanding (sometimes called cognitive structures or intelligence) in the process of 'going over' or 'internalizing' their experiences of physical actions on objects – hence the familiar Piagetian claim that thought is not possible without action. However, the development of more complex thinking, including symbolic thinking, depends on the gradual freeing of thought from its links with very specific actions and objects. Until this happens no generalized recall of past events or predictions into the future can be drawn on for continuous comparisons, guidance and anticipatory planning. For something like reflective and projective thinking to develop, there must be a means of holding on in the mind to actions, perceptions and events, after they have occurred.

This begins when the internalized imitations of actual actions, events and objects develop and start to evolve into recalled images of general features of the world. Images in the mind build on and extend the earliest action representations, but they do not totally replace them. The capacity for picturing or 'image-ining' the generalized features of the environment develops some time in the second year of life, perhaps even earlier. In terms of the growth of the representational and symbolizing activities that will eventually culminate in language, literacy and literature (and other expressive and cultural arts), the infant has made the crucial first moves in freeing its thinking from immediate stimuli, from its rootedness in the here and now.

Distanced or 'deferred' representational thinking is clearly happening when young children recognize pictures of cats, for example, in books, and name them or react by eagerly setting off to search for their own cat, or respond in the same way if they overhear the name of their pet cat in a general conversation, or are directly asked, 'Where's Sammy?' Being able to think about people, animals, objects and experiences in their absence means that, in a special way, we still have a hold on them. The hold is special because it is created mentally and is not totally subject to reality or present facts. Furthermore, we can experiment with these representations: we can play and pretend with them. Young children, from at least the second year of life, can say 'miaow' like a cat, or climb into the cat's basket and curl up to sleep. They can even label their own marks and drawings as 'cat' or 'Sammy'. In the latter case, this is not necessarily because the marks are attempts to produce a graphic image of a cat but may be because the actual making of the marks was a way of imitating with movement, gesture and a marker cat-like actions and their own feelings about 'Sammy'.

The repetition and playful trying-out of generalized representations or thoughts about the world of experiences is a process that actively constructs knowledge or the mind. Children show us that they know something by doing it, by creating or responding to a picture-image of it, or by using an abstract symbolic means such as number or language to represent it. Any discussion of writing development adds further complexity to this 'three-modes' view of the growth of thought – writing is really a system of symbolic representations of a system of symbolic representation! Spoken language uses words and syntax to symbolize people, objects, places, etc., but the written words and sentences that represent this speech are at a further remove. If this is complicated and confusing to read about in this context, how do we account for the 3- and 4-year-olds who confidently write a birthday letter to granny or create a name label for the gerbils' cage in the nursery? The answer seems to have at least two major components: the power of cultural influences in children's lives and the power of images and marks.

Symbols and the Creation of Meanings

At the heart of symbolic systems and behaviours as varied as pretending to be a cat or 'eating' Plasticine cakes is the human gift for making meanings out of essentially pointless and arbitrary movements, sounds, marks and gestures: there is nothing cat-like about the word 'cat' and cats do not actually say 'miaow'; moulded blobs of Plasticine are not at all cake-like and holding them near the mouth while making chewing movements with the jaws is not 'eating'. And as for language, 'What's in a name? That which we call a rose/By any other word would smell as sweet' (Shakespeare, *Romeo and Juliet*, II. ii. 43).

The possibility of meaning and communication in all these symbolizing activities is created by the human makers, children and adults alike.

The activity starts in the earliest months of life, most noticeably when the infant endows a soft toy or blanket, etc., with a great wealth of feeling and significance – so much so that comfort in stressful situations or in the minutes before falling asleep appear to depend on it utterly. This drive continues as children cuddle and talk to objects and toys, pretend to be things and try to interpret the marks they notice in their world. These behaviours are clearly reflections of children's ability to make meaning out of arbitrary signs.

We need to bear in mind that young children generalize experiences very readily. Young infants recognize significant people in many changing circumstances, movements, clothes and moods and go on to draw their first people as stylized signs with big heads and tail-like legs – the tadpoles. Western children live in a great variety of dwellings, and few have open coal fires, but the usual 'my house' drawing is a standardized square with windows in the corner angles, a central door and a chimney belching smoke. The person drawing and the house drawing do not appear to be attempts at artistic realism but are cultural signs, abstract representations of the meaning and significance of 'my dad' and 'my house'. This tendency to use a generalized sign is probably the bridging activity between thinking with actions, images and symbols and communicating through a conventional writing system. Perhaps the 'graphic potential of language' easily slots into the graphical representation systems of marks and drawings.

In the early years of childhood, drawings and writing are produced together and, like so much play and pretending, they may be doing many things: communicating messages or standing for experiences, ideas and sensations. Many researchers (for example, Bissex, 1980; Kress, 1982; Ferreiro and Teberosky, 1982) into early writing development emphasize the significance of the drawings that precede and then accompany writing. The importance of drawings lies partly in their contributions to the total meaning of children's written communications and also in their links with general cognitive strategies. In many ways children use drawing as a dynamic, exploratory problem-solving activity. The marks on the surface of paper, board, pavement or wall are creative: they are totally new in the world, they were brought into existence by the child. But, once made they are fixed, unlike actions or utterances, and can be worked on, repeated and altered in regular and economical ways.

Representations of a surprisingly regular kind emerge as children exploit the possibilities of drawing (see Matthews, 1994). Spaces can be enclosed by a drawn line and then adapted by the addition of certain minimal 'signs' into representations of people, animals or buildings. For example, circles with dots and dashes added become faces and human figures that can be minimally altered to represent fishes, cats and cows. However, the face 'sign' is just as easily changed into suns, flowers, balls and spiders, while the squared enclosure can be a car, a parcel, the park or a house. Other conventions for indicating space, location and boundaries become very familiar to observers of children's drawings: the marking out of earth and sky with parallel horizontal lines, for instance. Even complicated and intangible emotions are indicated in children's drawing systems by minimal marks: jagged, saw-like teeth suggest greed and ferocity but the upward curving ends of a line are the 'smiley' mouth of happiness.

These comments and examples are not in any way intended to be an analysis of the complex nature of young children's drawings – they are simply an attempt to remind ourselves of the sign-like and even 'writerly' aspects of an area of children's early representational thinking that is sometimes undervalued. We need to be aware that under fives are not unaccustomed to creating and working with their own graphical systems that use flexible signs; this is what drawing and mark making is, and its potential for supporting and extending writing competence has not yet been fully explored in educational practice.

Unfortunately, drawing as a creative, exploratory, problem-posing and problem-solving activity has been under threat in classrooms in recent years. At one time, a well-intentioned desire to extend the range of young children's drawing experiences put considerable emphasis on detailed observational drawing. Drawing from life such things as rocks, flowers and street furniture enjoyed great prestige and popularity. There was much to praise about this extension of art in the primary years, but the early-years educator should be wary – it is strangely reminiscent of the 'object-drawing lessons' of the Edwardian classroom. The most recent threat has come from the National Curriculum which has over-emphasized imitating the styles and achievements of mature artists; consequently, Key Stage 1 classrooms are too often full of rows of 'Sunflowers' and 'Bridges over Lily Ponds'. What value does such pedantic copying have in terms of very young children's individual development and creative symbolizing? Does it contribute in any way to early communication and thinking with signs?

Ironically, the interest in early, or developmental, writing has also had the effect of diminishing attention, support and resources for drawing in the early-years curriculum. Young children's pictures and experiments with markers are now scanned by teachers for letters, numerals and letter-like forms but their intrinsic value as drawings is in danger of being ignored. This is not just an early-childhood education issue – pressure for writing in the later primary years drives drawing out of the literacy curriculum. Older pupils in primary schools still need opportunities to draw their messages and extend the total impact of their writing by using imaginative illustrations, diagrams, some appropriate observational drawing and the range of graphical signs, logos and symbols found in a literate society.

As teachers of literacy we are helping children to develop just one part of a whole continuum of related activities which can range from talking to a soft toy and pretending that a saucepan is a hat, to carving a sacred image and singing a national anthem.

- The possibility of the emergence of writing is related to the prior formation of cognitive modes for representing and symbolizing actions and experiences.
- These modes of representation are developing rapidly during the first three or four years of life and build on the internalization of actions and images, becoming general symbolic categories for what were originally specific perceptions and events.

- The process of early representation enables a gradual freeing of thought from specific stimuli and circumstances and supports the symbolic systems of gesture and language, pretend play and drawing.
- The ability to hold on to experiences and feelings by means of internalized actions and images is also characterized by the development of a tendency to transfer strong feelings and associations to arbitrary or 'found' objects in the environment. Things, and even people, treated this way come to stand for whole sequences of emotions and experiences: they are symbols.
- Drawing and mark making are part of these complex developmental processes and form powerful links between early representation and the symbolic nature of written sign systems.
- Drawings and marks are 'writerly' in that they use arbitrary signs to communicate meanings and stand for experiences, ideas and sensations.
- Playing, pretending and spoken language are crucial symbolizing activities that support and share many characteristics with early writing development.

Emerging Writing[2]

Emerging writing is a phrase that places a clear emphasis on the process by which children investigate and exploit the possibilities of writing. The phrase is also used here to suggest links with the emergence of spoken language in infancy and the development of playful activities involving pretending and problem-solving. There are problems to be tackled in literacy learning, problems that arise mainly from the differences between spoken and written communication. However, the ways in which young children set about investigating the challenge of print should not be thought of as different in kind from their general strategies for thinking about and resolving other problems.

First, a general theory of 'making sense' (see Bruner, 1986; Bruner and Haste, 1987; Wells, 1987; Wood, 1988) in children's learning strategies is discussed, and the wide range of research evidence that supports this view as it applies to literacy is indicated. A discussion of possible implications and policies for early-years settings follows, and some comments on handwriting as a craft skill conclude the chapter.

Making Sense

The view that young children's learning and thinking is based on the construction of meanings, or making sense of things, is very prominent in developmental psychology and linguistic theory. The notes and references at the end of the chapter exemplify this approach, which often describes early learning in terms of strategies and processes that enable infants to sort out and to organize things that are new, important, appealing, strange and disturbing. The significant strategies in this learning include the careful observations of features of the environment (including print), and of human behaviour, including talking, writing and reading. Lengthy periods of observation by young children culminate in selective imitations of bits of the noticed world: for example, a gesture may be tried out or part of a word or phrase repeated. Similarly, there may be an attempt to draw a few letters or numerals.

On the other hand, very young children also pretend to perform a skill or activity in its entirety. This is obviously happening when an infant babbles a 'conversation' with all the meaningful nonverbal features of pauses, rising and falling pitch and the accompanying nods, smiles and gestures. We also see this totality of pretence and imitation in operation when a young child does pages of scribble writing, re-creating both the speed and the flow of the physical actions as well as the spiky, linear appearance of a written text. This pretending or approximating behaviour is the beginning of the hypothesis-forming activity that characterizes human thinking, even in early infancy.

Researchers describe children's emerging talking, writing and general problem-solving in terms of sequences of abstracting, hypothesizing, constructing and revising (Bissex, 1984, p. 101). Abstracting the essence, the distinctive core, of an event or feature of the world must be going on during the lengthy periods of observation and non-production that precede the emergence of many skills, including talk and writing. Abstracting probably plays an important part in the creation of mental representations of actions, persons and events. Hypothesizing and constructing are reflected in the highly selective imitating and pretending that follow from abstracting. Hypothesizing about 'what it is' and constructing 'ways of doing it' occur in early talking, drawing and writing, as well as in a whole range of playful activities.

Revising can be thought of as the re-shaping and improving of pretending, in the light of helpful feedback and closer observations of discrepancies and conflicts. This revising can go on indefinitely, until the pretence approximates more closely to the target behaviour, or satisfies the child's purposes and sense of 'rightness'. One example of revising in early language learning might be the process by which the flow of an infant's babbled 'talk' is gradually modified and shaped. Actual sound combinations occurring in the home language (or languages) are focused on and repeated by child and care-givers until real words are thought to be 'recognizable'. Similarly, in the young child's marks and drawings, approximate numeral and letter shapes identifiable in the culture are 'seen', praised and gradually come to be repeated intentionally by the child.

The active, thinking, hypothesizing child is one element in this complex learning equation but the other crucial element is the human social and cultural environment. Young children become thinking, communicating people because they are involved in the discourse of social life from birth – regardless of race and socio-economic class or status. Children's growth into spoken and then written communication can only be properly accounted for in terms of the support and the stimulation they find in their personal and cultural situations. This is highlighted by research that identifies three recurring features of this social discourse (Bruner and Haste, 1987, p. 21). First, older and 'wiser' people appear to support or 'scaffold' all aspects of the infant's learning in the culture, presenting just enough manageable stimulation and information, as well as demonstrating examples of how to react and what to do. Even older children can be as useful in this way as adults.

Second, meaning is mutually constructed or negotiated between infants and their care-givers. This implies that the child is learning to share references and meanings as an equal partner and, in doing so, is exposed to the agreed meanings of the particular culture. The third feature is the culturally specific nature of the values and the assumptions shared with very young children. Of course language, both spoken and written, will be a major carrier as well as a dynamic creator of these cultural values: we do not just tell babies how to say 'hello' and 'goodbye' – we demonstrate when, where and how the expressions are spoken and gestured in our particular social world, by being particularly attentive in our own greetings and farewells to babies.

The reason for this digression into a general theory of learning is to emphasize that children develop powerful strategies for thinking and problem-solving long before schooling starts. In fact, learning is what the mind does and it predates the social and political organization of schooling in societies (Bissex, 1984, pp. 91–101). Furthermore, studying language is one way of studying the mind, and children's earliest attempts at writing and reading give us extra insights into language and thinking. For these reasons, contemporary research often describes young children as behaving like 'teachers' and 'researchers' in their own early learning.

Research Evidence

Research evidence about young children's early literacy learning has accumulated steadily over the last two or three decades or so to the point where we can make some useful general claims. First, although literacy is rooted in spoken language communication it does present novice learners with special problems: they must come to relate all their experiences of meaningful spoken communications to the written sign system (or systems) they encounter. In fact, this whole discussion can be reduced to two questions that face the literacy beginner: how do I share meanings in this special system and who can help me? The crucial helpers for the child will still be older and wiser members of the community, but the question of meaning is closely tied to the problems raised by the differences between speech and writing.

A major area of difference between the two is centred on the process of language production – speech is experienced immediately and its physical production can be both heard and seen. It is also varied and coloured by accent, dialect, situation, etc., and spoken communications are further clarified by vocal emphasis, pauses and rhythm and so on. The immediate face-to-face nature of speech makes it highly flexible, changeable and responsive to feedback from others and to the total social context in which it occurs.

However, we should set against these positive advantages the fact that speech does not communicate over distances, nor over long periods of time and, as we all learn to our cost, spoken words cannot be unspoken, recalled or destroyed (although they may, in time, be forgotten or forgiven). Spoken language communicates meaning immediately, negotiating its difficulties and repairing its misunderstandings and confusions as it goes along.

Writing does not rely on a face-to-face situation – it must be self-sufficient and self-explanatory, carrying all its intended meanings in linguistic signs and conventions only. In written communication everything must be fairly explicitly stated; arguments and sequences of thinking must be logically set out and developed. These features and limitations make writing more formal and impersonal than speaking but they are also the source of its power. Writing communicates across space and time and it can be preserved, returned to and even re-organized. For the beginner, however, writing does mean that you are on your own, a difficult move from sharing and building a verbal interaction. Emerging writers are always in the process of learning to be alone and independent. At any time they are operating along a continuum, always being somewhere on the line from oral to graphic expression – from receiving the feedback of a conversational partner to developing the ability to be both sides of the communication, the teller and the told. It all seems overwhelmingly difficult, yet the observational evidence is clear: many very young children demonstrate a great deal of initiative, pleasure and creative experimentation in their encounters with print.

Young children's hypothesizing about print would appear to be powered by the desire to answer two questions (or question clusters): what is it for and what's in it for me? How do you do it and which marks really matter? Of course, these are over-simplifications, but they can help to get us into the crucial areas of composition and transcription, as they do for many young children. The question of what is composed in writing is a question about meaning and function – what is it for and what's it about? Many young children discover that writing carries messages and, although these kinds of messages have often been shared in verbal interactions, written messages really make people sit up and take notice, so, print is powerful as well as communicative. Some 2-year-olds start on written greetings, such as 'kisses' on notes to friends and family or 'welcome' banners. Some 3- and 4-year-olds progress to unconventional yet readable instructions and complaints: 'I HIVANT HAD A TR IN PAD (I haven't had a turn in playdough)' (Newkirk, 1984, p. 341).

In their homes and communities, young children may attempt to add the name of their favourite sweet or cereal to a shopping list, and they often recognize the names and logos of supermarkets and fast-food restaurants. Sometimes they discover that they can leave an important message for Mum (Figure 7.1 – I'm in the playground. Nicholas Lee).[3] This really is a remarkable discovery about writing: you can go away and leave it to speak for you. The ability to write messages defeats time and distance but it also brings personal independence.

Ownership, power and control over their own writing and, eventually, their own lives, rests with readers and writers: they are full members of the literacy club (Smith, 1988). This is what is meant when writing is equated with 'finding a voice' (Graves, 1983, 1984), and young children seem to be on their way to this conception when they ask us, 'what does that say?' Until these crucial links between print and the power of voicing meaningful messages are made, the learner-writer of any age will be merely copying without real purpose.

Central as these questions of 'what is it for' and 'what's in it for me' are, many young children do not wait passively for complete answers. They often settle for hunches about meaning while simultaneously investigating 'how do you do it?' In fact, young children's spontaneous learning strategies are rarely tidy or organized into neat hierarchical stages. With respect to literacy, it is important for adults to develop some awareness of the complex patterns of interaction between finding out that real writing means something important, and finding out how it is done and what counts as writing.

Figure 7.1 I'm in the playground. Nicholas Lee

Children demonstrate for us daily these networks of interrelated discoveries as they attempt to write their own names. Personal names are charged with meaning: they encapsulate our sense of self-worth and our place in the world. Furthermore, the adult community usually places great value on very young children's ability to write their own names and welcomes the achievement enthusiastically. For the child, the ability to recognize and write that name conventionally also gives some control over a set of known and meaningful letters that can be easily identified. This known set may stimulate a great deal of experimenting and theorizing about complex written conventions. One 4-year-old boy in a nursery class I was visiting wrote part of his name, Dennis, as a fairly random scatter of 'D' 'e' 'n' 'n'. He then stopped, turned to me and said, 'I can write my name, it's got two of those' (pointing to the second 'n'). He completed the writing with 'i' 's', including a second attempt at the 's' (Figure 7.2). Dennis was spontaneously demonstrating his knowledge of conventional orthography, as well as his interest in practising and improving his control and skill with the marker (a biro pen), and the formation of the challenging letter 's'.

The research literature offers many structured analyses of the ways in which children have experimented with actual transcription and conventional orthography, but there are fewer studies of meaning and communicating. This is not surprising – it is far easier to describe and evaluate actual marks made on paper than to speculate on the nature and function of meanings and communicative interactions. The most influential research in Britain and the USA may

Figure 7.2 Dennis: I can write my name, it's got two of those

be thought of as highlighting three closely connected aspects of early literacy learning. Some researchers have concentrated on issues and problems that surround the nature of writing systems: what is writing, what is 'readable' and what are sentences (Ferreiro and Teberosky, 1982; Kress, 1994)?

Other research has developed a particular focus on orthographic knowledge: the ways in which children come to know about the actual systems of signs, marks and spaces used in the writing they encounter and use (Clay, 1975; Bissex, 1980). Researchers have also looked closely at the development of spelling competence and the processes that seem to underlie children's attempts to represent spoken sounds by written symbols (Gentry, 1982; Read, 1986). The categorization of the research in this way is only a convenient way of summarizing it – all the research referred to is concerned with all the aspects of literacy mentioned. Similarly, all the thinking and writing strategies used by the young children studied occurred in the context of their powerful desires to communicate important personal messages.

Children Exploring Writing Systems

Research into children's understanding of the nature of writing systems has produced evidence of child hypotheses that are not conventional but are attempts at answering the crucial question, what is writing? Pre-school children in a very poor, urban, Spanish-speaking environment in South America (Ferreiro and Teberosky, 1982) apparently evolved a 'minimum quantity hypothesis'.

When deciding what was 'readable' these children theorized that a minimum of three graphic characters must be together if a piece of writing could be read, anything less was called a 'number'. However, this hypothesis was eventually abandoned because it did not account for all the one- and two-syllable words the children used regularly in Spanish, including their own names.

Literacy, however, is more than collections of words and word recognition. The gradual discovery of writing as a system different from speaking hinges on the ability to create and manipulate sentences. Sentences belong to writing (Kress, 1994) not speaking; they are the really significant chunks of text around which writing is organized and built up. We do not talk in sentences unless we are reading or reciting prepared statements, lectures, letters and stories. The significant unit for spoken utterances is not a sentence but the meaning-bearing clause that constructs shared understandings 'on the run', while we are thinking on our feet.

The constructed sentence of the written language features one main topic, and young children come to understand these differences if they are encouraged to play with the possibilities of creating their own statements about pictures, photographs and activities. Simple topic sentences in children's early writing may appear dreary and monotonous to adults, but many children are delighted to find they have discovered a sentence formula that can be exploited almost endlessly. In the early stages of writing it is appropriate and powerful to be able to generate lots of sentences of the 'I like my . . .' or 'we saw a . . .' type.

Children Exploring Conventional Graphics

This discussion has already indicated that children's unconventional hypotheses and constructive errors about writing present them with regular but highly stimulating conflicts. The processes of trial and error, feedback and reformulation also characterize children's experiments with all the conventions of mark making, letter formation and the spatial arrangements of print. Young children's written messages emerge gradually from scribbles and drawings that may contain attempts at letters and numerals.

In an analysis of this emergent writing, Clay (1975) identified stages in which children seem to be sorting out particular aspects or 'principles' of writing. The first step in recognizing and producing written forms is taken when the young child appears to be making a distinction between drawing or pattern making and writing. This indicates the emergence of the sign concept because it suggests some insight about writing as a system of signs. This concept would seem to be developing when distinctly letter-like forms appear in children's drawings and when strings of pretend writing are produced.

Some understanding that writing is a sign system for conveying messages and some skill in producing letter forms is a beginning, but the production of writing involves other important principles. Some of these principles are concerned with the conventions for combining individual letters to form words, sentences and continuous text. The recurring principle focuses on the way in which writing uses the same shapes or movements of a marker over and over again. This repetition of loops, circles, sticks, squiggles and crosses produces most of the conventional forms and, in children's early attempts, a few near misses or invented forms.

The generative principle highlights the fact that words and sentences may be produced *ad infinitum* by combining and re-combining a limited set of letter forms. The principle of flexibility imposes some limitations on the number of letter-like forms that are acceptable as signs. The invented letters children come up with will eventually have to be dropped from their written repertoires.

Children's early hypotheses about what is acceptable as letters may appear to be distractingly complicated by the many varied printed forms, typefaces and graphics they encounter. However, exposure to so many forms and variants tends to ensure a useful focusing on the really essential elements and distinctive features of letters. One important aid for the young investigator of writing is a set of known and meaningful letters that can be confidently identified. The best example of such a set is, of course, a child's own name. This significant word stimulates a great deal of experimenting and theorizing about writing, as the above incident with Dennis suggested.

A further group of principles is concerned with the conventions of page arrangements and the spatial orientation of print. It is possible to observe and describe young children's experiments with the directional flow of writing and reading, its distinctive linear organization and the conventional uses of spacing. At times some children appear to stumble upon solutions and conventions that have been, or still are, used by human groups in various parts of the world. For example, British and American children's writing can temporarily flow from right to left, as in modern Hebrew, or it may be written in vertical columns. Some young writers organize their script to move from left to right, right to left in the ancient Greek pattern known as boustrophedon. What more sensible solution to page limits and directional flow can there be, than moving to and fro across the page, in the manner of oxen ploughing a field?

The gradual discovery that conventions (such as the orientation of letters in space and the directional flow of the text) matter because they significantly affect the communication of meanings in a particular culture, occurs as a result of pretending, sharing and practising reading and writing. When children are given the opportunity to be highly active and exploratory in their early literacy they appear to behave more like teachers and researchers than passive pupils.

The work of professional researchers in the USA, South America and Britain has drawn attention to the 'scientific' ways in which young children formulate hypotheses about writing and demonstrate curiosity about the variety of written forms they meet. This is exemplified by a monolingual British 6-year-old, of Scottish descent, in an East-End school who was teaching herself to write the Bengali characters she encountered in the school and the community (Figure 7.3).

Children behave like teachers of writing, for themselves and for their peers. These teacher-like behaviours include self-imposed practice and self-correction and the re-drafting of drawings, writing and spellings. Some children even set out practice lists or inventories of what they know and can write confidently. Lists of known letters, numerals and favourite words appear frequently in some children's writings and seem to function as personal checklists. But it is in the context of learning about standardized spelling that children can behave like fairly independent teachers and researchers.

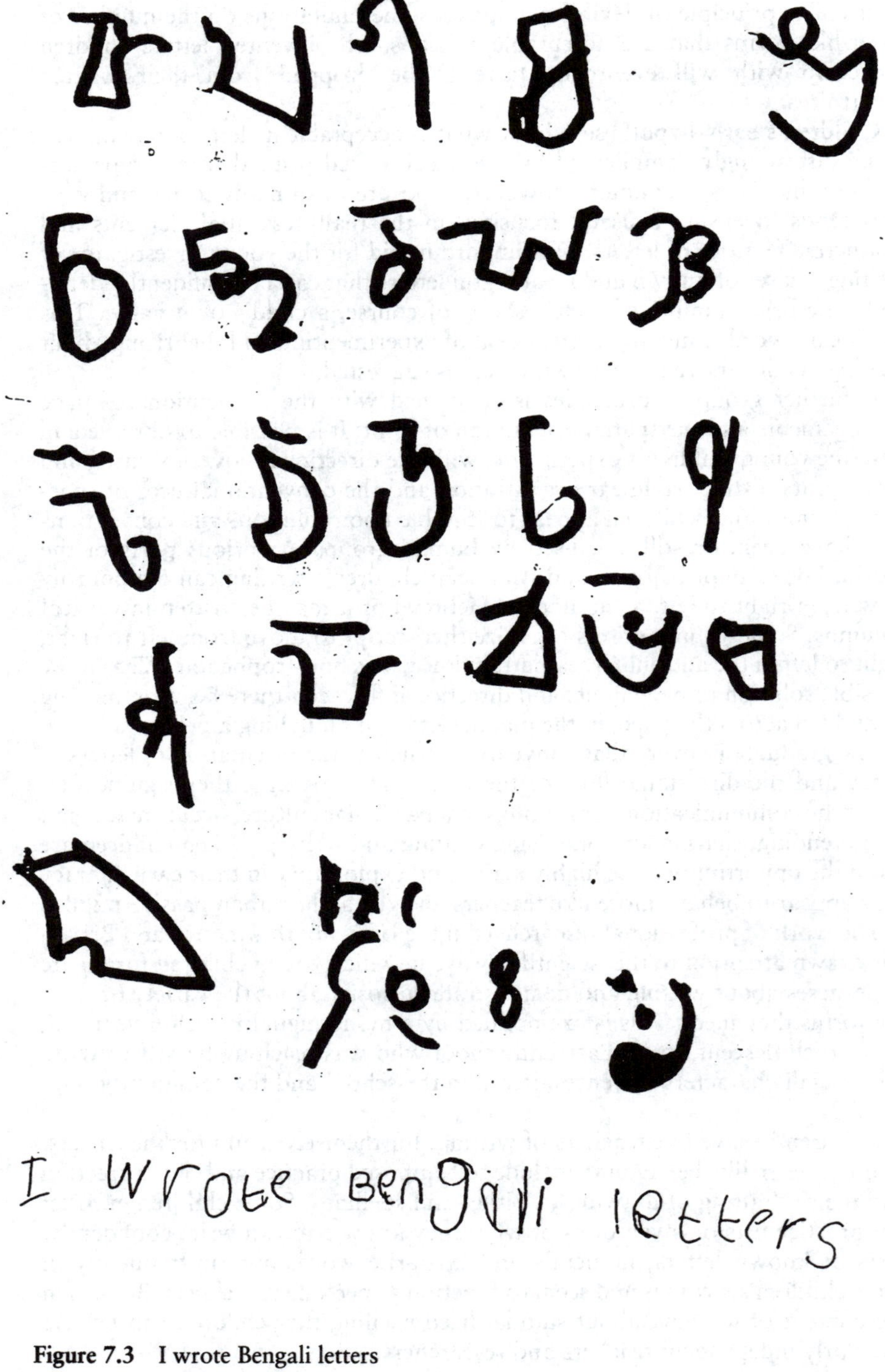

I wrote Bengali letters

Figure 7.3   I wrote Bengali letters

Children Exploring Spelling Systems

I used the phrase 'fairly independent' above in order to highlight the innovative approach young children often have towards the spelling system. This approach gives rise to non-conventional spellings but a closer analysis of these errors in English orthography indicates that they are real attempts to represent the sounds children utter and hear themselves, using the alphabetic names and sound symbols they know. Children's invented spellings reveal the extent, as well as the limitations, of their current knowledge of the sounds of their language, or languages, and the relationships of these sounds to an alphabetic system.

Read (1986) has described children's invented spelling as creative, systematic and highly phonetic. The strategy is creative in the sense that rather than copying or imitating a model, early spelling reflects children's own attempts to work out some systematic regularities and patterns that might underlie spelling. Children's initial hypotheses about spelling are phonetic judgements about sounds, the physical basis of speech, and how to represent them systematically. One detailed case study that illustrates just how very systematic children's invented spellings can be is Bissex's (1980) analysis of her own son's development as a writer. A clear pattern of developmental stages in spelling has been outlined by another researcher who re-analysed the material of the Bissex study (Gentry, 1982).

The research referred to does suggest that learning to use the standardized spelling system is rooted in the young child's desire to communicate messages and share in the general writing activities of the home and community. This drive to join in and share leads to the pre-communicative stage of spelling in which scribbles, numerals, letters or odd words are the pretend writing often found on shopping lists, labels, letters and story books.

The next stages in spelling development are semi-phonetic and phonetic and indicate a child's growing understanding that there are letter and sound relationships. The important principle being explored and exploited is that the names of the alphabet letters do themselves suggest speech sounds and syllables – the names of letters can be used to represent the sounds of spoken language. At first this is a fairly rough or semi-phonetic approximation, but it can produce such delightful examples as 'RUDF' ('are you deaf') (Bissex, 1980, p. 3) and 'PAULSTLEFNMBR' ('Paul's telephone number') (*ibid*. p. 7), written at the age 5 y. 1 m. In the phonetic stage a more complete attempt at representing all the sounds of words appears in the spellings, and the messages become more complicated and more confident: 'DO NAT DSTRB GNYS AT WRK' ('do not disturb genius at work') (*ibid*. p. 23), written at the age 5 y. 8 m. The highly phonetic nature of this strategy is tellingly revealed in the reflection of a particular pronunciation feature, the 'NAT' of standard American English.

The move from phonetic spelling to the stage of 'correct' or standardized spelling passes through a transitional phase. During this period some of the conventional and historical but not phonetic features of standard English spelling begin to appear in children's work. Increased experiences of reading add greatly to children's visual memories of many distinctive words, as well as commonly occurring digraphs, letter strings and word patterns. The work of Goswami and Bryant (1990) appears to confirm this view that school instruction in reading and writing alphabetic script helps children detect and recognize phonemes and this supports their early spelling strategies. It is only at a fairly late stage in spelling development that instruction will benefit children. This conclusion – that any formal teaching of spelling should be delayed until children have evolved their own strategies for understanding the nature of writing and spelling – brings the implications of research evidence for school and classroom practice into sharp focus. However, nothing in the National Curriculum requirements or the Desirable Outcomes directs practitioners to cut across young children's own sensible strategies for spelling unfamiliar words.

Practices and Policies

It is clear that very young children may learn far more about print and the functions of writing in their communities than has been acknowledged by traditional teaching approaches. However, opportunities to use and extend such out-of school learning within school or other early year settings are dependent on the attitudes of professional educators and carers. After all, it takes considerable professional confidence and courage to admit that the way in which we teach is not necessarily the way in which children learn (Clark, 1976). Self-directed, independent pupils who have the potential to function like teachers and researchers themselves need tolerant and flexible professional tutors – tutors who know that there is now a strong case for asserting that children may learn more about reading and writing from the captions, cartoons, signs, advertisements, labels and slogans of their environment than from the carefully controlled words in school primers and textbooks. Words in the environment are not graded and controlled but they are always purposeful: they carry real messages and are supported by a rich array of contextual clues.

Hence, we have to respect and extend not only the spoken language children bring to school but also the judgements and hypotheses they have constructed about written language. Failure to do this carries the risk of massively underestimating the experiences and abilities of young children. Furthermore, a complete break with the spontaneous processes of play, invention and experimentation, which characterize out-of-school learning, may leave young children helplessly confused in classrooms for weeks as they attempt to puzzle out the rules of the strange new regime. Practices and policies that avoid a damaging gulf between out-of-school and classroom- or group-based learning and that build on children's existing knowledge of language and literacy are the most appropriate professional responses to the research discussed.

What do such responses and policies look like in action? An appropriate set of guidelines for the teacher of early literacy must consider the issues of inspiration, real needs, supportive environments, informative feedback and new thinking skills. This may seem to be a surprising list because it appears to ignore the usual checklist topics, such as spelling, punctuation, sentence structure and handwriting. But these important areas are more usefully addressed and understood as intrinsic features of purposeful early literacy as it develops from the spoken language and social experiences of young children.

This claim has even greater urgency now that non-statutory early years settings are required to achieve 'desirable outcomes' (SCAA, 1996a) in

Language and Literacy which over-emphasize such matters as the appropriate use of upper and lower case letters.

Inspiration for Early Writing

Inspiration may seem an almost pretentious term to use in a discussion of writing in the early years, but arousing children's desire to write is an essential part of the literacy teacher's role. Wanting to write is a significant issue and should not be confused with the equally important business of needing to write.

The inspiration for writing arises partly from children's perceptions of it as a high-status activity – something that is done by significant people in their social world. This is one good reason for providing children with daily experiences of being at the elbows of important and admired persons who are writing for real. The potential of these experiences is enormous if we try to ensure that much of our genuine writing as professional educators is an open, public and educational activity. Young children might sometimes observe the writing up of records by teachers, nursery nurses and students, as well as being invited to choose examples of their own work to be dated, annotated and added to these records. We can arrange to plan and write letters, notes and invitations to 'outsiders', while children are around to comment and offer helpful suggestions. Occasionally the children can be taken on a writing expedition around the setting or school to discover other writers at work, in the kitchen, the medical room and the office. If the children rarely (if ever) see a professional writer or poet in their setting they can at least be given regular opportunities to hear and see the range of writing done by older children, as well as parents, helpers and teachers. These routine close contacts with more experienced writers may be thought of as the writing equivalents of the shared conversations that shaped and inspired the children's earliest spoken language learning.

Inspiration for young writers is furthered by providing a wide range of writing materials, some especially pleasant places to write in, and examples of 'writing' to investigate and try out. These could include the many kinds of print encountered every day, as well as varied scripts and writing systems, several styles of graphics, a selection of manuscripts, typescripts, print-outs and some different conventions of print and lay-outs in prose and verse.

A wide range of writing materials means much more than some regulation size school paper and thick pencils for young children. These basics have their place, but inspiration for real writers demands range and variety, according to need, function and even whim! The really stimulating writing area extends the possibilities of writing and of drawing with a range of markers and a variety of papers and surfaces.

A selection of printing devices in the early years setting can enlarge the potential for producing print repetitively and speedily; they also enable young children to produce what is beginning to look like 'real' published writing. Experiences of printing with oddments of scrap materials and cut vegetables are a traditional part of the early years curricular background and support children's understanding of the nature of print and printing technologies.

Inspiration for writing is fostered by an educational environment which acknowledges and extends the huge variety of scripts and writing technologies which exist in society, and introduces children to a new community of writers.

But progress in becoming a writer is intrinsically bound up with furthering the individual's need to write.

Real Needs for Early Writing

Real needs for writing in early childhood must be considered carefully and related to such broader literacy issues as the place of writing in a culture; the potential for social and political independence and choice that literacy can give individuals; and literacy as an extended way of thinking. These perspectives were outlined in the earlier sections of this chapter and should provide a rationale for daily decisions about writing and writing tasks in the early-years setting. However, approaches to writing at this stage of education should also be informed by a keen sense of the appropriate place for writing in the individual child's existing range of communicative skills.

Most children in playgroups or beginning nursery and infant schooling are already skilled communicators in the modes of gesture and body language, talking and listening, drawing, modelling and constructing and playing. It is misleading to think that teaching children to write is teaching them to communicate efficiently: writing should be seen as another means of enriching and extending children's existing communicative skills and satisfying their own felt needs for the tools of literacy.

In this respect it is important to be aware of the range of writing needs we as adults model for the children. Do we only write lists, memos, institutional notices, names on pictures and models, correct spellings and isolated demonstrations of good handwriting? Similarly, do the writing tasks we impose on the children amount to nothing more than redundant writing about already adequately expressive and communicative pictures and models or, worse still, very limited sentences about every single event, experience or outing shared by educators, carers and pupils? There are, of course, occasions when all these kinds of writing might be just the appropriate response for adults and individual children, but a simple blanket response of putting labels on everything and writing reports about everything trivializes writing and does not advance the development of young writers and thinkers.

Purposeful writing must encompass, at the very least, memory aids, records, communications, expressive and art-like functions. The use of lists, notes, Post-It pads and personal jottings, as memory aids, is part of many children's out-of-school culture and becomes a significant feature of later school-based literacy. The concept of a list often occurs naturally in play and pretend writing, particularly if home corners and dramatic play areas are thoughtfully equipped with pads and pens for shopping lists and till receipts, telephone messages and prescriptions. Lists occur spontaneously when some young children produce inventories or checklists of the words, letters and numerals they know and can write without help.

Encouraging children to jot down names, items, figures or words they like or need to remember can become a natural part of experiences inside and outside early years settings. For example, many different kinds of lists can be compiled and favourite words recorded.

Lists which spring from the children's lives and concerns in and out of early years settings, are not as banal as they may appear when suggested in cold print: they are examples of writing used to pin down and to remember; they also lay the foundations of ease and pleasure in amassing words, using the tools of writing and creating useful records of experiences and knowledge.

Some of the simple lists mentioned are already functioning as records. The beginnings of study skills, such as note-taking from books, can be found in the listed records of favourite story-book characters and incidents; the collection and discussion of strange, interesting and exciting words and phrases; and the noting of remarkable ideas. We cannot expect older primary children to be able to make useful notes from information books, as opposed to pointless copying of page after page, unless they have had this earlier background. Children should be helped to approach information texts with their own queries in mind (Mallett, 1992; Neate, 1992). In the early years these enquiries can start from lists of 'things to talk about' or 'things to find out' with such items as the following:

1. Siamese cats have blue eyes. Do *all* of them?
2. Do all dead creatures become fossils?
3. How many poisonous plants do you know?
4. Ask a very old person to tell you what they remember about going to school.

Several of these suggestions could be the beginnings of scientific records, but the last item extends the concept of written records to the notion of human memory, oral anecdotes, history and autobiography. Small children are already well initiated into this tradition: they frequently tell, draw, enact and sometimes dictate, personal narratives about their lives. These are inadequately described by the traditional school jargon of 'news'. Rather than pushing children and their families to concoct desperately novel items for the classroom rituals of sharing, talking and writing, we should be welcoming and transcribing those simple records of feelings, activities and thoughts that sustain all worthwhile writing.

Children reveal their understanding of the communicative function of the written record when they ask if they can take home a copy of a successful recipe or decide to copy out the words of a favourite song or poem to take home. These are good examples of writing as communication that satisfies real needs and crosses the home and education boundaries. These instances are far more significant, in communicative terms, for the individual writers than a compulsory sentence under every drawing or the copying of a class letter in order to learn letter-writing conventions.

Alternatively, real letters that really go by post (or sometimes by hand) to real recipients are potent and sensible motives for learning a society's highly conventional forms of personal address, as well as the crucial importance of accurately written envelopes. Real letters also reflect a whole range of possible styles, from affectionate and chatty notes through to formal and precise communications, and they introduce children to the notions of intended audience, purpose and appropriate form. We should ask of all the kinds of writing that go on in schools and group settings, at any age or stage of education, *what* is it for and *whom* is it for?

Writing is always directed towards someone, often a distant or even unknown other, but it must still be shaped and tried out by being rehearsed and planned. This preparation for writing happens inside our heads, is vocalized out loud, roughed out on paper, typed up on a screen or even tried out on a trusted listener. These trial runs are part of the process every writer must attempt of imagining an audience, but the effort brings a bonus. In the trying out and the shaping we find that we cannot just talk to ourselves, we can also write for ourselves as the intended audience. Writing as an expressive form, writing for the self in order to hold on to and understand experiences, it is hoped, joins the other early representational modes such as gesture, play, talk and drawing, already discussed. Opportunities to develop and extend this mode of writing into the art-like forms of stories, poetry and plays depend on the ethos created by professional educators. Respect for individual experiences and privacy; sensitivity to writing that demands a human response, prior to any correction and assessment; and the provision of a stimulating literacy environment are all part of a supportive and writerly classroom or group setting. From the educator's point of view, knowing when to intervene and how depends greatly on knowledge and insight about the varied functions and purposes of the children's writing. A sure sense of writing function, intended audiences and appropriate styles can probably only be developed by educators and carers who also try to be real writers themselves.

Supportive Environments and Feedback for Young Writers

Creating supportive environments also involves such issues as time and opportunities to write and rewrite, and the provision of informative feedback about writing. Time to write means ensuring that there are reasonably long and uninterrupted blocks of time in which writing and many other activities can go on. One of the most important reasons for resisting the increasing fragmentation of the early-childhood group and school day into rigid timetable slots is so that children may develop and sustain serious involvement with a wide range of curricular experiences. For the same reason, we need to look critically at the number of interruptions we allow for radio and television programmes, choir and assembly practices, or other worthy distractions.

If well-chosen and well set-out writing materials are available, as well as the time to become involved, children are able to exercise the independence and choice that characterize real writers, and they are more likely to be satisfying their own needs and finding their own writerly voices in the process. They are also more likely to explore and experiment with the actual nature and organization of print and texts, the pattern of narrative and the conventions of spelling. Children need opportunities for practising writing, but their own meaningful self-imposed tasks can be far more rigorous than any arbitrary exercises, as the example indicates (Figure 7.4). In this instance,[4] a child who enjoyed unpressured blocks of time, the security of a real writers' classroom and the appropriate materials (including scrap paper for rough work, as well as final draft sheets of paper), has been able to work through to the standard spellings of 'chips' and 'fish'. Clearly, lots of trying, looking at the visual patterns and rejecting some versions was involved. This is a particularly good example of a spontaneous approximation to one of the most reliable approaches (see Peters, 1985; Mudd, 1994) to learning standardized spellings: look, cover, write, check with the standard form, try again if necessary.

Chrisp

chisps

chsf

chips

fisth

fiht

fiths

fith

ftish

fisth

fish

Figure 7.4 Spelling 'chips' and 'fish'

A supportive environment for writing will be rich in examples and demonstrations of writing, as already indicated. However, we should note here the value of using not just print from the environment with young children, but linguistic materials, such as 'Breakthrough' (Mackay, Thompson and Schaub, 1978), which enable children to compose their own sentences and make the transition from spoken utterances to the sentence structures of writing.[5] Experiments with bits of printed language, as well as with different ways of saying and ways of writing, lead children and literacy teachers to the kinds of discussions and corrections termed informative feedback.

Beginning writers need feedback that is informative about writing and supportive of their own approximations and hypotheses. Professional educators need to know what children can do already, how they are thinking about language and literacy and what they are aiming to do next. The organization of groups and classrooms must be directed towards maximizing the time available for practitioners to talk to children, individually and in small groups. Such talk can focus on the messages intended and relate the attempted forms to known letters, words and texts. In a room full of meaningful writing about many things this should not be difficult. Sometimes the educator might write a word or two of comment and encouragement on a child's work. Gradually the discussions will involve the nature of some standardized spellings, as relevant, or conventional forms of sentence structure or syntax, and issues of presentation. This kind of feedback means spending time discussing children's work with them rather than accepting it in order to look at it later or even taking it away to mark. Demonstrating writing and discussing it with children is a top priority and might well replace some of the time spent on unproductive correct copying, routine 'writing-about everything' exercises and the traditional way of 'hearing' readers. The group setting and the classroom are potentially supportive writing communities and children usually take a great interest in each other's activities and investigations, so they too can be encouraged to help each other (see Chapter 8).

Research into early writing from several countries puts considerable emphasis on classroom writing conferences and the production of rough drafts rather than 'one-try-only' finished pieces. Writing conferences in which groups of children sit down, with or without a teacher, to discuss and edit their written drafts may be some years away from the earliest developmental stages of writing in playgroup and nursery and reception classes. However, something very like a writing conference happens for the younger children when the educator organizes a shared writing session, acting as scribe for a group, verbalizing a whole range of linguistic decisions and issues, pen in hand (see Chapter 8). Young children also enjoy just being with each other in attractive writing areas and at well-provisioned drawing tables.

In the early years of education there must be warm acceptance of tentative private writing and spontaneous, unpolished pieces which have clearly stretched the young child's resources. But to ensure literacy development, time must also be found for the regular discussion, drafting and editing of writing for publication in and around the setting or the school. When educators act as scribes and linguistic informants for young children they are tackling the young writer's greatest problem about getting started on independent writing – that the writing process involves both the physical business of transcription, and the language and thinking process of composition. In the early stages the two processes need to be clearly separated. Initially, the young writer must be released from the demands of conventional transcription and spelling and freed to concentrate on the cognitive and creative processes of composition. When this temporary separation is well handled and the adult–child writing partnership flourishes there is far more going on than the satisfying production of individual and group books, news-sheets and letters – important as these are. It is likely that children's thinking, their cognitive potential, is being changed and extended by the writing process.

New thinking has already been associated with the acquisition of literacy in the earlier discussion of the changes literacy brings about in a society. For the individual, particularly the young child, becoming a writer reflects a remarkable fusion of personal, individual experiences and needs with the symbolic communication system of the culture. But it is far from being a simple process of learning to use the written forms of the culture: writing, like talking, develops an inward-turning aspect, becoming a new means of organizing and restructuring thought – a new cognitive tool. The role of our earliest writing partners (parents, other people and professional educators) is as significant as that of our first conversational partners. In this respect, we should note the claims of L. S. Vygotsky, that the child's thinking potential is extended greatly in partnership with an adult (1978, pp. 84–91). It is as if the child is a head taller when working with an involved, supportive and more experienced adult. Children reading and writing in partnership with adults are thinking at full stretch.

Writing, by its nature, provides a way of holding on to experience, of going over it, shaping and evaluating. This is a special way of re-running experiences in order to understand them fully. Writing in process is also productive of totally new ideas and points of view, as experienced writers confirm. It is often in the act of writing about something that we are surprised by apparently new insights and conceptions that emerge on the paper. Writing as an act of externally forming and clarifying ideas is a virtual distancing of experience from ourselves. This may well allow for more efficient and perceptive contemplation and understanding.

Handwriting

Handwriting is a craft skill and should be stimulated and nurtured throughout the years of schooling, as a separate issue from becoming a writer. Of course, there is a link in that the thinking writer needs to evolve a personal handwriting style that communicates efficiently and pleasantly, but this is hardly a priority in the process of thinking and writing. After all, we know that handwriting suffers as our ideas flow and outpace the hand. In fact substantial writing of a professional, academic or commercial kind depends on the services of secretaries and machines. Perhaps we should try to free the issue of 'good' handwriting from all the moralistic and social etiquette associations it has acquired. The aesthetic quality of the handwriting is not a direct reflection of the quality of the ideas and thinking it encodes, even less is it a reflection of the worthwhileness of the person writing. Handwriting has possibly always been the literacy equivalent of Received Pronunciation (RP) in spoken language and the inclusion of a specific handwriting requirement in the revised National Curriculum for English is not unrelated to the widespread belief that good handwriting guarantees good content. Handwriting can provoke strong feelings that are closely associated with cultural attitudes and the assumptions we make about individuals (Sassoon, 1995).

A serious issue is involved here. If we make powerful sub-conscious judgements about writing, based on what it looks like, we are confusing the cognitive achievements of literacy with mere display and performance: literacy is the development of human mind and that is why we want children to be readers and writers. This is particularly important now that the rapidly developing technologies of wordprocessing and desk-top publishing remove the chores of transcription and place powerful new writing tools at our fingertips. What children and educators do with the new technology is dependent on their understanding of the interactive nature of language and literacy, of writing for real audiences and real purposes, and of using writing as an extension of thinking skills.

Bearing these issues in mind, we should still be concerned in the early years of education to lay the foundations of a personal handwriting style for our pupils. The National Curriculum English requirements for Key Stage 1 includes handwriting as a 'Key Skill' of the Writing component; they place considerable emphasis on neat presentation and direct instruction in correct letter formation, consistent letter size and spacing. These demands are best tackled at a general curricular level as well as by specific provision and activities. At the general level, all the materials and activities that support artistic, creative and physical education in the classroom also support the development of competent handwriting. General muscle tone, balance, eye and hand coordination and the fine muscle control of delicate finger and wrist movements are developed and sustained by brick construction, sand play, printing with junk materials, painting and drawing, and so on. Visual sensitivity to colour, spacing, harmony and aesthetic form is fostered by exposure to the displays, fabrics, pictures, artefacts and writing children see in their early years settings. If we cannot point to high standards of provision in all these areas of the curriculum and the educational environment, we cannot claim to be seriously concerned about handwriting.

Specific provision aimed at stimulating interest in the craft of handwriting and providing opportunities to practise it may be focused on a calligraphy area or small display. Even an attractive container of calligraphy materials and examples stored in the writing or language area of the classroom, or in a well-lit corridor display, can be a simple but adequate resource. The basic materials must satisfy two different purposes: first, to provide good examples and demonstrations of the craft; and, second, to provide the tools and materials for practising the skill. Examples of the craft should include well-mounted samples as well as illustrated books of different styles, including some traditional school classics such as Marion Richardson and italic, and examples of modern calligraphy on book-covers, documents and commercial material. There is also value in having cards of basic unadorned Roman script and examples of the other scripts used in the community and school.

If the school has adopted a particular handwriting style this should, of course, be prominent in the examples. Cards illustrating different writing styles should be attractive in appearance, sometimes featuring border decorations, drawings, photographs and decorated capitals. The meaning or content of the written material used as writing examples should have some intrinsic value, so that calligraphy is also a way of sharing a poem, a riddle, a proverb or counting rhyme. Some examples of complete alphabets and numerals, zero to nine, are also useful as stylistic guides.

Tools and materials for practising handwriting skills should include the usual variety of pencils, pens, felt markers and paper, including both rough draft and final draft qualities and firm clipboards and pads. In the early years, it is generally better to provide unlined paper for most writing as this is far more flexible for the children's own drawing and writing strategies. Delaying the introduction of lined paper fosters the development of the children's visual sensitivity to spacing, linearity and the impact of blocks of print and colour.

I am unconvinced of the usefulness of class-writing lessons from the chalk-board or of precipitous interference with the ways in which young children habitually hold their pencils and markers. There seems very little carry-over of such isolated interventions into the business of real writing for real purposes. The greatest spur to efficient handwriting is the desire to share and value an important message, and the most influential models of effective and pleasing personal handwriting are the early years educators children meet. However, educators should set aside time to talk about handwriting and demonstrate to individuals and small groups the most efficient ways of forming individual letters. This is not done by plodding illogically through the alphabet, but by taking groups of letters which are formed by similar strokes. A leading re-searcher into all aspects of handwriting in the early years, Rosemary Sassoon, advises that tuition in the early stages must be individual and 'little and often' (Sassoon, 1993, p. 193).

The excitement of this particular approach is in the emphasis on handwrit-ing as the visible trace of a hand movement; the links with other motor and artistic activities, the belief in finding comfortable and rapid personal styles; and the early introduction of 'exit strokes' to help the move to joined up writing (cursive). There is little support from this expert for the rigid imposi-tion of a whole school (or whole nation) script, or for imposed writing on lines for all young children. Flexibility is the best guide: handwriting teaching in the early years must be based on observing young children's writing experiments and practices and offering appropriate guidance and useful techniques.

- Young children's attempts to make sense of print are demonstrations of their powerful strategies for making sense of their lives and experiences. This problem-solving in early learning is characterized by active and cre-ative abstracting, hypothesizing, constructing and revising.
- Research evidence on young children's early literacy learning indicates the ways in which they tackle questions about the nature of print, how it works in their communities and how they themselves can use it. The research suggests that young children create reasonable hypotheses about print, spelling systems and texts, and modify and develop these hunches and experiments in the light of helpful feedback from models, demonstrations and talk with other writers.
- Practices and policies in early years settings must build on and extend children's existing knowledge of literacy and develop their strategies for experimenting, hypothesizing and making sense of new experiences and new materials.
- Teachers of early literacy need to give close attention, in their planning and provision, to inspiring children to write; to creating real needs for writing in their groups, schools and classrooms; and to providing supportive environ-ments and informative feedback about writing. Most important of all,

however, is the educators' understanding of the part played by the writing process in re-organizing and extending the thinking of children and adults.
● Handwriting or calligraphy is a craft skill and, although it can be stimulated and nurtured in the early-years curriculum, it must be treated as a separate skill from the process of becoming a thoughtful and communicative writer.

Teaching and Learning Suggestions

* Create an attractive and well-maintained writing area, corner or group of tables and provide a range of markers, papers, erasers, straight-edged rulers and sharpeners. Include fine pencils and biros as well as thick pencils and coloured felt and water-based pens; occasionally introduce inks, pens and small brushes.

* Vary the paper: children need small pieces for little notes and lists; large sheets which can be used flat on the floor, or fixed to walls and easels (giving them the experience of bold marking and writing); good-sized strips of paper that facilitate experiments with the linear organization of drawings and writing; and lightly tinted paper is a great attraction.

* Firm writing pads can be improvised by covering strong cardboard, or hardboard, with decorative wrapping paper or tinted brushwork paper. More experienced writers may need straight line guides and these can be made from strong white card with bold black lines drawn at the desired widths (the guides are placed beneath a child's writing paper and the dark lines show through).

* Other technologies for writing should also be provided: rubber stamps and ink pads, typewriters and computers with word-processing software and concept keyboards for the youngest children (these technologies extend children's alphabetic knowledge and awareness of punctuation, spacing and type-faces).

* Writing corners should stimulate children's interest in the range and functions of writing: help the children to collect samples of print from the environment (knitting patterns, recipes, haiku, invitations, greetings cards, postcards, bills, receipts, airmail envelopes, fast food take-away menus, carrier bags and photographs of street signs and shop logos). Arrange displays of scripts from several cultures and examples of messages, information and food packaging in many languages (involve families and all the members of the setting or school community in this).

* Extend the range of drawing, marking and messages in the setting: encourage spontaneous drawing (not just a matter of materials, but valuing and displaying drawings); provide a group/class message board for the use of children, adults and families; set up chalkboards and flipcharts for the younger children to draw, mark and write on. Focus on the use of lists and help the children to record such items as: names of children in the group, names of adult educators and carers, family members and friends; lists of favourite foods, pets, colours, clothes; names of local

streets and landmarks, favourite story-book characters; shopping and ingredients lists. Use these lists as counting and sorting data, as discussion points, and as the focus of alphabetic and phonological investigations and teaching

* Raise the literacy profile of all other curriculum areas: place writing materials (paper, pads, pens, crayons and pencils) in the outdoor area and with the science, maths, blockplay, home and role-play provision. Think of using magazines, newspapers and comics in these areas and providing written notices, guidelines, information and lists.

* Create a small workshop area (it can even be a well-organized box of materials) for the making of simple books. Provide paper, card, staples, glue, needles and thread and some basic instruction cards on 'How to make a stitched book', 'How to make a zig-zag book' etc. Think of the possibilities for making books 'across the curriculum': books about music, science, religious education, games, the garden, mathematics, computers, etc.

* Look at the setting/classroom/school as a rich source of words and information about writing and spelling. Let the children help in creating lists of words and phrases they use regularly, labels for displays and materials, name cards and notices. Prioritize daily 'shared writing' sessions (see Chapter 8) and maximize the roles of adults as scribes, secretaries, proof-readers, publishers and correspondents for the children.

* Maintain a focus on the craft of calligraphy: display examples of scripts (Italic, Sassoon, Marion Richardson, Roman) and illuminated letters – this can be an opportunity to write out some poems, rhymes and folk-sayings. Encourage the children to decorate their own writing and experiment with calligraphy. Provide some examples of modern styles (on documents, book-jackets and commercial material). Provide cards of the script taught in the school or setting and examples of numerals, zero to nine. Make specific opportunities for practising handwriting – according to the ages and stages of the children (the years 3 to 8 cover a vast developmental phase and generalizations about handwriting practice would be unhelpful).

Notes

1. These issues are fully explored in Ong (1982), Heath (1983), Goelman *et al.* (1984), Olson *et al.* (1985), Cook-Gumperz (1986) and Kress (1995).
2. Some of the issues raised in the following sections were originally discussed by the author in two previous articles (Whitehead, 1985; 1986).
3. I am grateful to my former colleague Jan Lee for providing this example. It was written by Nicolas (5y. 10m) and reflects his phonetic knowledge: the substitution of the sound symbol 'B' for 'p' is a feature of his own pronunciation (as well as creative ingenuity) using the known 'B' and 'g' sounds in 'playground' but indicating missing letters with dots. The capital 'A' (written over a lower case 'a') apparently represents the sound of the stressed 'm' in 'I'm'.
4. I am grateful to Miranda Higham for this example from her teaching-practice classroom and to my former colleague Gill Hilton for bringing it to my attention.

5. 'Breakthrough to Literacy' materials for the teaching of initial reading and writing were designed to overcome two major difficulties experienced by young children: their lack of manual dexterity in handling a writing tool and their difficulties with spelling (Mackay, Thompson, Schaub, 1978, p. 3). The teacher and the child have a card folder, called a 'Sentence Maker', of printed individual inserts of commonly used words, as well as blank inserts for making additional new-word items as required. There is a firm plastic stand in which words can be inserted and ordered to create free-standing sentences, phrases and labels. Other support materials and books of stories and poems are available.

Further Reading

Bissex, G.L. (1980) *GNYS AT WRK: A Child Learns to Write and Read*, Harvard University Press, Cambridge, Mass.

Browne, A. (1993) *Helping Children to Write*, Paul Chapman, London.

Clay, M.M. (1975) *What Did I Write?*, Heinemann, London.

Hall, N. (1987) *The Emergence of Literacy*, Hodder & Stoughton, Sevenoaks.

Hall, N. and Robinson, A. (1995) *Exploring Writing and Play in the Early Years*, David Fulton, London.

Mudd, N. (1994) *Effective Spelling. A practical guide for teachers*, Hodder & Stoughton, London.

Sassoon, R. (1990) *Handwriting: a new perspective*, Stanley Thornes, Cheltenham.

Sassoon, R. (1990) *Handwriting: the way to teach it*, Stanley Thornes, Cheltenham.

Smith, F. (1982) *Writing and the Writer*, Heinemann, London.

Temple, C.A., Nathan, R.G., Burris, N.A. and Temple, F. (1988) *The Beginnings of Writing (Second Edition)*, Allyn & Bacon, Boston, Mass.

8

Literacy and the early-years educator

The previous discussions have highlighted at least three major aspects of literacy: the complex interrelationship of listening, talking, reading and writing; the roots of literacy located in a general symbolizing development in infancy; and the function of this symbolizing power in the creation of meanings. These aspects of literacy are rarely acknowledged as such when literacy programmes or curricula for the early years are being devised. It is all too easy for early-years educators to set about choosing reading schemes, or comply with requirements for desirable learning outcomes and key stage levels, while ignoring questions as fundamental as, what is reading and writing really doing for readers and writers? Or why teach children to read and write at all? If these basic questions are rarely asked, it is hardly surprising that such complex matters as the interdependence of language modes and the roots of symbolizing activities are not considered at all. However, if we hope to foster early literacy we need to be sensitive to all these fundamental aspects of human development and learning.

Our studies of language and the role it plays in individual development and in education should convince us of at least one thing: language is all pervasive and bound up with much of what we think, feel and do as individuals and as members of particular social groups and communities. If it is difficult to untangle language from everything we experience as people, it is almost impossible to separate out the tight mesh of the four language modes of listening, talking, writing and reading. I would also argue that if we attempt to separate these forms of 'languaging' we do irreparable harm. At the best, a trivialization of language activities occurs when we begin to cast around for lists of things to do in daily listening or writing sessions (Whitehead, 1983a, pp. 60–1). At the worst, we facilitate the imposition of inappropriate checklists of achievements at certain ages in listening, reading, talking and writing 'skills'.

Level descriptions of what every 7-year-old should have achieved in English now exist (DFE, 1995), along with baseline targets for children on entry to primary school (SCAA, 1996b). However, the interrelatedness of the four language modes is not diminished by these official attainment proposals – it still renders some language assessment targets tentative, if not problematic. The complex interweaving of listening, talking, reading and writing must continue to be reflected not just in curriculum statements and teaching plans but in the human relationships and interactions we promote in early years settings and schools.

If the interrelated nature of talking and listening, reading and writing is sometimes lost in current practices, the connection between literacy and early symbolizing activities is rarely made and understood. Literacy is rooted in a general symbolizing capacity that develops in the first year of life and this ability is so distinctive of human thinking and behaviour that it can be thought of as the distinguishing feature of human development. This bold claim highlights the fact that the teacher of literacy is in the business of nurturing not just 'a language for life' (DES, 1975) but the very quality of life of the learner. We need to develop and value the many symbolizing activities which support and enrich early literacy, such as gesture, movement and dance; role play and dramatic representations; scribbling, drawing, painting and modelling; mapping, building and the construction of miniature worlds.

Our own understanding of the nature of symbolic representation is crucial. The point is not that we should always be able to interpret or share these complex symbolic representations but that we should respect them as powerful intellectual strategies. Symbolic activities are particularly interesting for the early-years educator because they are the fusion of the unique personal experiences and concepts of the individual with the systems of shared meanings specific to the culture. As an example, we all know what it means on occasions to have a struggle to put our own feelings and responses into the words and grammatical patterns of a particular language.

The interest for the educator lies in the analogy with the processes of literacy and education. They may be thought of as ways of expressing and developing the needs and purposes of the individual personality through public systems of shared understandings. In the case of education, the social and cognitive skills of the individual are extended by the acquisition of public forms of understanding. In the case of literacy, the conventional written systems of languages provide a rich extension of individual oral-language competence and a massive increase in social communicative power.

But these claims can become rather too generalized and abstract. What issues of specific relevance to early-years educators arise from the perspectives on literacy discussed so far? I have answered this by focusing on a total literacy approach rather than treating early writing and early reading separately. My approach tries to keep the web of language intact in all its intricacy. This necessitates a fair bit of overlap, as in all well-spun webs. However, it is the recurring features of the language pattern that interest me, not the naming of distinct rungs on a hypothetical ladder of language achievements.

The Literacy Approach

'Read them,' said the King.

The White Rabbit put on his spectacles. 'Where shall I begin, please your Majesty?' he asked.

'Begin at the beginning', the King said, very gravely, 'and go on till you come to the end: then stop'.

(Lewis Carroll, Chap. XII)

To begin at the beginning with literacy means going back to the earliest patterns of communication that can be observed in the 'conversation-like' behaviours of babies and their care-givers (see Chapter 3). I have argued elsewhere (Whitehead, 1983b) that the earliest interactions of babies with their care-givers establish not just language structures but the prototypes of narrative form and story-telling behaviours. But perhaps we can extend these ideas and see the very early prototypes of reading and writing as present in the beginnings of language. This is not such an extreme idea if we bear in mind the fact that it is now generally accepted that language begins with nonverbal communicative behaviours, and literacy is developed by the desire to communicate.

From the start, babies are 'reading' the eye contacts, faces, gestures and postures of those significant persons who care for them. This must involve scanning, focusing, anticipating and predicting responses and making contacts. The infant starts by 'reading' for emotional responsiveness and this is beautifully demonstrated by every baby who fixes an adult with a wide stare and accompanies this with appealing smiles and mouthing, and arm, leg and whole body movements.

Very young infants are also sensitive listeners and this supports their reading of persons and situations. The listening skills of newborn infants are highly developed, they are able to discriminate voices from other noise and rapidly come to recognize the particular voices of their constant care-givers. Again, it is emotional tone and mood that is picked up by the sensitive reading and listening infant. It is probable that patterns of intonation and emphasis are particularly important to young infants and help them focus on the meaning-bearing segments of speech, such as beginnings and endings, nouns and verbs. It is essential to think of young babies as 'reading' people and situations and listening for response and meaning in their earliest interactions because it establishes them as communicators and meaning-makers long before schooling.

However, it is equally important to note that infants are sensitive to words as pleasurable sounds and they delight in words linked with rhythmic movement, bouncing and rocking. So from the start it is not just words as messages that are attended to but words as poetic forms. Rhyme, rhythm and repetition are the earliest language play we can share with infants and, interestingly, are features of the earliest literature we share with children: the literature of nursery rhymes and songs. We begin, it seems, with play and learning thoroughly mixed up together.

The significance of talk for literacy cannot be overstated and it underlies all aspects of language discussed in this book. At this point, however, I want to emphasize its origins in shared conversations, its deep roots in powerful feelings and life-long relationships and its saturation with cultural ways of saying and doing.

These comments may seem to be taking us away from the concerns of the early-years teacher of literacy but they are the background to all that can be achieved in early years group settings and are the source of children's earliest understandings of literacy. With this in mind, we can consider what issues are particularly significant for literacy in early-childhood education.

I have grouped the issues under two broad headings, 'getting started' and 'emerging literacy'. Such an arrangement helps to free planning and thinking from the trap of always focusing on age-related norms and specific age-focused phases of education.

Getting Started

Getting started on literacy in the early years of education depends on the success children achieve in sharing meanings and becoming communicators. Research makes it clear that very young children are actively engaged in 'meaning': in investigating and questioning the significance of all human activities and responses. Such intellectual curiosity ranges from questions about where significant adults go to all day, to exhaustive interrogations about the economic basis of window-cleaning services in contemporary society (Tizard and Hughes, 1984, pp. 120–2). These lively explorations of the meaning of human behaviour and motivation need not be left at home, they should come into early years settings and be applied to the people, the talk, the literature and the other planned experiences of the early-years curriculum. If young children are to continue their development as communicators within group settings, they need an environment rich in opportunities for symbolic play and representation. Getting started on literacy comes down to sharing and negotiating meanings through the use of sounds, words, images, gestures, objects and signs. Learning to read and write, in and out of school or group settings, depends on involving young children in reading meanings and making messages.

Early education needs to create bridges between the common-sense, everyday shared meanings children have already explored and the specialized meanings framed in literary and other forms of knowledge. Young children know a great deal about their families, homes and communities but they need time and opportunities for relating this knowing and these meanings to the 'facts' of science, mathematics and book literature. Book language (the prestigious written form of the culture) is best introduced by pleasurable participation in rhythmic language games, rhymes and poems.

Telling Tales and Sharing Books

Early literacy thrives when it is nourished on a rich diet of gossip, anecdotes, reminiscences and story-telling. Oral story-telling is the oldest and most powerful way of sharing and passing on the knowledge, experiences and beliefs of a community. We all feel confident about launching into a good story about a professional 'hiccup', or a modern myth about the profligacy of local government, or the madness of eight-mile traffic jams. Yet we hesitate about risking a told story in the classroom. This can be overcome if we understand that it is legitimate to be as free with our own version of 'The Three Bears' as we are with our versions of 'The Night I Locked Myself out of my Own Car!' Furthermore, the use of story props (as described in Chapter 5) supports the concentration and the confidence of tellers and listeners, and the gains are incalculable. The total focus on establishing and maintaining a rapport between the teller, the tale and the listeners enriches classroom relationships,

nurtures listening skills and sensitizes young children to the rhythmic, for-
mulaic qualities of poetic language.

For young children, story-telling is also the best kind of introduction to the
features of extended, explicit prose: the 'book language' central to all further
literacy experiences. Oral story-telling leads children from the informal, face-
to-face qualities of everyday verbal interactions to the formally organized
patterns of the written language.

Many approaches to early literacy start with sharing picture books with
young children and the books certainly provide important experiences of listening to a tale told, hearing book language and looking at a story carried
forward by pictures as well as text. But the connections between the book and
the child's world need to be built by sensitive talk at the appropriate times.
Children need opportunities for conversations about books and stories and
time to examine books closely and sort out their feelings and responses to
them. Meanings are created in these ways and the layers of story or subtext are
gradually unpacked. Sometimes the picture tells one story and the text is less
explicit, as with *Rosie's Walk* (Hutchins, 1968).

If favourite books are available and in the hands of children, expectations
about them are not restricted to narrative form, plot and character. Close
textual investigations lead children to look at the black marks of text and to
discover familiar letters, repeated letters and even whole words they know.
The puzzling conventions of illustrations are also analysed as children learn
what is inside or outside the picture frame. Learning to read pictures is a
sophisticated skill and continues to develop as part of a general ability to 'read'
art, film and television images. But perhaps the most interesting and exciting
literacy development in these early stages comes when children begin to put
themselves and their worlds into the books, the excitement of knowing that
'My Nan's got one of those', or 'There's my baby's buggy!' or 'I ran away once
in the supermarket' is the motivation for going on looking at books. Books are
meaningful in human terms.

Sharing meanings is a richly complex feature of human behaviour and literacy will not be promoted by simply sticking to books and talk about books.
The experiences children bring to school and group settings and the new
experiences they find there must be re-enacted or tried out in many different
symbolic ways – drawing and painting materials, dressing-up clothes and play
artefacts, moulding and sculpting media and construction equipment and natural objects. These are the foundations of early literacy and not 'optional
extras' that might bridge the gap between home and playgroup or school and
help children settle in early. It is not the actual things that bridge the home–
school gap and make for emotional security, it is what children are doing with
and through them that enables the children to feel 'at home' in the world and
culture of school and group and make their own significant contributions to it.

Writing and Reading Messages
The children's contributions in the forms of stories, anecdotes and narratives
must not just be accepted, they must be very important components of the
early-years literacy programme. They are usually preserved as group-made
books of imaginative stories or accounts of shared experiences in and out of

the setting. From the start of early-years education, children's stories can be copied down by adults, taped for later transcription or the children's activities and outings can be recorded in sequences of photographs. These visual narratives can later have text added or, sometimes, be left as open-ended invitations to 'remember when, remember how?'

This sort of material may often be group inspired but highly personal stories fascinate both authors and classmates. It is often the case that families and neighbours are willing to make up simple books about their children and their daily lives and many schools have developed a policy for inviting families in to make such books with their children. Most practitioners who embark on a course of listening to very young children and inviting them to tell stories find that they have released a torrent of powerful material. Furthermore, the children become involved and proud collectors of stories; however, the proper respect due to their work must be reflected by careful transcribing and mounting, attractive display and suitable storage of all class narratives.

The most significant piece of meaningful writing in every child's life is probably her or his first name (see Chapter 7). 'Games with names' can be a powerful way into early writing and communication if we follow the children's developing interests and observations and provide ample examples of names in use. The obvious starting-point is the labelling of children's property and of the pictures and models they create. This can lead to the easy recognition of initial letters and children's names can be grouped according to these salient letters. Many children will point to letters in the environment and announce that 'I've got one of those', meaning that the letter occurs in their name. Other interesting features such as double letters in names seem to provoke considerable interest, as the previous chapter indicated.

This orthographic awareness can be extended by labelling children's own books, the seeds they plant in the garden, their seating places for meals, and so on. Names on cards can be sorted on a daily basis to 'record' who is here and who is away. Considerable enthusiasm and excitement is always generated by a display of mounted and named photographs of the children as babies, or photographed working in and around the building. The power of names is not to be under-estimated, whether written down or slipped into a familiar storytelling situation for fun. All the power of love and anger that focuses on the names of care-givers, siblings, friends and pets ensures their almost immediate recognition in spoken or written forms.

Children's interest in important words, words suffused with meaning and feeling, is usually accompanied by a desire to write or make them. Even if not positively helped or encouraged to do so, children make their marks in wet sand, mud, clay and dough, or with paints, pencils and crayons. These 'signatures' are often highly idiosyncratic, recognized immediately by families and professional staff, even if they are not in the full conventional form but just a promising initial or a scatter of the component letters. This attachment to the letters of a name is often expressed in terms of real affection and some young children will stroke certain letters and hug special pieces of text (Lierop, 1985).

This serves as a reminder that learning anything, but especially literacy, is bound up with feelings and emotions. In the later stages of education we go so far as to ask pupils to evaluate literature in terms of how they 'feel' about or 'like' or 'prefer' certain texts. However, it is unreasonable to expect such sensitive and feeling responses to literature at the later stages if the early processes of learning to read and write have undervalued feeling and caring about words and texts.

The excitement of children's own names as symbols of ownership and presence in the world should soon spill over into a delight in finding writing almost everywhere. Suddenly it seems that the whole world is neatly named: the inspection covers and drain grids in the outside areas, the fencing round the garden, the school or playgroup sign-board, the lavatory bowls, etc. Such varied but very informative writing from the environment should not be ignored. Many young children have learnt to write and read before schooling by investigating such materials and asking questions about them.

We can extend these discoveries by bringing into the early years setting collections of packages and cartons we can then 'read' in order to cook the food, make the model or grow the plants. We can share the children's delight in familiar advertisements, shop carrier-bags, rhyming or repetitive slogans and well-known logos and signs. These materials have real-world relevance and importance and they make bridges between home and educational settings. They encourage talk and play about the world of out-of-school learning and experiences. In terms of linguistics, such materials provide information about the features of letters, spaces, words and text and allow important insights into the symbol and sound correspondences of the alphabet. Furthermore, these materials are easily collected, easily replaced and perfect for endless play and manipulation.

With a little more effort, the early years practitioner can also make collections of texts and packages from other cultures that feature more than one language and even different sign systems or alphabets. 'What does this writing say?' is a particularly interesting question when the teacher does not know the answer! Literacy learning can make us all vulnerable and young children need to know that it is acceptable not to know about everything. Incidental demonstrations of powerful adults 'not knowing' may be very reassuring for many children. Responses such as 'How can we find out?' 'Could we guess?' 'Who can we ask?' 'Perhaps *x* will come to our school (or group) and tell us about the writing', are models of good education in action.

It is important to allow for a great variety and range of experiences and experiments in early literacy. While some children write their names and play with printing sets or plastic alphabet letters, others will create pages of pretend writing, fold sheets of paper into booklets and dash off linear-looking scribbles. Young children do need considerable supplies of paper and markers so that they can experiment with scribbled notes, doctor's prescriptions, books of stories, labels, warnings, welcome letters and even music.

Some children delight in cutting out and collecting scraps of printed text from magazines and newspapers; others play such games as looking for writing 'on me and my friends'. Many children are also aware that they see writing on the television and they recognize the names of programmes and products. Some children choose to write, over and over again, all the letters and even numerals that they can 'do'. This is a kind of inventory or checklist of all that they know and can write (see Chapter 7). Other children may have some experience of using a computer keyboard and will be ready to explore the potential of a simple word-processing program.

In the earliest stages of literacy many children will be aware of alphabets because families often buy them as posters and wall-charts to decorate children's rooms, as well as buying alphabet picture books. Alphabets are also displayed in clinics and many of the children's treatment areas in hospitals. The collection of alphabets in an educational setting should be as varied, appealing and relevant as possible. Children can be actively involved in creating their own exciting alphabets of such sets as 'our names'. Any gaps in a group alphabet provide a valuable, open-ended, problem-solving situation for children and educators: 'Do we know anyone with a "Z" in their name?' Favourite food makes a good subject for an 'ABC' and 'most-disliked' food is even greater fun. A more ambitious alphabet can illustrate the children's exploits in the local community, for example:

D is for Deptford Park where we can run round the track.
K is for Keston Ponds. We went pond-dipping and made our own nets.
T is for Totters. They have horses and carts and collect old junk.

All these suggestions for getting started reflect the varied interests and stages that children may go through. I stress that tentative 'may' because becoming a reader and writer is a very personal business and the ways to do it are unique as are the many cultural, ethnic and religious settings in which children get started. But the aim is clear: to get the young learners to a stage where they are saying or thinking 'what does that say?' And 'how do you write X?' Early literacy is dependent on asking the right questions about language and print and on using adults and other children as linguistic informants by directing questions to them. Literacy is also about feeling safe and confident enough to indicate one's ignorance or confusion but, above all, it is based on an unshakeable belief that writing and reading are always meaningful activities.

Emerging Literacy

Once we have helped to nurture in children a positive passion for stories, poems and books and an expectation that written language carries meaningful messages, we will need to support the development of specific aspects of literacy. In order to avoid any suggestion that literacy is first reading and then writing, with neat groups of hierarchical skills and orderly phases of progress, I have chosen four aspects of literacy that can be focused on in the early years of education: the roles of authors and readers; the significance of collaborative approaches to emerging literacy; the nature of written forms as both permanent and disposable; and, finally, the issues of independence and of written conventions. All the current statutory requirements for language and literacy (English) in the years 4–8 are covered by these aspects – only the labels and the philosophy are different.

Authors and Readers

The reason for discussing authors and readers is that from the earliest days of education, if not before, children can and should experience being in both roles. The author–reader relationship is not a one-sided affair in which the reader accepts passively the message given out by the author whose ownership of the text is emphasized by the high status of print. In the act of reading we are all authors as well as readers. Readers must use their knowledge of the world and their linguistic expectations to re-create actively the meanings implied in text and pictures. Readers also become authors when they respond to experiences, including reading and listening to literature, by writing about them.

These theoretical claims about the blurring of the author–reader role have implications for educational practices. If young children are to see themselves as potential writers and as active author-like readers they need to regard books as communications from real, knowable people. The idea that people write books is fostered initially by a plentiful source of stories made up and told by carers, teachers, other adults and children as well as heard from books, and by sharing close examinations of the texts and the pictures. The possibility of gradually building up a collection of favourite and 'known authors' is dependent on good book resources and pleasant settings for quiet browsing. Such approaches are enhanced if teachers, parents and helpers refer to the authors by name when sharing books and refer back to other books by the same writer and/or illustrator. Educators can also set up small displays of books by one author so that young children can 'tune in' to the quirky, idiosyncratic and recognizable style of the writer.

Particular authors and illustrators become known and loved by children. I visited a class of 6-year-olds who were so enchanted by the gorilla and chimpanzee characters created by the artist and writer Anthony Browne that the teacher and parents had organized a visit to a children's book fair so that the class could buy their own copies of the books. In another class of 8- and 9-year-olds the strangely punning and surrealistic illustrations of some of Anthony Browne's books had inspired working models and writing about fantasy playgrounds and parks. It is not uncommon for my students to find that their story-sharing sessions are interrupted as the name of the author is greeted by 'Where's her photo then?' This is surely a mark of appreciation for a particularly human and interesting publishers' convention?

Establishing authors as persons is now widely reflected in the valuable practice of inviting authors to visit schools and public book events on an *ad hoc* basis or as part of a 'writers and illustrators in schools' scheme. Early-years teachers and group leaders and their pupils are sometimes not considered to be interested in such schemes but this is a sad under-estimation of young children's fascination with people and their work. Young children in an infant school have, to my knowledge, baked and decorated a cake to celebrate the birthday of a favourite story-book character and invited the author to tea!

Supporting this sound appreciation of the person behind the text will be all the ways in which young children themselves take on the role of author. The planning, writing, illustrating and making of individual, small-group and class books provide essential insights into the nature of the writing process. This personal kind of reading material is highly motivating and allows for a sense of pride in ownership and early success in reading back what is known, expected and expressed in familiar language forms. Books made at home and at school develop from the spoken language forms children know and use confidently, but these books also highlight the nature of written text.

Children can learn an enormous amount about writing from reading. Initially, if teachers and adults write messages and stories for them, children learn that writing is different from talk. Subtle changes occur as the vocal pitch and intonation, the hesitations, repetitions, vocal 'noises' and throat clearings, self-corrections and body language of face-to-face talk are removed from the performance and only the words are retained. Even the difficulties of the adult–scribe, who cannot keep up with the pace of everything the child says, provide useful introductions to the differences between spoken and written language forms.

Young children beginning reading are not just reading words in order, they are reading groups of meanings blocked together in sentences and paragraphs. They are 'reading' that written words are separate and surrounded by space, in contrast to the continuous stream of sounds in speech. If children read and write with sensitive adults in unhurried situations where words are tasted on the tongue and discussed they also begin to experience the varied and complex relationships between sounds and their representation by means of letters. Good reading and writing experiences sensitize young children to initial letter sounds and to some interesting sound pairs or digraphs, such as '*ch*', '*sh*'and '*th*' and even to endings such as '-ing' and '-ed' (see Riley, 1996, for detailed advice on introducing phonemes and digraphs).

Making books involves a literacy partnership between children and supportive adults and the resulting texts can be 'published' for group, home and school use. Publication can be enhanced by children's illustrations, photography, word-processing and traditional book making techniques (Johnson, 1991). A major study of making books in educational settings (Smith, 1994) describes a triangular relationship between the composer/reader, the scribe/ good listener and the text which is written, read and edited. This study also has detailed advice on training other adults, parents and older children as scribes and listeners.

As children work with their own books they are increasingly keen to model them on the published books they read. This is another aspect of 'conventions' and of becoming an author, as the children move on from their initial pride and delight in simple ownership of their writing to a wish to see it look 'like a real book'. This leads to an interest in the clear separation of pictures from blocks of text and the idea of meaningful paragraphs is developed from decisions about 'what shall we say on this page or under this picture?' In this phase, title pages and authorial ownership take pride of place, as does an emphasis on 'The End'. Some children become fascinated by publishers' names and addresses and replicate these features with their own school or class identity. Pages become numbered as writing becomes more extended and the claim that this book is 'mine' or 'ours' is also reflected in a desire to use the conventional copyright logo. All this play and pretending is a powerful indicator of children's rapidly developing sense of the place of literacy in their culture and in their lives.

Collaborative Approaches

Literacy is learnt and used in collaborative ways in many cultures and its initial learning and use need not be restricted to childhood or to educational institutions. Adults as well as children engage in mutually supportive talk and explanations as they negotiate the meanings of written material. Just observe two or more people reading the instructions on a food package or on DIY equipment and materials! These shared readings are paralleled by collaborative writings, such as the joint writing of a report or mutual agonizing over a difficult letter of condolence or rejection. 'Two heads are better than one' (according to folk psychology), and this certainly applies to the sophisticated demands of literacy.

Life in educational settings provides many opportunities for such shared 'literacy events' (Heath, 1983), and children and adults should not stop at sharing story books and co-operative book making – there are also posters to design, invitations and acceptances to receive and send, as well as the sharing of greetings, enquiries, etc. Initially educators play a major supportive role as readers and linguistic informants for younger children, but as the children's own literacy skills develop they can be practised and extended in collaborative ways.

It is possible to boost greatly the amounts of writing and reading children do in school by encouraging them to share both their knowledge about writing and their reading abilities with their peers. Children can read to each other in attractive and informal book corners, library areas, sheltered gardens and playgrounds. This reading can be within their own class or age-range but it can also spread to reading to younger and older children, as appropriate.

Shared Reading

Another way of boosting daily reading is by the practice of 'shared reading' using 'big books'. Many children's books of high literary and artistic quality are produced in a 'big book' format which enables a large group of children to see the fine details of print and illustrations easily. In frequent shared reading sessions the teacher demonstrates all the skills and insights which an experienced reader brings to a text. This involves reading the text aloud to the group, first in one uninterrupted reading which establishes the plot of the story, the narrative style and the enjoyment of the illustrations. Second and subsequent readings will begin to engage the children more closely with the text as the adult points out the left to right flow of the printed words as they are spoken and highlights interesting book conventions (title pages, authors' and illustrators' names, publishing details, ISBN codes). Discussions of the plot, the characters and the tales being told by the illustrations develop the children's skills as discriminating and critical readers.

An ever closer focus on the print is ensured as the adult draws the children's attention to recurring names, repeated phrases, rhymes and words, some of which the children may know already from previous book readings, group and classroom word collections and labels, and the environmental print outside the setting. Shared talk about all these meaningful words will be an appropriate way of teaching phonological, alphabetic and orthographic awareness. Furthermore, initial letter combinations (digraphs); end (terminal) groups and rhymes; common patterns in English ('qu', 'ou'); and the double vowel sounds (as in 'sleep', 'moor', 'baa'), enable children to identify and group words in 'families'. This close focus on print also helps children and adults to talk about the nature and functions of punctuation as they encounter capital letters, full stops, commas, speech marks and the really exciting dashes, question marks and exclamation marks that occur in literature.

Writing

The biggest problem for the beginning writer is lack of information about words, their component sounds and how these are represented by conventional symbols or letters. Overcoming this difficulty is also the biggest problem for the teacher of beginning writers! The way out of the dilemma hinges on collaborative approaches and a special kind of division of labour. The complex tasks of transcription and composition must be clearly separated (Smith, 1982). Teachers and other adults have the transcription skills that enable them to write down the message in the conventional form, by hand or machine. Young emerging writers have the ideas, feelings and experiences they are composing or shaping into narrative forms, but they need scribes or secretaries to dictate to, and this is the significance of early book-making as a collaborative venture between child–author and adult teacher–secretary.

Gradually, children will take advantage of any other linguistic aids and props such as small collections of words linked to particular experiences or materials and presented in attractive containers. Personal word collections of the *Breakthrough to Literacy* type (Mackay, Thompson and Schaub, 1978) can develop from these word hoards. Other sources of information include other children who may know and 'own' words. Favourite books and areas of the school and classroom can be checked for 'that word' required. An inspiring account (Geekie and Raban, 1993) of this kind of approach in an Australian reception class charts the empowerment of young children who are taught to interrogate each other and their classroom setting in the dynamic pursuit of literacy. Verbal accounts may be recorded on tape and later transcribed by teachers and other assistants and the use of the wordprocessor can eventually lessen the children's dependence on an adult–scribe, although care is needed as laboriously printing up words letter by letter on the screen can become a tedious trap rather than a writing prop. This is a poor use of the new technologies, as is the uncritical reliance on 'reading books' on CD Rom that simply replicate dreary primers and mask meaningless text with visual tricks and loud music.

Shared Writing

Writing is not a simple matter of finding individual words: the child's lively and creative use of grammatical patterns and literary phrases is 'the writing' and it depends on the educator for its survival. Approaches that utilize the pleasure of savouring words, discussing problems and creating books together have come to be called 'shared writing'. Teachers and small groups of children jointly create large books that may be based on personal experiences, the adventures of a favourite story-book character, or some favourite poems and songs, or shared outings and classroom investigations. This approach maximizes the children's creative ideas and composing skills and also enables the teacher to share the processes and conventions of writing with several children at once.

The only tools required are a bold marker pen and a flipchart, or some large sheets of paper fixed to a small easel or chalkboard. The teacher/scribe writes at the dictation of the children, but talks herself and the children through every aspect of the process and draws the children's attention to the smallest details. This includes shaping the group discussion and fragments of talk into suitable passages for writing. At this level the children are helped to make the important and complex move from speaking to writing, learning in a meaningful context that writing is different from speech. The conventions of writing are taught as the teacher talks about, and invites the children to instruct her in, all the detailed decisions writers must make. For example, 'Where do we start on the paper?' 'Do we use a capital letter?' 'How do we spell that?' 'What letter does it start with – do we know a word like it; have we used this word before?' 'Is that the end of this part?' 'Do we use a full stop here?' 'How can we show that this is a question?' These questions lead to constant re-reading of the text and re-writing it, lots of linguistic talk and the energetic solving of genuine literacy problems (Geekie and Raban, 1993, p. 23); they also help children and teachers to engage with the range and key skills requirements of the National Curriculum for reading and writing.

Shared writing is also a way of preparing children to continue tackling their writing in collaborative ways at the later stages of education. In the later primary years a willingness to engage in shared writing conferences will be important. However, in the early stages of literacy writing is often a hard-won achievement for the child, as well as a spontaneous creative experience, and too much re-drafting is best avoided. The young child's pieces of writing are often treasured objects to be tucked away in secret places or, sometimes, a gift for a loved person and we need to exercise great sensitivity about re-working such material.

At the later stages of literacy development it is still advisable to provide time, space and materials for writing that is private and not subject to 'handing in' and marking. Of course, such writing might be shared voluntarily with a trusted adult who happens to be a teacher but this is a personal communication and should be responded to in an appropriate way.

Permanent and Disposable

There is a tendency in language study to make much of the importance of writing in terms of its permanence and, correspondingly, to neglect its equally important 'disposable' nature. We should remember that in one significant sense spoken language is permanent: it can never be 'unsaid' and has a terrible permanence in other minds. The neglect of writing as a disposable product has led to some foolish and 'unwriterly' practices in schools. For a start, there has been a reluctance to allow children to have second thoughts about a piece of writing, to erase sections of it or even throw it away and start a fresh sheet. But an interest in re-drafting and editing at the later stage of writing implies the tolerance of such messy but very writerly practices as cutting up sections, re-jigging them and pasting them down. Real writing involves using lots of scrap paper for headings and useful ideas and, of course, positively cultivating over-flowing waste-paper bins.

Writers, particularly young ones, also like to 'say it out loud', or whistle, wriggle and get up and walk about. But this is heady and revolutionary stuff, so let us simply admit that we do not often get writing 'right' first time and we should not expect children to do so!

The sort of permanence in writing which is highly significant for education is that which enables us to use writing as an extended way of thinking. Once the idea, experience or phrase is roughly written down it is captured. Ideas, implications and new connections begin to flow from the matter on the page or the screen. In this sense the permanence of writing is bound up with its alterability or total disposability, but it is also an interesting issue of power and control for writers. Who decides for beginning writers what they can keep, alter or destroy? It seems clear that if from the start the young writer has to give over this control to a teacher, then writing will never become a powerful mode of personal thinking, communication and a source of pleasure. Response to children's early writing must be sensitive and respectful. We should incorporate into our 'marking' such procedures as discussing and altering material with the child's agreement and active involvement. The mistakes made by children should be seen as a powerful teaching aid that enables the educator to have some insight into the child's progress and current strategies for understanding and using written forms.

Children's appreciation of the permanence of writing will be fostered by their awareness of it as a source of pleasure that is always there to go back to. It is a measure of our success when a child flicks excitedly through a book and says 'Where's that poem about . . .?' Or demands to know where we have put the story about, 'that dog who got all dirty so they didn't know he was really Harry and they put him in the bath'. Children also go home and recommend favourite books to friends and family, or demand that they buy them. And, over the years, no matter how many times we go away, we can always come back and the story is still there. John Brown lets Rose have her Midnight Cat (Wagner, 1977) and Nothing is restored to his family (Inkpen, 1995).

Writing is also a permanent record of facts, information and historical change. Books begin to work for children in the early stages of literacy as extra 'informants' or 'teachers' and the use of library collections and reference skills may start from the children's own group-made books. Educators, parents and children together can produce highly personal and relevant books about 'our gerbils', 'planting Pansy seeds' or 'the Avocado book', complete with recipe for making Guacamole![1] Such books form the nucleus of a classroom reference collection and are meaningful initiations into using the power of written language to get things done in the world.

Independence and Conventions

Getting things done in the world is one aspect of being independent and early literacy raises important issues of personal autonomy and the nature of conventions. It may seem a little odd to be linking issues of autonomy and conventions together, but many worrying and controversial aspects of early literacy teaching are rooted in misunderstandings about these related issues. Without in any way minimizing the significance for individuals and cultures of a sound mastery of conventional written language, we need to question the high priority still accorded to teaching and learning conventions in the early stages of literacy. History, research and classroom experience suggest that too much concern for the early teaching of conventions and rules, at the expense of independent and exploratory approaches to reading and writing, slows down children's progress and seriously undermines their desire to be readers and writers.

A first priority for early literacy and, indeed, an aim of education at any stage, must be personal autonomy: the clear establishment of a sense of control over one's life and learning experiences. If this sounds too grand and vague for the early years we should stop and consider the growing evidence of avoidable confusion and misunderstanding that assails young children in their first weeks and months in schools and has a detrimental effect on early literacy; (see, for example, King, 1978; Francis, 1982; Barrett, 1986; Riley, 1996). Sadly, it is often the areas of reading and writing in school that confront young children with meaningless tasks, pointless questions and unexplained activities. These practices are increasingly evident in nursery schools and playgroups. We need to question the usefulness of such activities as asking low level questions about perfectly obvious pictures, colouring in outline drawings of characters from primers, copying out trivial sentences from work books or learning to write letters and numerals by linking up dots, etc.

The writing that goes on in early-years settings between the children themselves and between teachers, other adults and the children should raise the questions that drive children to seek clearer and more effective writing strategies, that is, conventions. We need to raise the issue of writing functions: what is this piece of writing for? The answers will be as numerous and varied as human purposes, ranging from 'fun' to 'dire warnings'. My favourite example of the latter came from an infant classroom where the cleaner had pinned a hastily written note on the window for the children arriving that morning: 'The window ain't safe. Watch out for bits of glass'.

Our writing activities must also raise the question of audience. The teacher of literacy has a responsibility for using effort and ingenuity to ensure that children have a wide range of people and even institutions to write for. Children can, with teacher or other adult help in editing and typing (those significant conventions again), complain about the dogs fouling their local park or ask a local veterinarian to let them observe a routine surgery. Let us think less about 'marking' and more about writing back to our pupils with notes of encouragement or important information. Children's writing in the early years will be highly expressive, full of their personal stance in the world, their feeling responses and shared assumptions. If we try to eradicate from their writing how children feel about their experiences we are likely to eradicate any desire to write at all. The appropriate tone and style of a piece of writing is gained slowly and is a result of asking and answering for oneself, 'what is this for and whom is it for?'

Progress in writing is bound up with autonomy, and children need to be involved from the start in forming opinions and having views about their own writing successes and difficulties. This can be established by actually writing back to the children about their work, and also discussing with them the effectiveness of their writing for its purpose and audience.

Early reading also involves aspects of independence and early-years educators need to encourage those approaches that will ensure rapid and meaningful reading. Young children need to tackle reading globally, getting the gist of the message quickly, rather than attempting to decode every word and risking losing meaning. Any tendency to read alone or begin to read 'silently' should be positively supported. Considerable thought and flexibility should govern the teacher's approaches to the 'hearing' of young readers. Reading aloud to other adults, older children and visitors will help when children are suddenly racing away and anxious to practise their emerging competence. But the old tradition of hearing every child, every day, labouring through short and often meaningless snippets must be critically re-assessed.

Less frequent but far more intensive contacts with a teacher will probably set children off on fruitful meaning-making encounters with books and other written matter. The 'hearing reading', every day, approach effectively devalues all the other important reading for meaning that goes on in early-years classrooms.

As part of the process of encouraging independent reading, early years educators must find ways of developing children's self-correcting strategies and their self-assessment. If children are allowed to make minor mis-cues and even lose meaning they will learn, given a little time and a sense of self-confidence, to go back and self-correct or, at least, question the text and raise the issue of 'that doesn't make sense'. It all depends on the teachers' professional sensitivity and judgement about not rushing in too soon with a word-perfect correction but, equally importantly, not leaving a child floundering too long so that meaning and confidence evaporate.

Editing and Study Skills

We can begin to extend young children's understanding of the usefulness of written language conventions by introducing them to the process of editing writing and acquiring study skills. The success of editing depends on using the children's own writing, building on their developing insights into the differences between spoken and written forms and supporting their desire to communicate more effectively. Early work on editing will tend to focus on the conventions of standardized spelling and punctuation. Success in taking on the conventions of spelling seems to depend on a cumulative build-up of language experiences – a general background of listening carefully to language and playing with its sounds, rhythms and patterns.

Specific attention to spelling is most successful once children are confident readers and have a considerable experience of seeing written forms and writing themselves. Children also need plenty of opportunities for attempting spellings without being unduly constrained by the fear of getting it wrong. Attempts to spell 'as it sounds to you' encourage the investigation of the sound properties of language and the varied relationships between spoken forms and their written representations.

Careful examination of children's writing will reveal groups or patterns of non-standard forms. These can be discussed with individuals and small groups, related to words the children know by sight or to words in favourite books, poems and songs. Once the children are enthusiastic readers and writers they will enjoy linguistic games that involve collecting groups of words similar in appearance, sound or that have related meanings. Class and personal dictionaries can begin to be useful as children's writing and reading skills develop. They may be arranged thematically for some purposes, as well as alphabetically. Frequently encountered digraphs and strings of letters may be explored by making collections of them or building families of words that have these features.

These activities should be undertaken in exploratory ways and in meaningful contexts because they can easily become sterile exercises. Children's investigations of spelling should be pursued in a spirit of linguistic curiosity rather than with moralizing overtones about 'good' and 'bad' spellings. Spellings are neither good nor bad, they are standard or non-standard, but they are an important aspect of clear communication. Eventually the social and occupational well-being of those who are unable to spell in conventional and standardized ways is undermined.

Punctuation is bound up with two issues, the disembedded nature of written language and the concept of the sentence. It is often difficult for teachers, parents and other adults who have been writing successfully for years to realize that the sentence is not a natural feature of spoken language. It is true that the explicit sentence with its clear subject and predicate and its proper agreements of number, gender, and so on, as well as the cohesive devices which link the clauses, has migrated into some spoken forms. When we speak in our most formal registers, as in prepared speeches, we tend to use sentences because we are speaking aloud from the written form, but the language of social interaction and personal expressive talk is based on the unit of the meaning-bearing phrase. Daily language use is concerned with conveying and sharing meanings and it is embedded in obvious social contexts which make explicit verbal references and agreements less crucial. The implication is that children need many experiences of listening to book language and creating books and other pieces of text in shared-writing situations if they are to understand what is going on between the initial capital letter and the full stop.

It is much easier to approach the use of punctuation by way of the problems associated with the disembedded, or perhaps we might say 'unembodied', nature of written language. Punctuation partly compensates for the loss of much that is crucial in meaningful face-to-face communications. This includes indicators of units of meaning and their relationships and developments, as in sentences, paragraphs, phrases and clauses. Punctuation markers also replace the vocal intonation patterns and the pauses and changes of pitch we use to convey questions, statements and hesitations. The best way to develop children's sensitivity to these features of writing is to encourage the reading aloud and sharing of their written communications (an approach recommended at Key Stage 1 'Writing', DFE, 1995). Difficulties with phrasing, ambiguities and breathless unpunctuated continuity soon become obvious in interesting and unthreatening ways. Asking questions (such as 'What can we do?' 'How can we make this better?') is always wiser and more educationally useful than the silent condemnation of fairly meaningless red-ink corrections.

In the early years of education we can make a positive start on the teaching of a range of study skills. Good points of departure here are the children's interest in sorting and classifying the group or classroom collection of books, as well as experiences of looking things up in first reference books. Interest in different kinds of information books depends, of course, on there being a range of such books available. Interest is further stimulated by placing appropriate reference books next to thematic displays or collections of materials and artefacts. Thus, a collection of the musical instruments improvised and made by the children can be gathered together attractively and further enhanced by 'close at hand' books about singing games, musical instruments from other cultures, or an anthology of the children's own favourite songs. Similarly, a display of stones, pebbles and fossils does need one or two well-illustrated and accurately informative books to accompany it.

The skills of 'looking things up' and 'finding out about it' in reference books are extended by an introduction to the functions of a contents page, an index and the use of alphabetical order. The use of such books for searching, identifying and informing introduces the particular techniques of reading for information. This kind of reading is different from readerly approaches to narrative and poetic writing: the forms of imaginative literature need to be read in their entirety. However, reference material can be scanned and only the relevant sections attended to. Relevance here is judged in terms of the reader–researcher's question or problem. It is unnecessary to read the whole book, let alone copy it out word for word – a pointless practice often associated with the use of information books for projects in the later primary years. Approaches to early literacy that encourage autonomy, reflection and investigation are one way of ensuring that children use reference books as resources for answering their own independently formulated questions (see Mallett, 1992; Meek, 1996).

As they progress through the early years of schooling, children become increasingly interested in the variety and range of books provided for them. This interest can lead to a spontaneous sorting and classifying of the class book collection. If spontaneity appears to be missing it can be stimulated by the teacher's policy of displaying the children's own class-made books on special shelves, placing information books next to relevant resources, setting up collections of books by one author and organizing trips to the local public library. These kinds of initiatives often lead children to demand 'let's have a library'. Such a literacy role-play project teaches the children a great deal about the conventions and organization involved in the management of a wide range of books for borrowing. As well as deciding how to classify the available books the children have to organize ways of issuing borrowers' tickets and keeping a check on the books borrowed. Such problems challenge and extend children's understanding of alphabetical order, reading and writing for practical purposes, the classification and retrieval of information and the nature of 'subjects' or knowledge categories. To these complex study skills we might also add the very important interpersonal skills of courtesy, fairness and respect for shared resources.

Early Literacy and the Nursery Curriculum

The increasing emphasis on young children's potential interest in literacy and their experiments with significant marks and the possibilities of writing has aroused new interest in what goes on in playgroups, nursery schools and classes. In terms of teaching literacy, the centre of gravity has suddenly shifted to the 'early' early years and nursery teachers and nurses have to consider the issues that face all teachers of beginning writers and readers. These issues can no longer be left for the infant or first-school teachers to concentrate on (Campbell, 1996; Miller, 1996).

A few decades ago many 'progressive' or 'child-centred' nursery professionals would not write for children or allow writing and labelling around the nursery environment. This rather extreme and socially unrealistic position developed from a laudable reaction against the imposition of meaningless and regimented writing instruction on very young children. Is it now the case that young children's playful explorations of writing and message sharing are once again being channelled and distorted into another grim era of teacher-directed writing and copying lessons for 3- and 4-year-olds? Nothing but good can come from nursery professionals knowing more about the processes of writing and reading and the complexities of the issues involved in early literacy. However, the well-resourced nursery environment and the central focus on young children's development, thinking and exploration of their world must be safeguarded.

Young children bring to the educational process a considerable range of early learning achievements and many strategies for making sense of new experiences. Professional educators decide how to avoid presenting very young children with situations, dialogues and materials that are totally unrelated to all the learning they have accomplished out of nursery school. What patterns of organization and what structures of personal relationships in the nursery setting best support children's existing strategies for learning and meaning making? What crucial features can be identified in early learning experiences in infancy, particularly in early language learning? What do the recorded achievements of pre-5 writers and readers teach the professional educator?

One area of literacy learning in the nursery curriculum that has benefited from asking these sorts of questions and acting on the answers is early reading experiences with quality books. Opportunities to share books in intimate and relaxed ways with an adult are now a high priority for individual children and small groups in the good nursery. This practice has become firmly established, with cosy and well-stocked book areas, ample story props, audio and video story tapes and software. The renewed interest in the significance of poetry, rhyme and alliteration has also thrown a spotlight on pre-statutory school literacy (see Beard, 1995). These facts, plus the national requirements for desirable learning outcomes in language and literacy at age 4, prompt questions about the nature and role of early years education. How, in short, do we plan for literacy to be part of the nursery curriculum without it becoming a distorting factor?

Attempts to answer these questions will need to focus on the central issue of balance in the nursery curriculum. Literacy, as I have indicated, must not be concentrated on to the detriment of other aspects of the early-years learning environment. Indeed, literacy itself will suffer if it is not established on a broad and deep foundation of worthwhile experiences of symbolizing and representing meanings through nonverbal communication skills, gesture, movement, dance, music, listening, talking, drawing, painting, modelling, building, storytelling, poetry sharing, scientific and mathematical investigations, rituals and religious celebrations. Literacy in the written forms of a culture is only one sort of literacy: the long list above represents the other 'literacies' and many symbolic languages (Edwards, Gandini and Foreman, 1996) that early education must establish and build on. Such a balanced early-years education must be pursued in ways that are open-ended and sensitive to where the children are in their thinking and investigations.

If the approach of professional nursery educators is unpressured and reflects their confidence in children's abilities to think and to learn for themselves when supported by their peers and caring adults, there should be less danger of a work–play split in the nursery curriculum: one other possible danger inherent in explicitly locating literacy in the nursery curriculum is a denigration of all the central experiences of nursery education we label 'play'. What does the hidden curriculum of the nursery class or school signal about the teachers' beliefs with regard to 'work' and 'play'? 'Go and play outside, dear.' 'Wouldn't you like to do some work in the writing corner?' 'Tidy those bricks away now.' 'You can take your writing home to show your Mum what hard work you've been doing.' In the nursery years the choice is clearly between allowing children's playful explorations of literacy to enrich the curriculum and their lives or allowing the blight of meaningless tasks and bits of knowledge to trivialize the educational experience.

Parents, Families, Communities and Cultures

All the issues and choices raised in this book lack a crucial dimension if they are not shared with the families and communities who send their young children to us to be educated. Early years settings and schools are not educational service centres or supermarkets (despite pressure to describe parents as education 'consumers', DES, 1991), but they should be as open to the public they serve and as well-known and well used as any other community facilities. Ideas about open schools and group settings and partnership with parents have significant implications for many professional choices. Partnership involves genuine sharing of ideas and mutual support and this increasingly depends on the quality of the conversations parents and professional educators share. Professionals, for their part, need to formulate the principles on which they base their practices in sensible human terms. Do we talk mysteriously, of 'reading for meaning', using 'real books' and 'developmental writing' and leave it at that? Outside the institution these terms are ludicrously obvious or meaningless! What is a parent to make of 'learning from concrete experiences' or 'writing across the curriculum'? As well as saying exactly what we mean, rather than staying safely in the cocoon of professional jargon, we must help parents and the community to say what they mean.

A research project (Hughes, Wikeley and Nash, 1994) focused on Key Stage 1 revealed that parents choose schools (if they have the possibility of genuine 'choice') on the grounds of size and friendliness and that they appreciate their local schools and teachers. They find the National Curriculum basic and lacking in fun and are critical of the disruption caused to their children's education by SATs (Standard Assessment Tasks). However, many of the parents did not feel that they had enough information about what their children were learning in school, despite plentiful contacts. This suggests that all professional educators and carers must continue to work at true partnerships, real conversations and co-operation. Educators may talk of 'writing' and mean the processes of composition while, in the same discussion, 'writing' to the parents means neat handwriting and the conventions of spelling and punctuation. Parents' understandable anxieties about the formal achievements of 'correct' and well-presented English can only be alleviated if educators' priorities and their reasons are presented in unambiguous terms. The success of the many 'reading-with-parents' schemes has been instrumental in helping families to worry less about word-perfect barking at print. In fact, many families have been able to reclaim their pride in their under-5 children's skills of recognizing books, slogans, instructions, labels and names in all sorts of places and at all sorts of extraordinary angles. A rapidly increasing number of projects in the USA and Britain – for example Reading is Fundamental (RIF), and Families and Schools Together(FAST) – continue to extend the notion of partnership by sharing the excitement of books and literacy, and acknowledging that literacy begins at home and then 'goes to school' (Weinberger, 1996).

Parents and communities need to be constantly in and around early years settings because the telling is not enough – it is the showing by doing that enables parents to understand the ways in which professional educators try to support and extend young children's strategies for learning. So, for every practitioner there is one constant and testing question: 'what would an ordinary, sensible parent make of this practice, instruction or display?' Rather than being a daunting prospect, the question can be liberating. Suddenly we are free of the tyranny of 'colour tables'and 'messy areas' and 'busy books' – or are we?

True partnerships are rarely bland or comfortable all the time and parents and communities may appear to make demands that worry educators. Indeed, a school or early years setting may sometimes feel that a simple acquiescence in certain requests would damage its educational provision and curriculum policies. Parents may ask 'when are the children going to be taught the rules of spelling?' 'Why aren't they copying their letters?'. 'Why have the children not got reading books?' This is not necessarily a criticism of the early years setting. It is certainly a request for information and probably reflects an understandable fear of the disadvantages and inequalities suffered by those who are not functionally literate in society. It also indicates that not enough is being done to make families and communities feel that they are co-workers in every aspect of the education of their children (see Whalley, 1994). The unnerving questions about literacy teaching are indications of a need for regular practitioner–parent workshops and discussions about language, literature, literacy and child development.

Records and Assessment

Professional records of young children's developing literacy must be based on detailed observations that are carefully analysed in order to ensure 'feed forward', or appropriate decisions about what might come next. Something of this kind has been preserved in the Key Stage 1 English tasks for reading and writing, notably in the emphasis on talking to young children about their knowledge of literature and books; the guidance on making a running record of a child's reading of a passage (see Riley, 1996); and the use of descriptive levels for making summative assessments of children's achievements in speaking and listening, reading and writing. At least there is some room here for professional judgements by educators about children's attainments and learning strategies. Furthermore, the complexity of these judgements has encouraged many practitioners to develop procedures for pooling and moderating together their records and decisions before assigning 'levels' to children's work.

Practitioners can find good advice and models in many publications (Blenkin and Kelly, 1992; Bartholomew and Bruce, 1993; Gorman and Brooks, 1996; Hutchin, 1996). Many of these researchers base their work broadly on the practices for monitoring and assessing language and learning pioneered by the Primary Language Record (CLPE/ILEA, 1988). This remains a valuable guide because it goes well beyond simple summative assessments; it provides diagnostic insights for the practitioner; it reflects the richness and breadth of children's language experiences and potential; and it involves parents and carers directly in contributing to their children's cumulative language records.

All these good things are in danger of disappearing in the pre-5 years of education as we enter a period of checking up on desirable outcomes for language and literacy and baseline assessments on starting primary school. Yet research still tells us that young children's 'errors' in reading and writing are a source of valuable insights into their thinking processes. Research also tells us that learning is a matter of processes and potential, best assessed when children are working with an older and wiser tutor, but not necessarily tapped by one-off solitary performances.

Good literacy teachers must range widely in their assessments and build up records of children's responses and developments in talking, listening, stories, books, poetry, rhyme, play with language, music, dance, print, signs, drawing and pictures. Children and families too can be drawn into the assessment process at a very early stage. One valuable practice is building up folders of selections from the children's drawing and writing and letting the children nominate items for inclusion. These items should be dated and have the child's reasons for choosing them attached along with notes by the adults working with the child. I always included a few examples which gave a time sequence to the collection: the first drawing or writing the child did with me and some half-termly examples. The sense of progress in such a folder is exciting for parents and child to contemplate. The professional educator gains a new insight about the child's thinking as it is revealed in changing strategies and hypotheses for representing meanings and experiences.

Reading profiles kept by teachers must include notes on children's attitudes and approaches to texts and their knowledge of illustrations, print conventions and the clues offered by context, syntax, phonics and semantics. When children read aloud the teacher will need to note attempts at self-correction, questions about the text and other evidence of making sense of the task. However, complex as the teaching of reading is, there is still a place for children's own views about learning to read – self-assessment can start in the early years. With the help of the teacher's secretarial skills, young readers can keep personal records of what they read in and out of school, what they like and why, and what they have not enjoyed. They can be helped to talk about their reading aloud performance, what gives them trouble and what occasions have been successful. Many 'Infants' are asked to read aloud in school assemblies – do we follow this up with informal discussions on how the child felt about this as a reading activity? Independence in literacy is about encouraging children to express from the start their own needs, formulate their own questions and hypotheses, and evaluate their own progress. If this approach is established as a priority it will lead to a more meaningful focus on the conventions of written language.

The key question for evaluating records and assessment processes is, do they enhance children's learning and teachers' teaching (Hutchin, 1996)?

Finally, we have to think about the problems faced by children and their families when the process of literacy learning appears slow or impossible, and becomes a Special Educational Need. Before rushing to embrace ever bigger and brighter solutions, labels and diagnoses, we might check that the basic requirements for quality care, security and close adult professional relationships are in place for children in the early years. We must then be absolutely sure that all the enabling language and literacy factors discussed in this book are found in early years settings. We can then remind ourselves that the big breakthroughs in reading achievements seem to come, according to the research, when children have closely monitored one-to-one tuition; have approaches that are literacy oriented and involve writing; have meaningful material to read; and, perhaps most importantly, receive the powerful hidden messages that they are valued and respected.

Being a Literacy Teacher

Barthes (1986) writes of three educational practices, teaching, apprenticeship and mothering and, although he sees them as distinct choices, I would suggest that they are all used by the literacy teacher. Teaching is concerned with transmitting knowledge and uses spoken and written forms, books and lectures. In early-years education there is a place for telling and reading about some of the skills of literacy. Apprenticeship emphasizes demonstration by one who has acquired the skills and performs them alongside an apprentice who observes and assists as much as possible. Mothering is the least regarded and most exciting of the teaching practices. It does not use much telling or demonstration of skills but relies on inexhaustible support, encouragement and incitement to learn. Those who 'mother' desire the success and achievements of their charges and surround them with the incitement to succeed. It is not enough to teach and to demonstrate – being a literacy teacher also involves desiring the success of our young pupils and willing it.

Note

1. My thanks to Martha Boyd and her teaching-practice class for this delightful experience.

Further Reading

Blenkin, G.M. and Kelly, A.V. (eds.) (1992) *Assessment in Early Childhood Education*, Paul Chapman, London.

Blenkin, G.M. and Kelly, A.V. (eds.) (1994) *The National Curriculum and Early Learning. An evaluation*, Paul Chapman, London.

Blenkin, G.M. and Kelly, A.V. (eds.) (1996) *Early Childhood Education: A developmental curriculum (Second Edition)*, Paul Chapman, London.

Browne, A. (1996) *Developing Language and Literacy 3–8*, Paul Chapman, London.

Bruner, J.S. (1986) *Actual Minds, Possible Worlds*, Harvard University Press, Cambridge, Mass.

Campbell, R. (1990) *Reading Together*, Open University Press, Milton Keynes.

Campbell, R. (1996) *Literacy in Nursery Education*, Trentham Books, Stoke-on-Trent.

Geekie, P. and Raban, B. (1993) *Learning to Read and Write Through Classroom Talk*, Warwick Papers on Education Policy No. 2, Trentham Books, Stoke-on-Trent.

Goelman, H., Oberg, A. and Smith, F. (eds.) (1984) *Awakening to Literacy*, Heinemann, London.

Millard, E. (1997) *Differently Literate. Boys, Girls and the Schooling of Literacy*, Taylor & Francis, Basingstoke.

Smith, B. (1994) *Through Writing to Reading. Classroom strategies for supporting literacy*, Routledge, London.

Weinberger, J. (1996) *Literacy Goes to School. The parents' role in young children's literacy learning*, Paul Chapman, London.

Whitehead, M. (1996) *The Development of Language and Literacy*, Hodder & Stoughton, London.

References

Adams, M.J. (1990a) *Beginning to Read: Thinking and learning about print*, MIT, Cambridge, Mass.

Adams, M.J. (1990b) Why not phonics and whole language? Paper prepared for the Symposium on Whole Language and Phonics, Orton Dyslexia Society, Minneapolis, Minnesota, March.

Aitchison, J. (1989) *The Articulate Mammal: An introduction to psycholinguistics (3rd edn.)*, Routledge, London.

Aitchison, J. (1991) *Language Change: Progress or Decay? (2nd edn.)*, Cambridge University Press.

Aitchison, J. (1994) *Words in the Mind: An introduction to the mental lexicon (2nd edn.)*, Blackwell, Oxford.

Aitchison, J. (1996) *The Seeds of Speech. Language origin and evolution*, Cambridge University Press.

Aitchison, J. (1997) *The Language Web (1996 BBC Reith Lectures)*, Cambridge University Press.

Andersson, L. and Trudgill, P. (1990) *Bad Language*, Blackwell, Oxford.

Arnberg, L. (1987) *Raising Children Bilingually: The Pre-School Years*, Multilingual Matters, Clevedon.

Austin, J.L. (1962) *How to do Things with Words*, Clarendon, Oxford.

Ayto, J. (1989) *The Longman Register of New Words*, Longman, Harlow.

Baddeley, P. and Eddershaw, C. (1994) *Not So Simple Picture Books. Developing responses to literature with 4–12 year olds*, Trentham, Stoke-on-Trent.

Baker, C. (1993; 1996) *Foundations of Bilingual Education and Bilingualism*, Multilingual Matters, Clevedon.

Baker, C. (1995) *A Parents' and Teachers' Guide to Bilingualism*, Multilingual Matters, Clevedon.

Barrett, G. (1986) *Starting School: An Evaluation of the Experience*, AMMA/UEA, Norwich.

Barratt-Pugh, C. (1994) 'We only speak English here, don't we?' Supporting language development in a multilingual context, in L. Abbott and R. Rodgers (eds.) *Quality Education in the Early Years*, Open University, Buckingham.

Barthes, R. (1974) *S/Z*, Hill & Wang, New York (originally published 1970), Seuil, Paris.

Barthes, R. (1986) *The Rustle of Language*, Blackwell, Oxford.

Bartholomew, L., and Bruce, T. (1993) *Getting to Know You. A guide to record-keeping in early childhood education and care*, Hodder and Stoughton, London.

Beard, R. (ed.) (1995) *Rhyme, Reading and Writing*, Hodder and Stoughton, London.

Bennett, M. (ed.) (1993) *The Child as Psychologist. An introduction to the development of social cognition*, Harvester Wheatsheaf, Hemel Hempstead.

Bielby, J. (1994) *Making Sense of Reading. The new phonics and its practical implications*, Scholastic, Leamington.

Bissex, G.L. (1980) *GNYS AT WRK, A Child Learns to Write and Read*, Harvard University Press.

Bissex, G.L. (1984) The Child as Teacher, in H. Goelman, A. Oberg and F. Smith (eds.), op.cit., pp. 87–101.

Blenkin, G.M. and Kelly, A.V. (eds.) (1983) *The Primary Curriculum in Action*, Harper & Row, London.

Blenkin, G.M. and Kelly, A.V. (eds.) (1992) *Assessment in Early Childhood Education*, Paul Chapman, London.

Blenkin, G.M. and Kelly, A.V. (eds.) (1994) *The National Curriculum and Early Learning. An evaluation*, Paul Chapman, London.

Blenkin, G.M. and Kelly, A.V. (eds.) (1996) *Early Childhood Education (2nd edn.)*, Paul Chapman, London.

Bridges, A., Sinha, C. and Walkerdine, V. (1981) The development of comprehension, in G. Wells (ed.) op.cit., pp. 116–56.

Britton, J.N. (1970; 1992) *Language and Learning*, Allen Lane, Penguin, Harmondsworth.

Brown, R. (1973) *A First Language*, Penguin, Harmondsworth.

Brown, R. (1977) Introduction, in C.E. Snow and C.A. Ferguson (eds.) op.cit., pp. 1–27.

Browne, A. (1993) *Helping Children to Write*, Paul Chapman, London.

Browne, A. (1996) *Developing Language and Literacy 3–8*, Paul Chapman, London.

Bruner, J.S. (1962) Introduction, in L.S. Vygotsky, *Thought and Language*, MIT, Cambridge, Mass.

Bruner, J.S. (1975) The ontogenesis of speech acts, *Journal of Child Language*, Vol. 2, pp. 1–19.

Bruner, J.S. (1983) *Child's Talk: Learning to Use Language*, Oxford University Press.

Bruner, J.S. (1986) *Actual Minds, Possible Worlds*, Harvard University Press.

Bruner, J.S. (1990) *Acts of Meaning*, Harvard University Press.

Bruner, J.S., Olver, R.R., and Greenfield, P.M. *et al.*, (1966) *Studies in Cognitive Growth*, Wiley, New York.

Bruner, J.S. and Haste, H. (eds.) (1987) *Making Sense. The Child's Construction of the World*, Methuen, London.

Bryant, P.E. and Bradley, L. (1985) *Children's Reading Problems*, Blackwell, Oxford.

Burchfield, R.W. (ed.) (1996) *The New Fowler's Modern English Usage (3rd edn.)*, Clarendon, Oxford.

Butler, D. (1979) *Cushla and Her Books*, Hodder & Stoughton, Sevenoaks.

Cameron, D. and Bourne, J. (1989) *Grammar, Nation and Citizenship: Kingman in Linguistic and Historical Perspective*. Occasional Paper No. 1, Dept. of English and Media Studies, Institute of Education, University of London.

Cameron, D. (1995) *Verbal Hygiene*, Routledge, London.

Campbell, R. (1990) *Reading Together*, Open University Press, Milton Keynes.

Campbell, R. (1992) *Reading Real Books*, Open University Press, Buckingham.

Campbell, R. (1996) *Literacy in Nursery Education*, Trentham Books, Stoke-on-Trent.

Carter, R. (ed.) (1990) *Knowledge about Language and the Curriculum: The LINC Reader*, Hodder and Stoughton, London.

Causley, C. (1988), Story and symbol, *Times Educational Supplement*, 22 January, p. 26.

Centre for Language in Primary Education/Inner London Education Authority (1988) *The Primary Language Record. Handbook for Teachers*, CLPE, London.

Chall, J.S. (1967) *Learning to Read: The Great Debate*, McGraw-Hill, New York.

Chomsky, N. (1957) *Syntactic Structures*, Mouton, The Hague.

Chomsky, N. (1965) *Aspects of the Theory of Syntax*, MIT, Cambridge, Mass.

Chukovsky, K. (1963) *From Two to Five*, University of California Press.

Clark, E.V. (1982) The young word maker: a case study of innovation in the child's lexicon, in E. Wanner and L.R. Gleitman (eds.) op.cit., pp. 390–425.

Clark, E.V. (1993) *The Lexicon in Acquisition*, Cambridge University Press.

Clark, M.M. (1976) *Young Fluent Readers*, Heinemann, London.

Clark, M.M. (ed.) (1985) *New Directions in the Study of Reading*, Falmer, Lewes.

Clay, M.M. (1975) *What Did I Write?*, Heinemann, London.

Cochran-Smith, M. (1984) *The Making of a Reader*, Ablex, New Jersey.

Conti-Ramsden, G. and Snow, C.E. (eds.) (1990) *Children's Language, Vol. 17*, Lawrence Erlbaum, New Jersey.

Cook-Gumperz, J. (ed.) (1986) *The Social Construction of Literacy*, Cambridge University Press.

Cromer, R.F. (1974) The development of language and cognition: the cognition hypothesis, in B. Foss (ed.) op.cit., pp. 184–252.

Crystal, D. (1987; 1997) *The Cambridge Encyclopedia of Language*, Cambridge University Press.

Crystal, D. (1995) *The Cambridge Encyclopedia of the English Language*, Cambridge University Press.

Culler, J. (1974) Introduction, in F. de Saussure, op.cit., pp. xi–xxv.

Department of Education and Science (1975) *A Language for Life (the Bullock Report)*, HMSO, London.

Department of Education and Science (1985) *English from 5–16: curriculum matters 1*, HMSO, London.

Department of Education and Science (1986) *English from 5–16: the responses to curriculum matters 1*, HMSO, London.

Department of Education and Science (1988a) *Report of the Committee of Inquiry into the Teaching of English Language (the Kingman Report)*, HMSO, London.

Department of Education and Science (1988b) *English for ages 5–11. Proposals of the Secretaries of State (the Cox Report)*, NCC/HMSO, London.

Department of Education and Science (1991) *The Parent's Charter*, DES, London.

Department for Education (1995) *English in the National Curriculum, (Revised National Curriculum for English)*, HMSO London.

De Villiers, P.A. and de Villiers, J.G. (1979) *Early Language*, Fontana, London.

De Vries, R. and Kohlberg, L. (1987) *Programs of Early Education, The Constructivist View*, Longman, New York and London.

Donaldson, M. (1978) *Children's Minds*, Fontana/Collins, Glasgow.

Doonan, J. (1993) *Looking at Pictures in Picture Books*, Thimble, Stroud.

Edwards, A.D. (1976) *Language in Culture and Class*, Heinemann, London.

Edwards, C., Gandini, L. and Foreman, G. (eds.) (1996) *The Hundred Languages of Children*, Ablex, London.

Egan, K. and Nadaner, D. (eds.) (1988) *Imagination and Education*, Open University, Milton Keynes.

Engel, D.M. and Whitehead, M.R. (1993) More First Words: A comparative study of bilingual siblings, *Early Years*, Autumn, 14, 1. pp. 27–35.

Engel, D.M. and Whitehead, M.R. (1996) Which English? Standard English and language variety: some educational perspectives, *English in Education*, Vol. 30, no. 1, Spring.

Engel, S. (1995) *The Stories Children Tell. Making sense of the narratives of childhood*, W.H. Freeman, New York.

Ferreiro, E. and Teberosky, A. (1982) *Literacy Before Schooling*, Heinemann, London.

Fisher, R. (1992) *Early Literacy and the Teacher*, Hodder and Stoughton/UKRA London.

Foss, B. (ed.) (1974) *New Perspectives in Child Development*, Penguin, Harmondsworth.

Fox, C. (1993) *At the Very Edge of the Forest. The influence of literature on storytelling by children*, Cassell, London.

Fox, G., Hammond, G., Jones, T., Smith, F. and Sterck, K. (eds.) (1976) *Writers, Critics and Children*, Heinemann, London.

Francis, H. (1982) *Learning to Read: Literate Behaviour and Orthographic Knowledge*, Allen & Unwin, London.

Freire, P. and Macedo, D. (1987) *Literacy. Reading the Word and the World*, Routledge and Kegan Paul, London.

Gallaway, C. and Richards, B.J. (eds.) (1994) *Input and Interaction in Language Acquisition*, Cambridge University Press.

Gardner, H. (1980) *Artful Scribbles. The significance of children's drawings*, Jill Norman, London.

Gentry, J.R. (1982) An analysis of developmental spelling in GNYS AT WRK, *The Reading Teacher*, November, pp. 192–200.

Geekie, P. and Raban, B. (1993) *Learning to Write and Read Through Classroom Talk*, Warwick Papers on Education Policy No. 2, Trentham Books, Stoke-on-Trent.

Goelman, H., Oberg, A. and Smith, F. (eds.) (1984) *Awakening to Literacy, The University of Victoria Symposium on Children's Responses to a Literate Environment: Literacy before Schooling*, Heinemann, London.

Gorman, T. and Brooks, G. (1996) *Assessing Young Children's Writing. A step by step guide*, The Basic Skills Agency/INFER, London.

Goswami, U. and Bryant, P.E. (1990) *Phonological Skills and Learning to Read*, Lawrence Erlbaum, Hove.

Graham, J. (1990) *Pictures on the Page*, NATE, Sheffield.

Graves, D. (1983) *Writing: Teachers and Children at Work*, Heinemann, London.

Graves, D. (1984) *A Researcher Learns to WRITE*, Heinemann, London.

Gregory, E. (1996) *Making Sense of a New World. Learning to read in a second language*, Paul Chapman, London.

Gregory, R.L. (1977) Psychology: towards a science of fiction, in M. Meek, A. Warlow and G. Barton (eds.) op.cit., pp. 393–8.

Hall, E.T. (1973) *The Silent Language*, Anchor, New York.

Hall, N. (1987) *The Emergence of Literacy*, Hodder & Stoughton, Sevenoaks.

Hall, N. and Martello, J. (eds.) (1996) *Listening to Children Talk: exploring talk in the early years*, Hodder and Stoughton, London.

Hall, N. and Robinson, A. (1995) *Exploring Writing and Play in the Early Years*, David Fulton, London.

Halliday, M.A.K. (1975) *Learning How to Mean. Explorations in the Development of Language*, Arnold, London.

Harding, D.W. (1937) The role of the onlooker, *Scrutiny*, Vol. VI, pp. 247–58.

Harding, D.W. (1977) Response to literature, in M. Meek, A. Warlow and G. Barton (eds.) op.cit., pp. 379–92.

Hardy, B. (1977) Towards a poetics of fiction: an approach through narrative, in M. Meek, A. Warlow and G. Barton (eds.) op.cit., pp. 12–23.

Harris, M. (1992) *Language Experience and Early Language Development*, Lawrence Erlbaumn, Hove.

Heath, S.B. (1983) *Ways with Words, Language, Life and Work in Communities and Classrooms*, Cambridge University Press.

Hewins, A. (ed.) (1981) *The Dillen: Memories of a Man of Stratford-upon-Avon*, Elm Tree Books, London.

Hockett, C.F. (1960) The origin of speech, *Scientific American*, 203, September.

Hoffman, C. (1991) *An Introduction to Bilingualism*, Longman, London.

Holdaway, D. (1979) *The Foundations of Literacy*, Ashton Scholastic, London.

Holmes, G. (1977) *The Idiot Teacher. A Book about Prestolee School and its Headmaster*, Spokesman, London.

Howard, P. (1984) *The State of the Language. English Observed*, Hamish Hamilton, London.

Hughes, T. (1988) Myth and Education, in K. Egan and D. Nadaner (eds.) op.cit. pp. 30–44.

Hughes, M., Wikeley, F. and Nash, T. (1994) *Parents and their Children's Schools*, Blackwell, Oxford.

Hunt, P. (1991) *Criticism, Theory, and Children's Literature*, Blackwell, Oxford.

Hunt, P. (1994) *An Introduction to Children's Literature*, Oxford University Press.

Hutchin, V. (1996) *Tracking Significant Development in the Early Years*, Hodder and Stoughton, London.

Hymes, D.H. (1971) On Communicative Competence, in J.B. Pride and J. Holmes (eds.) (1972) op.cit., pp. 269–293.

Jackson, M. (1993) *Literacy*, David Fulton, London.

Johnson, P. (1991) *A Book of One's Own*, Hodder and Stoughton, London.

Jones, R. (1996) *Emerging Patterns of Literacy. A multidisciplinary perspective*, Routledge, London.

King, R. (1978) (1978) *All Things Bright and Beautiful? A Sociological Study of Infants' Classrooms*, Wiley, Chichester.

Kozulin, A. (1986) Vygotsky in Context, in L.S. Vygotsky, op.cit. pp. xi–Lvi.

Kress, G. (1994) *Learning to Write (2nd edn.)*, Routledge and Kegan Paul, London.

Kress, G. (1995) *Writing the Future, English and the making of a culture of innovation*, NATE, Sheffield.

Labov, W. (1966) *The Social Stratification of English in New York City*, Centre for Applied Linguistics, Washington.

Labov, W. (1972) *Sociolinguistic Patterns*, Pennsylvania University Press.

Labov, W. and Waletzky, J. (1985) 'The baddest girl in the neighbourhood', in L. Polanyi, op.cit., p. 22.

Lake, M. (1991) Surveying all the factors. Reading research, *Language and Learning*, 6, pp. 8–13.

Le Guin, U.K. (1980, 81) It was a dark and stormy night: or why are we huddling about the camp fire?, in W.J.T. Mitchell (ed.) op.cit., pp. 187–95.

Lewis, D. (1990) The constructedness of texts: picture books and the metafictive, *Signal* 62, pp. 131–146.

Lierop, M. van (1985) Predisposing factors in early literacy: a case study, in M.M. Clark (ed.) op.cit., pp. 64–80.

Lindqvist, G. (1995) *The Aesthetics of Play. A didactic study of play and culture in preschools*, Uppsala Studies in Education 62, University of Uppsala.

Luria, A.R. and Yudovich, F.I. (1971) *Speech and the Development of Mental Processes in the Child*, Penguin, Harmondsworth.

Mackay, D., Thompson, B. and Schaub, P. (1978) *Breakthrough to Literacy*, Longman, London.

Macnamara, J. (ed.) (1977) *Language, Learning and Thought*, Academic, London.

Mallett, M. (1992) *Making Facts Matter. Reading non-fiction 5–11*, Paul Chapman, London.

Marriott, S. (1991) *Picture Books in the Primary Classroom*, Paul Chapman, London.

Martin-Jones, M. and Romaine, S. (1986) Semilingualism: A Half-Baked Theory of Communicative Competence, *Applied Linguistics*, Vol. 7, no. 1, pp. 22–38.

Matthews, J. (1994) *Helping Children to Draw and Paint in Early Childhood. Children and visual representation*, Hodder and Stoughton, London.

Meadows, S. (1993) *The Child as Thinker. The development and acquisition of cognition in childhood*, Routledge, London.

Meek, M., Warlow, A. and Barton, G. (eds.) (1977) *The Cool Web. The Pattern of Children's Reading*, Bodley Head, London.

Meek, M. (1982) *Learning to Read*, Bodley Head, London.

Meek, M. (ed.) (1983) *Opening Moves*, Bedford Way Papers 17, London.

Meek, M. (1988) *How Texts Teach What Readers Learn*, Thimble, Stroud.

Meek, M. (1996) *Information and Book Learning*, Thimble, Stroud.

Michael, S. (1986) Narrative presentations: an oral preparation for literacy with first graders, in J. Cook-Gumperz (ed.) op.cit., pp.94–116.

Michaels, W. and Walsh, M. (1990) *Up and Away. Using picture books*, Oxford University Press.

Millard, E. (1997) *Differently Literate. Boys, Girls and the Schooling of Literacy*, Taylor and Francis, Basingstoke.

Miller, L. (1996) *Towards Reading. Literacy development in the pre-school years*, Open University Press, Buckingham.

Mills, R.W. and Mills, J. (1993) *Bilingualism in the Primary School. A handbook for teachers*, Routledge, London.

Milroy, J. and Milroy, L. (1985) *Authority in Language. Investigating language prescription and standardisation*. Routledge and Kegan Paul, London.

Minns, H. (1991) *Language, Literacy and Gender*, Hodder and Stoughton, London.

Mitchell, W.J.T. (ed.) (1980, 1981) *On Narrative*, University of Chicago Press.

Mudd, N. (1994) *Effective Spelling. A practical guide for teachers*, Hodder and Stoughton, London.

Neate, B. (1992) *Finding Out About Finding Out: a practical guide to children's information books*, Hodder and Stoughton/UKRA, London.

Nelson, K. (1989) *Narratives from the Crib*, Harvard University Press, Cambridge, Mass.

Newkirk, T. (1984) Archimedes' Dream, *Language Arts*, Vol. 61, no. 4, pp. 341–350.

Nutbrown, C. (1994) *Threads of Thinking. Young children learning and the role of early education*, Paul Chapman, London.

Olson, D.R., Torrance, N. and Hildyard, A. (eds.) (1985) *Literacy, Language and Learning. The Nature and Consequences of Reading and Writing*, Cambridge University Press.

Ong, W.J. (1982) *Orality and Literacy. The technologizing of the word*, Methuen, London.

Opie, I. and Opie, P. (1980) *A Nursery Companion*, Oxford University Press.

Paley, V.G. (1981) *Wally's Stories. Conversations in the Kindergarten*, Harvard University Press.

Paley, V.G. (1986) *Mollie is Three. Growing up in school*, University of Chicago.

Payton, S. (1984) Developing awareness of print. A young child's first steps towards literacy, *Education Review Offset Publication, No. 2*, University of Birmingham.

Perera, K. (1987) *Understanding Language*, NATE, Sheffield.

Perera, K., Collis, G. and Richards, B. (eds.) (1994) *Growing Points in Child Language*, Cambridge University Press.

Piaget, J. (1926) *The Language and Thought of the Child*, Routledge & Kegan Paul, London.

Pinker, S. (1994) *The Language Instinct. The new science of language and mind*, Allen Lane/Penguin, Harmondsworth.

Pinsent, P. (ed.) (1992) *Language, Culture and Young Children*, David Fulton/Roehampton Institute, London.

Polanyi, L. (1985) *Telling the American Story. A Structural and Cultural Analysis of Conversational Storytelling*, Ablex, New Jersey.

Pride, J.B. and Holmes, J. (eds.) (1972) *Sociolinguistics*, Penguin, Harmondsworth.

Read, C. (1986) *Children's Creative Spelling*, Routledge and Kegan Paul, London.

Reddy, V. (1991) Playing with others' expectations: teasing and mucking about in the first year, in A. Whiten (ed.) *Natural Theories of Mind*, Blackwell, Oxford, pp. 145–158.

Riley, J. (1996) *The Teaching of Reading. The development of literacy in the early years of school*, Paul Chapman, London.

Romaine, S. (1984) *The Language of Children and Adolescents*, Blackwell, Oxford.

Rosen, B. (1991) *Shapers and Polishers. Teachers as storytellers*, Mary Glasgow, London.

Rosen, H. (1984) *Stories and Meanings*, NATE, Sheffield.

Sassoon, R. (1990a) *Handwriting: the way to teach it*, Stanley Thornes, Cheltenham.

Sassoon, R. (1990b) *Handwriting: a new perspective*, Stanley Thornes, Cheltenham.

Sassoon, R. (1993) Handwriting, in R. Beard (ed.) *Teaching Literacy: Balancing Perspectives*, Hodder and Stoughton, London, pp. 187–201.

Sassoon, R. (1995) *The Acquisition of a Second Writing System*, Intellect, Oxford.

Saunders, G. (1988) *Bilingual Children. From Birth to Teens*, Multilingual Matters, Clevedon.

Saussure, F. de, (1974) *Course in General Linguistics*, Collins, Glasgow, (originally published 1915, Payot, Paris).

Schaffer, H.R. (ed.) (1977) *Studies in Mother–Infant Interaction*, Academic Press, London.

School Curriculum and Assessment Authority (1996a) *Nursery Education. Desirable Outcomes for Children's Learning on entering compulsory education*, SCAA, London.

School Curriculum and Assessment Authority (1996b) *Baseline Assessment. Draft proposals*, SCAA, London.

Scollon, R. and Scollon, S.B.K. (1981) *Narrative, Literacy and Face in Inter-ethnic Communication*, Ablex, New Jersey.

Sealey, A. (1996) *Learning about Language. Issues for primary teachers*, Open University Press, Buckingham.

Selinker, L. (1992) *Rediscovering Interlanguage*, Longman, London.

Sendak, M. (1977) Questions to an artist who is also an author, in M. Meek, A. Warlow and G. Barton (eds.) op.cit., pp. 241–56.

Sheridan, D. (1979) 'Flopsy, Mopsy and Tooth': the storytelling of preschoolers, *Language Arts*, Vol. 56, no. 1, pp. 10–15.

Siegal, M. (1991) *Knowing Children. Experiments in conversation and cognition*, Lawrence Erlbaum, Hove.

Slobin, D. (1979) *Psycholinguistics* (2nd edn.), Scott Foresman, Illinois.

Slobin, D. (1982) Universal and particular in the acquisition of language, in E. Wanner and L.R. Gleitman (eds.) op.cit.

Smith, B., (1994) *Through Writing to Reading. Classroom strategies for supporting literacy*, Routledge, London.

Smith, B.H. (1980, 1981) Narrative versions, narrative theories, in W.J.T. Mitchell (ed.) op.cit., pp. 209–32.

Smith, F. (1982) *Writing and the Writer*, Holt, Rinehart & Winston, New York.

Smith, F. (1983) *Essays into Literacy*, Heinemann, London.

Smith, F. (1988) *Joining the Literacy Club*, Heinemann, London.

Smith, F. (1992) *To Think. In language, learning and education*, Routledge, London.

Smith, F. (1994) *Understanding Reading. A psycholinguistic analysis of reading and learning to read* (5th edn.), Lawrence Erlbaum, New Jersey.

Snow, C.E. (1977) The development of conversation between mothers and babies, *Journal of Child Language*, Vol. 4, pp. 1–22.

Snow, C.E. and Ferguson, C.A. (eds.) (1977) *Talking to Children: Language Input and Acquisition*, Cambridge University Press.

Snow, C.E., Barnes, W.S., Chandler, J., Goodman, I.F., Hemphill, L. (1991) *Unfulfilled Expectations. Home and school influences on literacy*, Harvard University Press, Cambridge, Mass.

Stanzel, F.K. (1984) *A Theory of Narrative*, Cambridge University Press.

Steedman, C. (1982) *The Tidy House. Little Girls Writing*, Virago, London.

Stephens, J. (1992) *Language and Ideology in Children's Fiction*, Longman, London.

Stern, D. (1977) *The First Relationship: Infant and Mother*, Fontana, London.

Stubbs, M. (1986) *Educational Linguistics*, Blackwell, Oxford.

Styles, M., Bearne, E., Watson, V. (eds.) (1992) *After Alice. Exploring children's literature*, Cassell, London.

Styles, M., Bearne, E., Watson, V. (eds.) (1994) *The Prose and the Passion. Children and their reading*, Cassell, London.

Styles, M., Bearne, E., Watson, V. (eds.) (1996) *Voices Off. Texts, contexts and readers*, Cassell, London.

Sutton-Smith, B. (1981) *The Folkstories of Children*, University of Pennsylvania Press.

Temple, C.A., Nathan, R.G., Burris, N.A. and Temple, F. (1988) *The Beginnings of Writing* (2nd edn.), Allyn & Bacon, Boston, Mass.

Thornton, G. (1986) *Language, Ignorance and Education*, Arnold, London.

Tizard, B. and Hughes, M. (1984) *Young Children Learning: Talking and Thinking at Home and at School*, Fontana, London.

Trevarthen, C. (1993) Playing into reality : conversations with the infant communicator, *Winnicott Studies*, 7, Spring, pp. 67–84.

Trudgill, P. (1974) *The Social Differentiation of English in Norwich*, Cambridge University Press.
Trudgill, P. (1978) *Sociolinguistic Patterns in British English*, Arnold, London.
Trudgill, P. (1994) *Dialects*, Routledge, London.
Vygotsky, L.S. (1978) *Mind in Society. The development of higher psychological processes*, Harvard University Press.
Vygotsky, L.S. (1986) *Thought and Language*, MIT, Cambridge, Mass., (Revised and edited by A. Kozulin).
Wade, B. and Moore, M. (1993) *Bookstart in Birmingham. A description and evaluation of an exploratory British project to encourage sharing books with babies*, Book Trust Report 2, Book Trust, London.
Wade, B. and Moore, M. (1996) Babies brought to book, *Times Educational Supplement*, Extra Early Years, 28 June, p. iv.
Wanner, E. and Gleitman, L.R. (eds.) (1982) *Language Acquisition: the state of the art*, Cambridge University Press.
Waterland, L. (ed.) (1989) *Apprenticeship in Action, Teachers write about 'Read with Me'*, Thimble, Stroud.
Watson, V. and Styles, M. (eds.) (1996) *Talking Pictures. Pictorial texts and young readers*, Hodder and Stoughton, London.
Weinberger, J. (1996) *Literacy goes to School. The parents' role in young children's literacy learning*, Paul Chapman, London.
Weir, R.H. (1962) *Language in the Crib*, Mouton, The Hague.
Wells, G. (ed.) (1981) *Learning Through Interaction. The Study of Language Development*, Cambridge University Press.
Wells, G. (1985) *Language, Learning and Education*, NFER/Nelson, Windsor.
Wells, G. (1987) *The Meaning Makers: Children Learning Language and Using Language to Learn*, Hodder & Stoughton, London.
Wertsch, J.V. (1985) *Vygotsky and the Social Formation of Mind*, Harvard University Press.
Whalley, M. (1994) *Learning to be Strong. Setting up a neighbourhood service for under-fives and their families*, Hodder and Stoughton, London.
White, D. (1954) *Books before Five*. Council for Educational Research, New Zealand.
Whitehead, M.R. (1983a) Language Development and the Primary Curriculum, in G.M. Blenkin and A.V. Kelly, (eds.) op.cit., pp. 57–80.
Whitehead, M.R. (1983b) Proto-narrative Moves in Early Conversations, in M. Meek (ed.) op.cit., pp. 44–55.
Whitehead, M.R. (1985) On Learning to Write. Recent Research and Developmental Writing, *Curriculum*, Vol .6, no. 2, pp. 12–19.
Whitehead, M.R. (1986) 'Breakthrough' Revisited. Some thoughts on 'Breakthrough to Literacy' and developmental writing, *Curriculum*, Vol. 7, n o. 1, pp. 26–32.
Whitehead, M.R. (1990) First Words. The language diary of a bilingual child's early speech, *Early Years*, Vol. 10, no. 2, Spring, pp. 53–57.
Whitehead, M.R. (1995) Nonsense, rhyme and word play in young children, in R. Beard (ed.) *Rhyme, Reading and Writing*, Hodder and Stoughton, London, pp. 42–61.
Whitehead, M.R. (1996) Narrative stories and the world of literature, in G.M. Blenkin and A.V. Kelly (eds.) op. cit.
Whitehead, M.R. (1996) *The Development of Language and Literacy*, Hodder and Stoughton, London.
Whitman, W. (1885; 1984) *Slang in America*, quoted in P. Howard, op.cit., p. vii.
Whorf, B.L. (1956) *Language, Thought and Reality, Selected Writings of B.L. Whorf*, Wiley, New York.
Winnicott, D.W. (1971) *Playing and Reality*, Penguin, Harmondsworth.
Wolfendale, S. and Topping, K. (eds.) (1996) *Family Involvement in Literacy. Effective partnerships in education*, Cassell, London.
Wood, D. (1988) *How Children Think and Learn*, Blackwell, Oxford.
Yule, G. (1985; 1996) *The Study of Language*, Cambridge University Press.

Literature referred to in the text

Agard, J. (1983) *I Din Do Nuttin*, Bodley Head, London.
Ahlberg, J. and Ahlberg, A. (1977a) *Burglar Bill*, Heinemann, London.
Ahlberg, J. and Ahlberg, A. (1977b) *Each Peach Pear Plum*, Kestrel/Penguin, Harmondsworth.
Ahlberg, J. and Ahlberg, A. (1978) *Cops and Robbers*, Heinemann, London.
Ahlberg, J. and Ahlberg, A. (1981) *Peepo*, Kestrel/Penguin, Harmondsworth.
Ahlberg, J. and Ahlberg, A. (1982) *The Baby's Catalogue*, Kestrel/Penguin, Harmondsworth.
Ahlberg, J. and Ahlberg, A. (1986) *The Jolly Postman or Other People's Letters*, Heinemann, London.
Ahlberg, J. and Ahlberg, A. (1995)*The Jolly Pocket Postman*, Heinemann, London.
Angelou, M. (1984) *I Know Why the Caged Bird Sings*, Virago, London.
Anno, M. (1979) *Anno's Italy*, Bodley Head, London.
Atwood, M. (1987) *The Handmaid's Tale*, Virago, London.
Barber, A. and Bayley, N. (1990) *The Mousehole Cat*, Walker, London.
Berridge, C. (1975) *Runaway Danny*, Deutsch, London.
Breinburg, P. (1973) *My Brother Sean*, Bodley, London.
Briggs, R. (1973) *Father Christmas*, Hamish Hamilton, London.
Briggs, R. (1978) *The Snowman*, Hamish Hamilton, London.
Briggs, R. (1983) *When the Wind Blows*, Penguin, Harmondsworth.
Briggs, R. (1984) *The Tin-Pot Foreign General and the Old Iron Woman*, Hamish Hamilton, London.
Browne, A. (1981) *Hansel and Gretel* (The Brothers Grimm), Julia MacRae, London.
Browne, A. (1983) *Gorilla*, Julia MacRae, London.
Browne, A. (1986) *Piggybook*, Julia MacRae, London.
Browne, E. (1994) *Handa's Surprise*, Walker, London.
Bruna, D. (1967) *b is for bear, an abc*, Methuen, London.
Burgess, A. (1987) *The Pianoplayers*, Arrow, London.
Burningham, J. (1970) *Mr. Gumpy's Outing*, Cape, London.
Burningham, J. (1977) *Come Away from the Water, Shirley*, Cape, London.
Burningham, J. (1980) *The Shopping Basket*, Cape, London.
Burningham, J. (1982) *Avocado Baby*, Cape, London.
Carle, E. (1970) *The Very Hungry Caterpillar*, Hamish Hamilton, London.
Carroll, L. (1988) *Alice's Adventures in Wonderland*, illustrated by Anthony Browne, Julia MacRae, London.
Cooper, H. (1993) *The Bear Under the Stairs*, Doubleday/Picture Corgi, London.
Cope, W. (1986) *Making Cocoa for Kingsley Amis*, Faber, London.
Cutler, I. (1971) *Meal One*, Heinemann, London.

De La Mare, W. (1962) *Poems*, Penguin, Harmondsworth.
Felix, M. (1975) *Another Story of . . . The Little Mouse Trapped in a Book*, Methuen, London.
Fine, A. (1992) *Flour Babies*, Hamish Hamilton, London.
Frank, A. (1954) *The Diary of Anne Frank*, Pan, London.
Furchgott, T. and Dawson, L. (1977) *Phoebe and the Hot Water Bottles*, Deutsch, London.
Hardy, T. (1902) *The Life and Death of the Mayor of Casterbridge*, Macmillan, London.
Hersom, K. (1981) *Maybe it's Tiger*, Macmillan, London.
Hill, E. (1980) *Where's Spot?* Heinemann, London.
Holman, F. (1974) *Slake's Limbo*, Scribner, New York, (1980, Macmillan, London).
Hughes, S. (1981) *Alfie Gets in First*, Bodley Head, London.
Hutchins, P. (1968) *Rosie's Walk*, Bodley Head, London.
Hutchins, P. (1972) *Titch*, Bodley Head, London.
Hutchins, P. (1976) *Don't Forget the Bacon*, Bodley Head, London.
Ingpen, R. (1986) *The Idle Bear*, Blackie, London.
Inkpen, M. (1995) *Nothing*, Hodder Headline, London.
Keats, E.J. (1970) *Goggles*, Bodley Head, London.
Keller, H. (1984) *Geraldine's Blanket*, Julie MacRae, London.
Kent, J. (1972) *The Fat Cat*, Hamish Hamilton, London.
Kerr, J. (1968) *The Tiger who Came to Tea*, Collins, Glasgow.
Kipling, R. (1986) *Just So Stories*, Macmillan, London.
Kitamura, S. (1985) *What's Inside? The Alphabet Book*, A. & C. Black, London.
Lewis, C.S. (1959) *The Lion, the Witch and the Wardrobe*, Penguin, Harmondsworth.
Lloyd, E. (1978) *Nini at Carnival*, Bodley Head, London.
McKee, D. (1980) *Not Now, Bernard*, Andersen, London.
McKee, D. (1988) *Who's a Clever Baby Then?*, Andersen, London.
McKissack, P.C. and Isadora, R. (1986) *Flossie and the Fox*, Viking Kestrel, London.
Mahy, M. (1986) *A Lion in the Meadow*, Dent, London.
Nicholl, H. and Pienkowski, J. (1972) *Meg and Mog*, Heinemann, London.
Opie, I. and Opie, P. (eds.) (1951) *The Oxford Dictionary of Nursery Rhymes*, Oxford University Press.
Opie, I. and Opie, P. (eds.) (1973) *The Oxford Book of Children's Verse*, Oxford University Press.
Oxenbury, H. and Tolstoy, A. (1968) *The Great Big Enormous Turnip*, Heinemann, London.
Parish, P. (1963) *Amelia Bedelia*, Scholastic Books, New York.
Patterson, G. (1986) *The Goose that laid the Golden Egg*, retold from Aesop, Deutsch, London.
Pearce, P. (1983) *The Way to Sattin Shore*, Kestrel/Penguin, Harmondsworth.
Pilling, A. (1985) *Henry's Leg*, Viking/Kestrel, Harmondsworth.
Provenson, A. and Provenson, M. (1984) *Leonardo de Vinci*, Hutchinson, London.
Rayner, M. (1976) *Mr and Mrs Pig's Evening Out*, Macmillan, London.
Rosen, M. (1983) *Quick, Let's Get Out of Here*, Deutsch, London.
Rosen, M. and Oxenbury, H. (1989) *We're Going on a Bear Hunt*, Walker, London.
Sendak, M. (1967) *Where the Wild Things Are*, Bodley Head, London.
Sendak, M. (1971) *In the Night Kitchen*, Bodley Head, London.
Seuss, Dr. (1984) *The Butter Battle Book*, Collins, Glasgow.
Simmonds, P. (1995) *F-Freezing ABC*, Jonathan Cape, London.
Taylor, J. (1973) The Star, in I. Opie and P. Opie (eds.) op.cit., p. 122.
Thwaite, A. and Mills, E. (1996) *The Horse at Hilly Fields*, Scholastic, Leamington.
Vipont, E. (1969) *The Elephant and the Bad Baby*, Hamish Hamilton, London.
Walsh, J.P. (1982) *Babylon*, Deutsch, London.
Wagner, J. (1977) *John Brown, Rose and The Midnight Cat*, Kestrel/Penguin, Harmondsworth.

Wells, R. (1977) *Benjamin and Tulip*, Penguin, Harmondsworth.

Wells, R. (1978) *Noisy Norah*, Collins, Glasgow.

Zacharias, T. and Zacharias, W. (1965) *But Where is the Green Parrot?*, Chatto & Windus, London.

Zion, G. (1960) *Harry the Dirty Dog*, Bodley Head, London.

Zolotow, C. and Sendak, M. (1968) *Mr. Rabbit and the Lovely Present*, Bodley Head, London.

Subject Index